PRAISE FOR

Arnie

"A comprehensive and engaging look at a man who was one of America's biggest sports personalities." —*Forbes*

"A biography so rich in anecdotes it begs to be savored like a box of chocolates." —*New York Times*

"Mr. Callahan has teed up a different sort of biography and knocked it dead center down the fairway." —*Wall Street Journal*

"Remarkable." —Associated Press

"Not just another of the Palmer biographies . . . Callahan's new book is bursting with creativity and research. . . . He deftly weaves stories that start with Palmer into great ones about other golfers such as Jack Nicklaus, Julius Boros, and Doug Sanders."
—*Augusta Chronicle*

"Before I played in a Masters or U.S. Open, I played golf with Tom Callahan in Pretoria. So we go back a ways. In my first American major, I was paired with Arnold Palmer. Now Tom and Arnold are paired forever." —Ernie Els

"Under Tom Callahan's spell, words soar, spin, and do the samba on the head of a matchstick. There's nobody better."
—Rick Reilly

"Tom knows the game of golf as well as anyone in the business. A lot of years, not just a lot of nights, went into this."
—Jack Nicklaus

"Tom has been a good friend and a respected journalist in golf for a very long time. . . . [He] has a special way of getting to the heart of the story." —Gary Player

"Tom Callahan writing about anything is like Julia Child saying, 'If you don't have any plans, stick around and I'll make you dinner.'" —Tony Kornheiser

"Written in an energetic fashion by a man who shares with us his in-depth, insider's view. . . . (Callahan) knows enough about Palmer's friends to fill a TV documentary." —*Florida Times-Union*

"A joyful, definitive biography. . . . Callahan shows obvious affection for Palmer, [and] successfully argues that Palmer's seemingly charmed life included great difficulty even as he revolutionized golf." —*Publishers Weekly*

"Callahan's lively and brisk writing style makes for an eminently readable book jam-packed with anecdotes and stories golfers will love." —*Kirkus Reviews*

"Consider this laudatory biography to be the screenplay for the movie." —*Library Journal*

"It is a good story in a good book about a good guy who did a lot of good things, and also played a real good game of golf . . . a delightful read." —*Weekly Standard*

ARNIE

ALSO BY TOM CALLAHAN

———

His Father's Son: Earl and Tiger Woods

*The GM: The Inside Story of a Dream Job and
the Nightmares That Go with It*

Johnny U: The Life and Times of John Unitas

Dancing with Sonny Liston

The Bases Were Loaded (and So Was I)

*In Search of Tiger: A Journey Through Golf
with Tiger Woods*

Around the World in 18 Holes (coauthor David Kindred)

ARNIE

THE LIFE OF ARNOLD PALMER

TOM CALLAHAN

HARPER

NEW YORK · LONDON · TORONTO · SYDNEY

For his ownself, Dan Jenkins

HARPER

A hardcover edition of this book was published in 2017 by Harper, an imprint of HarperCollins Publishers.

ARNIE. Copyright © 2017 by Tom Callahan. All rights reserved. Printed in the United States of America. No part of this book may be used or reproduced in any manner whatsoever without written permission except in the case of brief quotations embodied in critical articles and reviews. For information, address HarperCollins Publishers, 195 Broadway, New York, NY 10007.

HarperCollins books may be purchased for educational, business, or sales promotional use. For information, please e-mail the Special Markets Department at SPsales@harpercollins.com.

FIRST HARPER PAPERBACK EDITION PUBLISHED 2018.

Designed by William Ruoto

Title page credit: E. Knoblock/AP/REX/Shutterstock

Library of Congress Cataloging-in-Publication Data has been applied for.

ISBN 978-0-06-243974-1 (pbk.)

18 19 20 21 22 LSC 10 9 8 7 6 5 4 3 2 1

CONTENTS

PREFACE

My first year at the Masters was 1972. Only two players broke 70 on Thursday: the eventual winner, Jack Nicklaus, and Sam Snead, who turned 60 years old a month later. Arnold Palmer shot 70.

In the interview room (the Charles Bartlett Lounge) of the old green Quonset hut that housed the press in those days, a nervous reporter put an awkward question to Nicklaus, who made a little joke at the fellow's expense, then answered it. Something similar happened during Palmer's birdies-and-bogeys session, except, this time, when a rattled kid started to fall off the ledge, Palmer reached out with that strong forearm, steadied him, saved him, reworded the question, and answered it before anyone in the room knew what happened. I remember thinking, *It's a natural grace.*

The first time I had Palmer to myself was in Cincinnati during the early 1970s at a one-day charity event.

"What's the charity getting and what are you getting?" I asked him. His eyebrows shot up.

"You'll have to see [agent Mark] McCormack about the charity," he said. "I'm getting twelve thousand dollars, Gary Player's getting eight thousand, and everyone else is getting a grand apiece [even the winner, Hubert Green]. Anything else you want to know?"

"Sorry," I said.

"Don't ever apologize for doing your job," he told me.

Throughout the years, I watched him at many tournaments on both sides of the Atlantic Ocean. I was at Oakmont in Pennsylvania when, with six holes left to play, Palmer was sure he was winning the U.S. Open only to hear the thunder of Johnny Miller's 63 up ahead. I was at Medinah in Illinois when the vinegar between Arnold and Jack finally spilled out. I was at Muirfield Village in Ohio when they reconciled. And I was at Augusta in Georgia on the Wednesday when they played their first practice round with 20-year-old amateur Tiger Woods.

For *Golf Digest*, I went to Latrobe, Pennsylvania, to write "Arnie turns 60," "Arnie turns 70," and "Arnie turns 80" pieces. Sitting at his office desk with his adjutant, Doc Giffin, on the couch, Palmer talked his life story to me in three volumes and complete chapters too detailed to fit in *Golf Digest*. Like the nightmare of being taken by a highway patrolman to identify best friend and roommate Bud Worsham's body at Wake Forest College.

Giffin had been the tour's traveling press secretary in the '60s, driving from tournament to tournament, hauling all the decimal points in the backseat. At the Western Open in Chicago, Doc witnessed a tableau that changed his life. A college journalist weighed down by a bulky tape recorder requested a sit-down interview with Palmer, who said fine. After they finished, the student realized to his horror that he had neglected to turn on the machine. "That's all right," Arnold said. "Let's start over and do it again." Later, when Palmer asked Giffin to throw in with him, the incident of the tape recorder swayed him.

Along the way, I discussed Palmer with Nicklaus, Player, Snead, Byron Nelson, Dow Finsterwald, Ken Venturi, Tom Watson, Lee Trevino, Raymond Floyd (I think Floyd would tell you we've talked more about Palmer than we have about Floyd)—everyone but Ben Hogan. The only time I ever spoke with Hogan, at Shady Oaks Country Club in Fort Worth, Texas, Arnold wasn't mentioned, which would have come as no surprise to Palmer. "Hogan never called me by my name," he said coldly. "Never."

After Nicklaus and I finished an afternoon-long hit-and-run conversation on a bustling workday at his Florida office (considerately, Jack had said, "I'll keep leaving and coming back; you keep asking questions"), he kicked off a shoe to show me his hammer-toe. Only Nicklaus would think anyone could find his hammertoe interesting. Too casually he mentioned "one of those old *Shell's Wonderful World of Golf* things is on TV tonight: me and [Ben] Crenshaw."

"Let me guess," I said. "*You* won."

He laughed. "I suppose we're all a little like that," he said, "even Palmer."

Snead and Nelson kept score by Hogan; Nicklaus and Player by Palmer.

"And Hogan was there . . . and Hogan was there . . . and Hogan was there . . . ," said Lord Byron, recapping 1945 for me, the barely believable year when Nelson won 18 tournaments, 11 in a row. Hogan, Snead, and Nelson were all born in 1912, Byron first. "I was alive when the *Titanic* went down," he said triumphantly. "*Hogan* wasn't!"

I could have made my own way to Player's farm north of Johannesburg, but, being a courtly host, he sent a car to my hotel (appropriately enough, a Volkswagen Golf). The driver was a young black man named David. Leaving the city behind, where the newspapers were throbbing with a black-on-white commando attack at the King William's Town Golf Club (four dead, 20 wounded), we rolled into the countryside on a shiny Sunday.

"It sounds bad," David said. "It *is* bad. But it's getting better." This was the mantra of South Africa.

At a sign that said "Blair Atholl" we veered onto a dark path that led to a beautiful little forest, then to a creek and an entrance-way where a brightly uniformed sentry popped out of a box like someone out of Joseph Conrad's imagination. "Sometimes," David said, "when you come to a place like this, it's like you mustn't go away again."

Five hundred black children went to school every day at Gary and Vivienne's home. It started with their workers' children, and grew. Singing filled the property. "Listen," Player whispered. Accompanying the song was the squeak of gumboot dancing and the smoke of learning. "Isn't it lovely? Education is the light. South Africa is at a crossroads and the children are the key. They'll lead, as usual. Look at them: some barefoot but all in a jacket and tie."

With intense eyes, black as coal, Player told me, "I loved it when Jack and Arnie were partners. I hated it when they got so competitive—too competitive. But I knew they were both very good men. I just waited the cold spell out."

In this modest account (personalized, too, I hope you don't mind), you should know that on the frequent occasions where Palmer was simply holding forth, he was at his office desk in Latrobe, surrounded by mementos (for instance, a baseball signed by Pirates second baseman Bill Mazeroski) but only one loving cup, the Canadian Open trophy, representing the first of Palmer's 92 professional victories. (He is cuddling it on the cover of this book.) It came in 1955 along with a check for $2,400, a typical winner's share then.

On a corner of the desk crouched a silver cigarette case, a gift from the Augusta National Golf Club to all of the competitors' wives, badly dented when Arnold threw his spikes at it in anger after blowing the tournament. He kept the bashed little box on shameful display as a perpetual reminder to himself.

A low circular table of worn and faded walnut was the room's most distinctive furnishing, inlaid under glass with four gold medals from the Masters, two from the Open Championship, one from the U.S. Open, one from the U.S. Amateur, and none from the PGA Championship, together with a score of silver medals from all four majors (no fewer than four second places from the U.S. Open alone, three of those coming in 18-hole playoffs.) Three blank circles stood out in green. Were they ever filled, he'd have immediately drilled a few more. "Don't you always want to leave a little space," he told me, "for the future?"

Prominent among the photographs crowding the walls was one of Babe Didrikson Zaharias, the Olympic hurdler (Gold), javelin thrower (Gold), and high jumper (Bronze), Ladies Professional Golf Association co-founder, 41-time tournament winner, three-time U.S. Women's Open champion, six-time Associated Press female athlete of the year, and member of the World Golf Hall of Fame, who died at 45. She won all of her Opens by at least eight strokes, the last by 12, one month after colon cancer surgery, wearing a colostomy bag. The most telling and least told of her many bequests to the world was the effect she had on Palmer and therefore the effect she had on golf and sports, especially in the '50s, '60s, and '70s.

"She came to Latrobe [tiny Latrobe], believe it or not, for an exhibition," he said. "I was about thirteen. We played golf with her, my father and I. Babe had a lot of game, but she had even more showmanship ['Pardon me, folks, while I loosen my girdle'], which was a revelation to me. Up until then, I had my head down, competing. I just wanted to win. But, while watching her showing off—both her skills and her personality—it occurred to me that I was a showoff, too. I wanted to entertain the people and earn their cheers. Those weren't just strangers standing there; they were part of it. Babe taught me that."

A bathroom was handy to his left, a metal shop just a few steps

away, with an iron vise clamped to a rugged workbench stacked
with leaded tape, lacquer, shafts, heads, grips, epoxies, hammers,
saws, rasps, wrenches, and all the other accouterments for fiddling
with golf clubs.

Now and then he'd get up and do so, still talking. "This is my
lair," he said. A tablet hanging near a cuckoo clock read in part:

> *If you think you are beaten, you are.*
> *If you dare not, you don't.*
> *If you'd like to win but think you can't,*
> *It's almost certain you won't.*
> *Life's battles don't always go*
> *To the strongest or fastest man,*
> *But sooner or later the man who wins*
> *Is the man who thinks he can.*

Absent friends like Dave Marr, Bob Rosburg, Herb Wind,
and Bob Drum were of supreme help here without knowing it.
The Drummer, a perfectly named percussion instrument, was boy
Palmer's Boswell/town crier at the *Pittsburgh Press.* "Bob was on the
case when Arnold was a freshman or sophomore in high school,"
said Giffin, a Pittsburgher himself, "and by the time Arnold won
the West Penn Junior at seventeen, everyone in town was convinced, including me."

In the fedora ranks at the 1960 U.S. Open, Drum and Dan
Jenkins of the *Fort Worth Press* were an entry, 1 and 1A. Born in
December of 1929, sixty-four days after Palmer, my friend Dan
was a rich source and an ideal sounding board. This book is dedicated to him.

ARNIE

1

1960

WINNER:

Bob Hope Desert Classic

Texas Open

Baton Rouge Open

Pensacola Open

Masters

U.S. Open

Insurance City Open

Mobile Open

Canada Cup (with Sam Snead)

"Fancy meeting you guys here."

Palmer didn't formally become Palmer until the 1960 U.S. Open at Cherry Hills Country Club near Denver. There were other applicants, including Mike Souchak, a muscleman himself, and Ken

Venturi, the betting favorite to succeed Ben Hogan atop golf. (Hogan's favorite, too.) But a couple of months earlier, as Palmer was playing his final two holes at the Masters, something happened.

Venturi had completed his round and was leading Palmer by a stroke as Arnold knelt behind a 40-foot birdie putt at 17. "Maybe it only *seems* that long now," he said. "Let's say thirty-something anyway." It was one of those putts you had to slug to make, at the risk of wandering by and three-putting. Playing for a playoff made more sense: lagging short, accepting a par, staying alive for a birdie at 18 that would tie Venturi and force an 18-hole showdown the next day.

Play for a tie? Palmer thought as he stepped knock-kneed and pigeon-toed into the putt. *Hell.* He rolled it in for birdie. In his mind's eye, the ball clanged the back rim of the cup, jumping straight up in the air like Dick Fosbury and flopping over backward into the hole. In fact, it just made it to the hole. But now a closing birdie would win.

After bending right to left all day, Augusta National leans left to right at the end. Toeing one foot slightly inward as an extra precaution against pine trees on the right (the bunkers on the left hadn't yet been installed), Palmer thought of his father, whom he called "Pap," and Pap's formula for swinging a golf club under pressure: *"Start deliberate, go slow on the backswing—slower, SLOWER! GODDAMMIT!—then on the downswing give it absolutely everything you've got."*

The ball flew uphill about 270 yards, lighting on the left side of the fairway. With a 6-iron, Palmer homed in on the pin instead of the green, prompting himself: *Hit through it now. Stay down. Let the crowd tell you where it goes.* Five feet. He was distracted momentarily by the whispered commentary of television broadcaster Jim McKay, but he made it. He won. Incidentally, TV and golf were fairly new to each other in 1960. As photogenic as Palmer had always been in the old newspapers, he was even more telegenic in the new medium.

In a manner of speaking, Arnold Palmer was delivered with the first sets.

"You'd think any five-footer in that situation might feel a little jumpy," he said, "but it didn't. The six-iron was the shot, one of the best of my career. The putt felt automatic to me. Automatic. Playing the seventeenth hole, I'd heard Winnie's voice in the gallery, saying something encouraging, keeping just ahead of me as she walked. Having tuned out Jim [McKay] and everybody else, I looked at the back of the ball and thought of the day Win and I applied for our marriage license. [Wouldn't every professional athlete like to have a wife who answered to 'Win?'] We forgot to bring her parents' signed permission; she was only twenty, you know, and her father hated my ass. I was sitting in the license bureau, trying to sound confident ['Oh, she's twenty-one all right'], praying for the clerk to hurry up and stamp the form when—I made the putt."

He tossed his head back and laughed.

"If I had to have one putt for my life," Augusta founder Bobby Jones said that evening, "I'd rather have Palmer putt it for me than anybody I ever saw."

"From that Masters on," Arnold said, "I had a philosophy of golf: when you miss a conservative shot, you're in just as much trouble as when you miss a bold one."

The first hole at Cherry Hills embodied this philosophy, which didn't keep him from butchering it Thursday, Friday, and Saturday morning in that era of 36-hole final days at the Open: "Open Saturdays." Souchak, a former football end at Duke, led the first round by a stroke, the second by three, and the third by two, despite double-bogeying 18 Saturday morning after flinching at a camera click—a camera click that might have changed everything—and hitting his ball out of bounds. Palmer stood a full seven shots and 14 players behind—tied, in fact, for 15th place. In all of the prior Opens, no one had ever made up that much ground in a concluding round, and nobody has done it since.

In the lunchroom, Palmer grabbed a hamburger and joined Venturi, reigning PGA champion Bob Rosburg, Dan Jenkins, and Bob Drum. "What would sixty-five do this afternoon?" he asked his friend Drum, an oversized personality, a big man in every way, louder than a checkered sports jacket. As Palmer liked to say of the Pittsburgh newspaperman, "If Drum was there, you *knew* he was there."

"It wouldn't do *YOU* any good!" Drum bellowed in reply. "You're out of it! Done! Cooked! Stick a fork in yourself!"

"That would make my score two-eighty," Palmer continued undaunted. "Doesn't two-eighty win Opens?"

"Yeah," Jenkins said, "when Hogan shoots them."

"Besides," Drum said, "only one guy ever shot sixty-five in the final round of an Open. Walter Burkemo."

Jenkins was astounded Bob had this statistic at the ready. The Drummer wasn't exactly a stats man. Actually, Dan doubted it was true. But it was.

"I still think I can drive that first green," Palmer said.

"Go ahead, and make another double-bogey while you're at it," Drum told him. "Why don't you play the hole like a pro for a change, tee off with an iron for placement, guarantee yourself at least a par, and still have a putt for birdie?" Leaving the hamburger uneaten, Palmer stormed out. "I was hot," he said.

The first at Cherry Hills, a 346-yard par 4, was the kind of hole golfers say "is right there in front of you." You could see everything from the tee. "Elevated tee," Palmer said, "with a severe drop. Trees on the left, ditch on the right, a trickling stream—that's where the members usually ended up. That's where I went on Thursday, making six. Serious USGA [United States Golf Association] rough fronting the green. A real bunker there, too, with grass growing in it. My second day, a bogey. That morning, a par. But I was still convinced it was an eagle hole. We're at altitude, remember. Mile high."

He was drop-kicking his driver slightly in those days. "Just microscopically," he said, but enough to lessen backspin. "No good on a rock-hard U.S. Open green three hundred and fifty yards away. But I'd arrived in Denver figuring if you could bounce your ball through the rough in front of that green [instead of flying it over], maybe the grass would kill it enough so it wouldn't race away."

The time was 1:44 when he pulled his driver out of the bag. Not that he was wearing a watch. "Never have worn one playing golf," Palmer said. "I see them on players' wrists today, but I don't get it. Just one more potential distraction while you're addressing the ball, one more little inhibitor to the free flow of a golf swing."

The sun was so bright, it made slits of his eyes. "The arc of the ball was perfect," he said. "It slowed down in the grass and stopped in the middle of the green [twenty feet away]. I missed it. But you can't tell me the birdie I made there was the equivalent of the birdie I might have made the 'pro' way, as Drum described it, because it wasn't. This was boldness over meticulousness [Hogan], and boldness was going to carry the day."

He missed the second green but chipped in from 30 feet for another birdie. "I birdied the third, too, and the fourth," he said, curling in about a 20-footer there. "Maybe it was shorter; felt longer. Birdied the sixth as well, and the seventh. [Six under par for seven holes.] When did Jenkins tell you he and Drum showed up?"

About then. They came galloping over the hill, wheezing like sportswriters. Before hitting his drive at the 10th hole, Palmer walked over to where the two men stood at the tree line, and, without a word, fished a pack of Winstons out of Dan's breast pocket. Lighting up and striding back to the tee, he said, "Fancy meeting you guys here," and kept the whole pack.

Palmer went out in 30. "Damn!" he said. "If I hadn't bogeyed eight [blasting from a greenside bunker, missing a three-and-a-half-footer], it would have been twenty-nine. I'd have been the first man ever to do it in an Open." He caught Souchak at the 10th. Soon the pars began. Move over, Walter Burkemo. Palmer shot 65. Two-eighty *does* win U.S. Opens.

Most of the crowd's attention that Saturday was focused on 47-year-old Hogan, the four-time Open champion, and 20-year-old Jack Nicklaus, paired together for rounds three and four. Nicklaus said, "My dad came to me Friday night and told me, 'Guess what, Jack. You're playing with Hogan tomorrow.' I couldn't believe it."

All week Charlie Nicklaus, a Columbus pharmacist and former Ohio State and semipro lineman, had the company of his irascible friend Woody Hayes, the Buckeyes football coach, who, offended by the short shrift Charlie's boy was getting from Hogan's galleries, invented marshaling; also, Woody called in the birdies and bogeys each night to the sports desks of the *Columbus Dispatch* and the *Columbus Citizen-Journal*, both unable to afford the fare to Colorado.

Hogan held a piece of the lead in the late afternoon when he reached the 17th hole, a par 5 with a moat guarding the green. In his impeccable manner, he had hit all 34 greens in regulation that day. But for some reason—perhaps because he hadn't been putting especially well for a considerable while (it was beginning to take him 12, 13, 14 seconds just to draw the putter blade back from the ball, and the tentative prod he employed in bungling a 10-foot birdie putt at 16 actually made young Nicklaus shiver), or maybe because Ben knew Palmer was somewhere behind him and wouldn't be playing safe at 17—he took a chance at spinning his third shot close and screwed a half wedge off the far bank into the front of the moat. Removing his right shoe and sock, rolling up the one pant leg, he stepped down into the water and, teetering like an uncertain flamingo, manufactured a commendable recovery but just for a two-putt bogey. Following a crooked tee-ball into another water hazard at 18, he was done. The three putts that topped off a triple-bogey 7 didn't matter.

"After he gambled and lost at seventeen," Nicklaus said, "he just went flat. He was completely drained—of drive, energy, concentration. It was all he could do to finish the round. Everyone knew the Hogan way was never to take on the odds in pressure situations. Let the other fellow make the crucial mistake [a system Jack co-opted as his own]. What got into Hogan at Cherry Hills? Palmer, I guess."

Sometime later, back in that 17th fairway, amateur Don Cherry stood over a perfect drive, waiting to go for the green in two. Sam Snead, who had shot his way out of contention by then, sidled up to his playing partner and drawled, "Son, you're gonna win the U.S. Open."

In 1976, I was playing an Ohio course called Beckett Ridge with an old National Football League flanker named Billy Gambrell. A single joined us: bald, short, 50-ish, bowlegged. After eight holes, I realized he hadn't missed any fairways, hadn't missed any greens, and had two-putted everything. "Give me your name one more time," I said.

Don Cherry.

"When Sam came over to me to say, 'Son, you're gonna win the U.S. Open,' I promise you, I don't remember a single thing that happened after that."

"He did it on purpose, you know."

"Of course."

Cherry said, "Can you imagine what winning the Open would have meant to me? An amateur. An amateur in show business. An amateur in show business married to Miss America. An amateur in show business married to Miss America and with a top-five record, 'Band of Gold,' on *Your Hit Parade*. *'I've never wanted wealth untold / My life has*

one design / A simple little band of gold / To prove that you are mine . . ."'
Dorothy Collins and Snooky Lanson had sung so many different vari-
ations of it, week after week for Lucky Strike cigarettes, the public had
begun to think it was *their* hit.

"Most of all," Cherry said, "can you imagine what it would have
meant to my sponsors?"

"Who were your sponsors?"

"The Mafia."

Cherry also hit the moat. He would have needed a 68 to tie Palmer.
Instead he shot 72 to tie Hogan. With a 71, Nicklaus finished second
to Arnold, two strokes back. They had begun. "If I could have done
the thinking for that kid I played with today," Hogan said, "he'd
have won by ten shots."

"If I'd have putted for Mr. Hogan," Nicklaus said, "*he'd* have
won by ten." Even at the age of 20, Jack had to have the final word.

"Charge!"—once the bugle call of Teddy Roosevelt and the U.S.
Cavalry—entered the lexicon of golf. The game had changed: from
meticulous to bold. An 11-year-old named Skip Manning retrieved
the red visor Palmer spun into the gallery in celebration. Manning
returned it 48 years later.

Jerry Barber, who was in second place after each of the first three
rounds but fell to ninth at the end, had the most memorable line of
the inquest. "Arnold Palmer," he said in a tone of wonder, "isn't at
all impressed with the fact that he is Arnold Palmer." Subsequently,
Herbert Warren Wind put the same sentiment slightly differently in
the *New Yorker*:

> His ability to perform wonders is based on the honest conviction
> that they are not wonders at all. In a recent conversation with

some friends, more or less as an aside, he announced that he felt his game had progressed to the point where, as often as not, he could get a birdie on any hole where he had to. Palmer, however, hasn't a drop of arrogance in his makeup, and when he is seen in action in the final clutch, what most forcibly impresses the spectator is his completely unfeigned confidence that almost nothing is beyond him. He moves down the fairway toward the ball in long eager strides, a cigarette in his hand, his eyes on the distant green as he considers every aspect of his coming approach shot. They are eyes with warmth and humor in them as well as determination, for this is a mild and pleasant man. Palmer's chief attraction is his dashing style of play. He is always attacking the course, being temperamentally incapable of playing it safe instead of shooting directly at the flag. His addiction to this sort of gambling, coupled with his love of hard hitting, can make Palmer's rounds, when his timing is off, one long, enervating sequence of sprayed drives and hazardous recoveries from trouble.

Drum's terser account for the *Pittsburgh Press* ran not on the front page of the sports section but on page one of the paper: "DENVER, June 18—Arnold Palmer, who had wrestled with the Cherry Hills golf course for three rounds, caught it in a stranglehold on the final 18 today and pulled off one of the most unbelievable victories in National Open history. . . ." While inserting extra facts in the story and generally dulling it up for page one, copy editors inadvertently dropped Drum's byline. But drinkers at Dante's or in the Travel Bar at the Pittsburgher Hotel recognized their friend's voice. He had signed it with his style. "Do you know how many Arnold Palmer stories I wrote?" Drum said years later. "Five thousand, quoting him in every one. And half the time I couldn't find him. Palmer still thinks he said all those things."

A month later, with the Masters and U.S. Open in his pocket, Arnold felt obligated to make his first bid for an Open Championship, what only America calls "the British Open." "That explains the *timing* of my first trip over," he said, "but I always knew I'd be going eventually. The reason was my father. [He was the reason for almost everything.] Pap told me, 'Boy, if you're going to be a golfer, you have no choice but to be a *world* golfer, because golf is a *world* game.'" In that spirit, Palmer flew to Ireland directly from Denver to partner with Snead in a Canada Cup at Portmarnock, which they won. "Drum was along," Arnold said (on a busman's holiday, after his paper recoiled at the estimated cost). "Bob and I were drinking on the plane, big surprise. We were talking about Bobby Jones and his amateur Grand Slam, the Impregnable Quadrilateral [British Open and Amateur, U.S. Open and Amateur, all in 1930]. One of us, I think it was me, said, 'Why don't we invent a new, *professional* Grand Slam [the Masters, U.S. Open, British Open, and PGA]?' We drank to it."

No one is exactly sure where or when golf was born, though the Romans, Dutch, Chinese, and a few others have been willing to accept partial responsibility. The consensus is, it came from Scotland. So, whatever their ancestry, golfers are disposed to believe that, in some essential way, they did, too. Palmer certainly thought so. Pap was Scotch-Irish.

For the Open Championship's centenary renewal in 1960, the pinwheel had spun back around to golf's capital, St. Andrews, in the county and kingdom of Fife. St. Andrews is a windblown and pewter-gray university town with Baskervillean spires, ruined turrets, and students wearing tattered red academic gowns by the North Sea. It smells like Cape Cod. The stations of the cross are the Swilcan Burn and Bridge, the Principal's Nose, the Beardies, the Coffins, Granny Clark's Wynd, Hell Bunker, Strath Bunker, the Road Hole, and the Valley of Sin. On the 18th green, the ghost of Doug Sanders is frozen forever in a magenta sweater over a 30-inch putt.

At first glance, the Old Course at St. Andrews (the *New* Course turned 100 years old in 1995) is an unimpressive muni congested and clogged with bracken and broom. At a 100th glance, a 1,000th, it's a basilica. By the likes of Mary Queen of Scots, golf has been perpetrated there for 600 years.

"Snead won his Open Championship at St. Andrews," Palmer said. "To Sam it looked like an abandoned golf course. That's what he told the Fleet Street press, pissing off all the locals. But I could see what he meant."

The first thing Arnold did was hire a second-generation St. Andrews caddie named Tip. Tip Anderson.

"Excuse me," Tip said several years later, tilting back a 16-ounce can of McEwan's Export ale at 7:00 in the morning, "I'm just having my breakfast." He was a tall man, slender as a 1-iron, white-headed under a cap with a beak instead of a bill that suggested a fisherman before a golfer. Anderson wore a tan windbreaker with a military cut of the kind TV anchormen rock on location. Under tufted brows, he had attentive eyes. His nose was a veiny purple masterpiece.

Palmer seemed partial to caddies whose noses could light the way back to the clubhouse in the dark. One of his domestic bagmen, Creamy Carolan, had a red rubber ball in the center of his face like the sorrowful Ringling Bros. and Barnum & Bailey clown Emmett Kelly. Tip was the opposite of sorrowful.

"My father," Anderson said, "was a caddie before me who packed for Walter Hagen and Henry Cotton—*Sir* Henry Cotton—but never won an Open Championship [though those two, between them, won seven]. He was 'Tip,' too; that is, he wasn't 'Jim,' either. I was an observant kid. I listened. They don't listen, these boys. That's the way in all trades now, all over the world, I suppose."

Once a junior champion, Anderson carried a 3 handicap in 1960.

"It was funny," he said, "but I was exactly two clubs shorter than Arnie. To the foot, maybe even the inch. My three-iron was his five-. We didn't chart yardages back then. We eyeballed it. He and I got along brilliantly."

They made a ragged start, though. "Oh, dear, disastrous," Tip said. "Our first practice round in bad weather. He shot eighty-seven. Bloody hell! You know, until the wind whips up off the Firth of Tay, Americans are forever mistaking this for an easy golf course. Arnie did, too. But now it was blowing a hoolie, at least fifty, maybe sixty miles an hour. No exaggeration. We were playing with Roberto De Vicenzo, the Senor, and Arnie was full of temper and wanting to quit mid-round. 'C'mon, stop your crying,' I said. 'You've come all the way to St. Andrews to win the Open.' He took that from me. What a grand man he is.

"Well, we got beat one shot by Kel Nagle [an elegant Australian, who required nine fewer putts, four to Palmer's 10 at the Road Hole alone. "Three three-putts," Arnold said contemptuously. "I should have played that hole in an ambulance."]. But we would win the next two Opens, at Royal Birkdale and Troon. From day one at Birkdale, a Wednesday start back then, we were locked up with Dai Rees [the Welshman, runner-up to Hogan at Carnoustie in 1953 and to Peter Thomson at Birkdale in 1954]. As usual, the last thirty-six holes were scheduled for Friday."

But what Tip called "a Brobdingnagian gale" blew the froth off the Irish Sea, and the R&A postponed the final two rounds until Saturday with a flat proviso: "The Championship Committee of the Royal and Ancient Golf Club have decided that the 1961 Open Championship must end on Saturday whether four rounds have been completed or not. If it is impossible to complete the four rounds, the 1961 Championship will be declared void, and neither the cup nor the medals will be presented."

"So even as it was continuing," Tip said, "nobody knew if the tournament was going to count. *Our* tournament, Arnie's and mine, seemed to take place entirely on the sixteenth hole, a three-hundred-seventy-yard par four. In a greenside bunker the second day, Arnie had already twisted his nails into the sand and was halfway into his swing when a puff of wind hit the ball. Not only was the shot ruined, a penalty stroke had to be added later, turning a double bogey into a seven. But, considering we caught the worst of the conditions, seventy-three was still a hell of a score. That tied us with Nagle a shot behind Rees and Harold Henning at the halfway point."

At the sixteenth again, the rain was lighter but the wind was severe. Tip said, "Arnie tried to hit an even lower drive than his usual, but the wind swept it away like a leaf, nearly out of bounds."

Palmer beat Tip to the ball, blinking out of the underbrush, only 125 yards from the green but with a wall of gorse blocking the way. "Too tall to go over," Anderson said, "too thick to go through. I asked him, 'Is there an opening?'

"'Tip,' he said, 'there's always an opening—if you can see it.'

"'Shouldn't we play safe and try to punch out to the fairway?'

"'No,' he said, 'we shouldn't.'

"'Coming out of that tangle, the ball could go anywhere.'

"He didn't say anything to that. After what seemed like five minutes' deliberation, Arnie yanked out a six-iron—nearly clouting me in the face with it. He choked up considerably. With just the proper degree of loft, the precise amount of dig, coiling and uncoiling every grain of his power, he smashed the ball through the smallest little stained-glass window I've ever seen in a bush—in fact, I didn't see it. But I heard the click, followed by the roar. Hitting the wet green, the ball stopped dead. We'd two-putt it. Simultaneously our eyes went to the scar on the ground and then to each other. There's a plaque there today. There is. Truly. You could go find it."

Wind-worn, sandblasted, and as mossy-green as the neglected headstone of a forgotten man, it reads:

ARNOLD PALMER
The Open Championship
14th July 1961

(The wrong date, by the way. The rained-out day was the 14th.)

"Executing a golf shot is the craft," Palmer said, seated at his desk. "Seeing it is the art."

Tip continued:

"I know in the end we pipped Rees by only the solitary stroke. [The Welshman had to come home in 31 to make it that close.] Still, after our miraculous six-iron, I didn't for one second think we were going to lose, and neither did Arnie."

Palmer said, "I can't tell you exactly what I did to make that shot come off, because I don't know. I really don't. First, I imagined what it would look like in flight. Next, I felt it in my hands. It's a hard thing to explain to people, but, from all the golf shots I had hit in my life, my hands just knew what to do on their own."

A year later, Troon.

"Oh, I've never witnessed golf like that at Troon," Tip said. "I don't think anyone has. The first day, on his way to an eighty, Nicklaus carded a ten at the eleventh hole, the Railway. Par five [at the time, par four now]. Four hundred and eighty yards. Short as par fives go, but with a landing area off the tee too pinched in for any kind of safe wood shot. One day Arnie reached the green with a pair of one-irons—or maybe it was a one-iron and a two-iron. Either way, the second was longer than the first, and he holed a twenty-five-footer for eagle three. I told him, 'Now, that's just not fair.' What a smile he gave me. We built a ten-shot lead in the final round, then took the commercial road home for a sixty-nine."

Palmer won by six strokes over Nagle. "Winning the Open Championship, and then winning it again," Arnold said, "you don't even dare to *dream* things like that." No American had done it since Hagen in 1928 and '29. *The Haig*. First Yank ever to win an Open Championship. "Winnie told me about Hagen before I teed off in the final round," Palmer said. "One of the writers had told her. She always figured I could use a little added incentive. You know, I ended up receiving a congratulatory phone call from Hagen, who was seventy." From his Michigan home, Hagen told *Golf World* magazine, "Palmer is one of the best players we ever had. Troon is a tricky course, and you have to have great knowledge and ability to beat it. You can't say enough about his ability, his will to win, his concentration. He's worthy of everything that is going to come to him now."

With a 276 total, Palmer trimmed two strokes off the tournament record. For the rest of his life, at any time of the night or day, he had it in his power to call back the sensation of being engulfed by what seemed like all of Scotland as he walked the last hole in their company. Breaking out of the crush and into the clear, he staggered like a happy drunk, almost going to his knees a couple of times.

"I was at Royal Troon in sixty-two," said the Scottish journalist Renton Laidlaw, then of the *London Evening Standard*, later of the British Broadcasting Company. "Well, it wasn't *Royal* Troon then, it was just Troon. I was in the middle of that mob scene. Poor Kel Nagle was trapped in the tide, too. So many people wanted to touch Palmer that day. He was like the Pied Piper, struggling to push his way through the masses and loving every minute of it. All of the United Kingdom embraced him, many literally. They thought he could do anything. He played golf just the way they themselves wanted to. As everyone knows, you've got to be hard to win these tournaments, and a wee bit selfish at times. But he was such a pleasant character, so humble, that the Scots in particular were happy to see him as one of them. From then on, he didn't belong only to America. He was ours, too."

"Good old Tip," Palmer said, "did more than just lead me around all the courses over there; he marched me through all the history at the same time. In St. Andrews, I stayed at the Rusacks Hotel right off the eighteenth fairway, just a short walk from the cathedral bell tower and the graveyard where Old Tom Morris and Young Tom Morris [winners of eight of the first 12 Open Championships] are buried. Tip took me up and down the rows of tombstones, pointing out the monuments for the likes of Allan Robertson [the estimable player and nonpareil club maker], and telling me everyone's stories as vividly as if Tip had been there in the early eighteen hundreds. Maybe he was. How can a golfer not be moved by all of that?"

In 1964, when next the rota twirled around to St. Andrews, Palmer was feeling exhausted back home ("fried" was his word) and reluctantly sent regrets. "But he also sent me Tony Lema," Anderson said. "That is, he lent Tony two of his most valuable possessions: one of Arnie's favorite old putters, and me. Lovely Tony. He and I [and the enchanted putter] beat Nicklaus by five. So, over a stretch of five years, I had three gold medals and a silver in the tournament my dad never won. They can't take that away from me, can they?"

No, they can't.

"As I keep telling Arnie, 'You've won two Open Championships; I've won three.' He takes that from me. What a grand man he is."

In a way, Palmer's pal Lema was a creation of Arnold's aide, Doc Giffin, going back to Doc's public relations days with the tour. At the Orange County Open in Costa Mesa, looking for his first official PGA victory, the 28-year-old Californian Lema dipped into the press cooler, raised a bottle of beer to the four or five reporters present, and said, "If I win tomorrow, men, we're having champagne."

A lightbulb came on over Doc's head. "I got ahold of the club manager," he said, "and he got ahold of the wine." The next day

Bob Rosburg was defeated in a playoff and "Champagne Tony Lema" was born. (Shortly Doc secured him an endorsement deal with Moët.) Lema and his wife, Betty, died in 1966 when a small airplane crashed into the Lansing Sportsman's Club golf course in Illinois. They were on their way to an outing that paid him $2,000 and came with a complimentary plane ride.

"Lovely Tony," Tip whispered. "All that champagne down the drain."

In the fourth leg of the new Grand Slam, the 1960 PGA Championship at Firestone Country Club in Akron, Palmer shot a 3-under-par 67 to lead the first round and Snead by a stroke. But a three-footer he had missed for eagle at two was still in his craw when he double-bogeyed three. In fact, it was still there when he triple-bogeyed 16 on Sunday. Palmer tied for seventh place five strokes behind the winner, Jay Hebert. By a total of six shots, he missed the Slam.

Arnie's final port of call for the year was the Hickok Belt banquet in Rochester, New York, where the professional athlete of 1960 would be named and awarded $10,000. Nominee Roger Maris of the New York Yankees was expecting to see teammate Mickey Mantle and football players Sam Huff, Kyle Rote, and Johnny Unitas but was surprised to find a golfer among his competition. Looking Palmer up and down, he said, "What the *fuck* are you doing here?"

Later, the Masters and U.S. Open champion just happened to be standing next to the outfielder when the winner was announced— *Arnold Palmer.* "I leaned over," Palmer said with a twinkle, "and whispered, 'What the *fuck* are you doing here?'"

Maris won the Belt in 1961 after beating Babe Ruth's home run record. "We ended up friends," Arnold said. The way almost everyone ended up with Arnie.

Sports Illustrated looked past Bill Mazeroski, Norm Van Brocklin, Bill Russell, Gordie Howe, Joe Bellino, Jerry Lucas, Pelé, Neale

Fraser, Bill Hartack, Floyd Patterson, and all of the Olympic heroes from Wilma Rudolph and Rafer Johnson to Cassius Clay and Oscar Robertson and Carol Heiss, crowning Palmer Sportsman of the Year. The presentation was made on a Sunday night, live on *The Ed Sullivan Show.*

For dominating the game of golf with a bold determination while adding to its splendor with genuine graciousness and charm, the editors of Sports Illustrated *award the Grecian amphora, a classic symbol of pure excellence. . . .*

Staffer Ray Cave wrote in the magazine:

Nowhere did a 1960 sports personality command his field with quite the overwhelming ability and natural charm of that 31-year-old golf professional from Latrobe, Pa., Arnold Daniel Palmer. Early in the year he won three tournaments in a row, the first time that has been done since 1952. [The Texas Open, the Baton Rouge Open, and the Pensacola Open, three first-place checks that totaled $6,800.] Then in April he came from behind to win the Masters by getting birdies on the last two holes in one of his typical final-day rushes to victory. Having hit, Palmer is down the fairway at a pace that leaves followers panting behind. He is literally racing to the next shot. His stride as much as says, "You think that shot was something? Watch this one."

In June he won the National Open, starting the last 18 holes with a prodigious 346-yard drive to the first green at Colorado's Cherry Hills Country Club . . . lost the British Open at St. Andrews by a single stroke when another driving finish fell just short. [Four shots behind Nagle with six holes to play, Palmer all but got there.] The British were as much impressed with his graciousness after what must have been a disappointing loss as they were with his excellent play. . . . Thus he has ended his sport's long wait for a fresh, vibrant personality, bringing a new age to golf: The Palmer Era.

Winning eight tournaments (40 years would go by before someone—you might be able to guess who—won nine), Arnold earned a record $80,738 in official prize money (some $30,000 more than second place, bettering Ted Kroll's $72,836 from 1956). At the same time, he became a staple in the top five. With Heinz ketchup (headquartered in Pittsburgh), L&M cigarettes, Munsingwear sports shirts, and (just as odd as it sounds) a string of laundry and dry-cleaning franchises, super-agent-to-be Mark McCormack boosted Palmer's total income for the year to around $190,000.

Arnie appeared on *What's My Line?* Because his name was thought to be a bigger tip-off than his face, he signed in on the chalkboard as "X." "Frankly, had he had a hat on," panelist Martin Gabel later told moderator John Daly (not the golfer), "I would have known him." After Bennett Cerf narrowed the inquiry to sports and then golf, Gabel, Arlene Francis, and Dorothy Kilgallen sang out together: "Are you Arnold Palmer?"

Almost.

2

1929

"Taking the honey out, putting the sugar back in."

"LATROBE ISN'T JUST THE place where I'm from," Palmer said. "It's who I am."

He made his entrance on September 10, 1929. The Roaring '20s and Jazz Age were going out, the Great Depression was coming in. And Bobby Jones was just about to win everything.

Palmer was really from two places: Latrobe and, three or four miles south, Youngstown, where he went to grade school (in a two-room schoolhouse) and did most of his adolescent carousing; three places, if you count Pittsburgh, 40 miles to the west, where the main exports were steel and quarterbacks.

Johnny Unitas, Joe Montana, Dan Marino, Joe Namath, Jim Kelly, George Blanda, Babe Parilli, Johnny Lujack . . . Palmer shared traits with all of them. "Arnie plays golf," Johnny Miller said, "like others play football." Palmer played a little football himself, in junior high, unconventionally marrying the positions of offensive halfback and defensive tackle, until golf preoccupied him.

He seemed to favor every Pittsburgh sports legend: the light-heavyweight boxer Billy Conn, a steamfitter's son (clocking in at five ten and a half, 175 pounds in his prime, Palmer had the easy grace and natural slouch of a prizefighter); the burly tight end Mike Ditka, a welder's boy; the resolute shortstop Honus Wagner, whose father and brothers were coal miners. Palmer was as indigenous to the region as the Mellons, Carnegies, and Rooneys. He was loamy meadows and smoky skies. He fit right in with the dancer Gene Kelly; the historian David McCullough; Sean Thornton, hero of *The Quiet Man* ("Steel, Michaeleen, steel in pig iron furnaces so hot a man forgets his fear of hell"); and Bob Drum.

"Pittsburgh was hard work, hard work, hard work," said Jim Kelly on the telephone. "My father held down three jobs at a time. He worked in the mills. He was a machinist. He did pretty much everything. If you checked his hands, you'd know what I'm talking about. Those sandpaper hands." Namath said, "All of Western Pennsylvania was blue-collar territory, certainly in the forties and fifties, when the steel mills and the coal mines were going full blast." "The kids got out of the mills and mines," Parilli said, "but they stayed mills and mines kids."

Montana and Kelly joked that it was the beer. "Joe says Rolling Rock," Kelly said. "I say Iron City." (Palmer's brand was Rolling Rock.) Their folks drank one or the other, and out of all those suds came all of these quarterbacks. "From Lujack to Marc Bulger," said Kelly. "Don't forget Bulger. And Notre Dame would say don't forget Terry Hanratty, either."

If it wasn't the beer, might it have been something just as golden and even more homegrown? Like an entire community founded on a single proposition, that *what you get out of anything depends on what you put into it.* "We were all raised on that," Kelly said. Arnie, too.

His father Milfred (Deacon to most, Deke to some, Pap to Arnold) was a workingman like the others—same as his own father, a housepainter. Arnie's paternal great-grandfather, who married for a third time at the age of 70, was a farmer who settled the Palmers in Latrobe. Most visitors took it for an exceedingly unremarkable black-and-white town of work-a-day people and honest grime. But a few could see a full-color cover painting by Norman Rockwell for the *Saturday Evening Post*. At Strickler's drugstore, the banana split was invented in 1904. In 1974, 80-year-old Rockwell painted a portrait of Arnie.

With his own sandpaper hands Deacon built first a golf course and then a golfer in the shade of the Alleghenies. Latrobe is usually described as "nestled in the foothills of the Allegheny Mountains," though there is no sensation of a mountain, or even a foothill, just a leafy and rolling green expanse of lush countryside and riotous red pheasant colors in the fall. During the tightest years, for an additional paycheck, Deacon put in some nights and off-seasons dodging molten sparks in the factories, but far preferred moonlighting as manager of the poolroom at the Youngstown Hotel. He liked running things. He liked the rough-and-tumble of the billiard parlor. He liked bouncing the occasional idiot. And he loved boilermakers. Arnie's father had a bit of a thirst.

As a boy, Deacon was bedridden with polio. Small towns weren't overflowing with medical specialists or rehab centers for invalids. So, on his own, he just got up one day and, for the second time, taught himself how to walk. With torturous calisthenics, chinning himself first with one arm and then the other, he retooled his upper body into an engine block while ignoring a deformed foot. He bobbled gently, like an uneven table, but nobody ever looked at him and saw a cripple.

He had a corkscrew golf swing entirely of his own design that minimized his legs and produced low, hard draws that a tall center fielder might have caught. And he knew how to get the ball in the hole.

At the age of 16, Deacon was one of the original roustabouts who dug out the boulders and helped shape the routing of the nine-hole Latrobe Country Club course that opened for play in 1921. Civic leaders conceived the course in response to and out of admiration for Jones. Five years later Deacon was appointed greenkeeper; seven years after that, greenkeeper/pro (though still mostly greenkeeper). He was much more fairway tractor driver than pro shop shirt sales-man. "They hired me for both jobs," he told Drum in 1962, "be-cause they had to cut expenses during the Depression. They said it was just until things got better. It's funny, though—I still hold both positions. Guess the Depression is still on."

From Pap, Arnie learned many important things, like integrity and how to hold a golf club. Pap installed English professional Harry Vardon's overlapping system and bolted it down before a baseball bat could corrupt the boy. Arnold said, "He put my hands on the club, well, just the way they are now, and told me in no uncertain terms, 'Don't you ever change this,' and I never really did. To most people, a proper golf grip is awkward as hell at first. But I was lucky. My hands were placed on the club so early that it always felt second nature to me. Thanks to Pap, I never had to unlearn anything."

The contribution of his mother, who came from railroading stock, made all the difference. Doris Morrison was as light and del-icate as a scarf, ready company, and a natural communicator. She liked people and they liked her. ("She was a ham," Winnie Palmer said. "Arnie's a ham.") Pap was always prodding his son to be tougher and try harder and succeed more. But whatever the boy did pleased Doris, provided he was kind. "No player ever had a more nurtur-ing golf mom," he said. "Her mellowness, willingness to feel things and to *show* her feelings, was a salvation for me. She was a gentle, generous person, but I never felt as if I was being soft by going to her. I sought her out because she was the counterbalance I needed to Pap, who was tough and hard-core and refused to give me a compliment. I was always afraid to lose because of my father's reaction, but I never felt that way about my mother. No matter what, she was the one who understood. She always took up for me. All that was so important—much more important than I realized at the time."

In the earliest days his waist and hips were so narrow they could barely sustain his trousers. Evenings, after dinner, he trailed behind Doris as she played twilight golf (not particularly well) with two neighborhood friends. She would chide her son as they walked, "Yank up those britches now before they fall off." The way Arnie hitched at his pants in mid-stride became a nervous habit, and a trademark.

"I used to get so tired of hearing my father telling me what to do," he said, "how to hold my knife, fork, and spoon, and leave the table if you're going to sneeze. *You don't sneeze at the table!* I used to think, *Isn't he ever going to get off my back?* And, at the same time, all of those things at some point made me love him more."

Arnie didn't have to be taught to love golf. "Arnold never caught the golf bug," said the British writer Peter Dobereiner. "He was born with it like a hereditary disease."

Using a sawed-off women's brassie (2-wood) he began to play at the age of three and turned pro at seven when Latrobe member Helen Fritz offered him a nickel to hit her drive over a ditch at the sixth hole, not too far from the small first white- and then green-frame house (only two rooms with heat) that the club provided the Palmers. After adjusting a cap pistol strapped to one hip, he took a whirling cut that brought to mind a finish-line flagman or a revolving lawn sprinkler. High forehead. Dented nose. Look of eagles. Mrs. Fritz's ball floated down like a paratrooper onto the fairway. Every Tuesday morning thereafter (Ladies Day at Latrobe), leaning against a tree in his backyard, he was available to belt dowagers' drives for five cents. "Some of them," he said, "were slow to pay."

He sat in his father's lap as Deacon steered the tractor, dragging multiple mowers. Then, almost before he was big enough or strong enough to manage it, Arnold drove the machine alone. He had to stand up for leverage and wrangle the wheel like a rodeo bulldogger twisting the horns of a rank steer. As a result, his arms puffed out into parts of a much larger boy.

A sister, Lois Jean (called Cheech), followed him by a couple of years. They weren't Jem and Scout, but as she said appreciatively, "Arnie took care of me." He included her in as many of his adventures as possible. Living on a golf course where you're not a member carries with it a definite feeling of isolation and loneliness. "We played cowboys and Indians," Cheech said. She was the Indians. After a gap of a decade and a half, a brother and another sister came late. "Arnie was fifteen years older than I," brother Jerry said, "so our parents in effect had two families." Because of that timing, and because of his connection to Pap, Arnie operated like an only child, or at least a special son.

"Just where we are now is a history in itself," Palmer said in his office, spinning his chair around and gazing out the window. "When I learned to shoot a shotgun, my father and I—he taught me—we walked that hillside over there and shot pheasants and rabbits and squirrels, and took them down and cleaned them in a stream right over here about two hundred yards away. My mother would soak them in salt water overnight, and we'd have them for supper the next day.

"Right here, right on the edge of this rise, an old oak tree fell over, like that one over there. See the squirrel climbing up? The trunk was rotten—I'll never forget this. A bunch of honeybees had moved in. Have you ever seen a honeycomb? Well, this one was full of honey. I mean, absolutely, like *that* . . ." Mimicking an exaggerating fisherman, he spread his hands wide, massive hands right out of

Winesburg, Ohio or *Of Mice and Men*. "A blacksmith's hands, a timber cutter's arms," Deacon would say years later. "There are only two ways to get hands and arms like that, swinging an ax or swinging a golf club."

". . . and my dad says, 'Now, Arnie, we're going to take this honey home and give it to your mother, and we're going to eat it. But we've got to get two five-pound bags of sugar. When we take the honey out, we're going to put those two bags of sugar right there, so the bees can have their food.' By God, we did it. I was about seven or eight years old."

Palmer would spend his entire life taking the honey out and putting the sugar back in.

"My father taught me discipline," he said, "before he taught me golf." Deacon was fanatical about good manners, deportment, honesty, and good manners again. *Tyrannical* isn't a bad word, either. Largely out of loyalty to Pap, young Arnie loved and loathed Latrobe Country Club. That is, he loved the golf course and loathed the club. Deacon was treated like an employee, and he treated himself that way. He took his lunch in the kitchen. Arnold said, "My father never set foot in the locker room, dining room, or bar without the expressed permission of a member." (Until 1971, that is, when Arnie bought the course and club—lock, stock, and a subdivision of houses. Everything from the airport to the phone book came to bear his name. Like Mr. Potter in Bedford Falls, but a benevolent version, he seemed to own the whole town.)

"I wasn't permitted to swim in the club pool or to play with the members' children," he said. Instead he swam (with the snakes) in a rocky creek that was the source of the pool's water, "and peed in it, too," he said, "a little present for the country club kids." He could caddie, even compete in the caddies' tournaments—and he won more than a few of them. "But my father wouldn't let me take the trophies home. 'They're for other men's sons,' he said."

Palmer's favorite boyhood memory was of a day in the pro shop when one of the club's grandees was chewing him out for being underfoot, and assuring Deacon that any number of servile positions could be arranged for Arnie in the mills. "Pap lit into this guy, taking up for me—and, the way I looked at it, taking up for himself." More than one member expressed the view that Deacon was making a mistake teaching his son to hit the ball so hard. (Sometimes both feet left the ground.) Deacon's philosophy was: *Knock the hell out of it, go and find it, then knock the hell out of it again.* Arnie said, "He told all of the critics the same thing: 'You take care of yourself, I'll take care of my boy.'" That phrase, *my boy*, meant everything to Arnie. "Funny, I never did hit the ball hard enough to suit Pap," he said.

On Mondays, when the course was closed, he was cleared to play, and at the age of 12 he broke 40. ("I was seven when I broke fifty-five. Then I went after fifty, then forty-five, and finally forty.") On the other days, before the members arrived and after they departed, he could practice, but exclusively in the rough ("in among the elms and oaks," as he said). Pap didn't allow pitching or chipping to the greens, and at that time the course had no bunkers to speak of. Sand was too expensive to maintain. "Because of the course he grew up on, I'm sure," Gary Player said, "Arnold was an incredible driver of the golf ball and a tremendous iron player, but a crappy wedge player. Crappy! And a terrible bunker player. But, oh, man, what a great driver! Maybe the best driver the world ever knew. I remember a number one wood he had, the most wicked-looking thing you ever saw in your life. It must have had eleven degrees of loft, and of course he needed it—he was a very shut-faced player. I tell you, he could hit that thing so straight and so far. Such a magnificent driver. Such a wonderful putter, too. I've seen other players who weren't afraid to knock the ball five and six feet past, who trusted themselves to hole those comebackers one after another after another. But none of them could touch Palmer. He was the inventor.

"Just as he won some tournaments taking unnecessary gambles, he lost some tournaments taking unnecessary gambles. But that was Arnold. That was the endearment. He did absolutely everything the same damn way. It wasn't his nature to lag a putt because it wasn't his nature to lag period. He woke up charging, charging, charging. He fell out of bed with this tremendous charisma, just fell out of bed with it. And I'll tell you something else: the rough was his friend."

Palmer made up games in the Latrobe rough, like Phil Mickelson in his backyard in San Diego, concocting unplayable lies and then playing them. "I'd have two or three balls going at a time," Palmer said, "make a tournament of it. One ball would be Byron Nelson's, my favorite golfer, another would be Ben Hogan's, and the third would be mine. You might not be surprised to hear, mine was usually the best."

Thinking of radio but eerily anticipating television, Arnie delivered a hushed play-by-play as he zigzagged through his father's rough, copying the staccato, mile-a-minute delivery of the political commentator H. V. Kaltenborn: "Now, Palmer-settles-into-his-stance. He can't-even-*see*-the-ball, yet-he-must-get-down-in-two-to-win-the-UUUU-nited-States-OOOO-pen."

"Watch me, Pap!" he pleaded. "Look at me hit this one!" But Deacon didn't have time for watching and wasn't that kind of instructor anyway. He believed in snappy lessons, and now go work it out for yourself. "I hired Arnie as caddie master when he was a teenager," Deacon told Drum, "but I was forced to fire him. He was the worst caddie master I ever had. His mind was always someplace else. I knew where it was, if I wasn't always sure where *he* was. His thoughts were on his own game."

Arnie wasn't overly successful as a caddie, either. He never meant to show disrespect to his clients, but that expressive putty face of his couldn't hide his disagreement with club selections—even from the club champion—or his disgust with wrongheaded strategies. It couldn't hide anything. This turned into a plus later on.

Deacon taught him how to install fresh grips and repair or renovate old shafts and club heads. Arnie enjoyed working with his hands and knew even touring pros were expected to be artisans in the off-seasons. "Whenever Arnie wanted help with his game or anything to do with the game," Deacon said, "he always came to me. I never went to Arnold."

As land became more available and affordable, Latrobe's par of 34 stretched out to 36, and then to 18 holes. Deacon planted every pine, starting with none and ending with thousands. To Arnie, the course was a living, breathing, agronomical edition of his dad. The snowy months in Latrobe, as glorious as they could sometimes be, depressed Arnie. He liked Christmases well enough, especially the mixed aroma of hot chocolate for the children and warm whiskey for the adults, but he couldn't wait for the ice to melt and the slope of the 7th hole to stop doubling as a ski run and get back to being a fairway. "I played golf in my head," he said, "if I couldn't play it any other way."

Always Deacon, occasionally the entire family, accompanied 14-year-old Arnie to his first junior and schoolboy tournaments. Bill Yates, Palmer's high school golf coach, said, "I didn't teach him anything. He knew more about golf as a freshman than anyone in school. He taught the team; I managed it. If he hit a bad five-iron shot in practice, he'd let everybody go ahead. Then he'd get a bag of fifty balls and bang away with a five-iron until the problem was solved."

Arnie's first formal opponent was "a lefty, kid by the name of Danko, Bill Danko, from Jeannette [sixteen miles west of Latrobe], who became a doctor." The uncanny way chess grandmaster Bobby Fischer had of pulling out a miniature magnetized set from his inside breast pocket and replicating white-piece-by-black-piece boyhood speed matches from years before (inconsequential "skittles" games dashed off by the hundreds at summer camps), Palmer was able to re-create stroke by stroke every one of his formative rounds, like the 71 he shot to beat Danko.

At age 15 or so, while playing another match he had reason to remember, Arnie pulled a Rumpelstiltskin over a botched putt that climaxed with him whirlybirding the putter over a poplar tree. "I won that match," he said, "but on the car ride home nobody would talk to me until Pap finally growled, 'If you ever throw another club like that in my presence or while you're living in my house, you'll never play another game of golf.' Period."

It's remarkable how many pros tell the equivalent story. Mickelson's father had one overriding commandment on the golf course (which described his son's game forever): "Whatever else golf can be, it has to be fun." After eight-year-old Phil Jr. slammed his club against the ground in a fury, Phil Sr. demoted him to spectator for several holes until the boy spoke up in a contrite whisper, "Dad, I think I can have fun now." Almost universally, golf is a father's game. If TV cameras zoomed in on golfers the way they do football players, nobody would say, "Hi Mom."

Around Youngstown, Palmer was a two-fisted boy who had his share of fights. Truth be told, he enjoyed them. ("I was a hell-raiser," he admitted.) Like many a two-fisted boy (Bill Clinton comes to mind), he eventually raised his hands to the old man, who, under the influence of shots-and-beers at the pool hall and firehouse was being ugly to Doris. "Leave her alone!" Arnie shouted in the kitchen. No punches were landed, but the two of them crashed into a stovepipe, flattening it. That night, Arnie ran away from home (without his golf clubs), but after walking the course for hours in the dark, he let himself back in the house and went to bed. The incident was never repeated or referred to again. It was his 16th birthday.

Among Arnie's neighborhood friends was Fred Rogers, who

would grow up to be a television host, Mister Rogers, with his own "*Neighborhood*." "Fred was a year ahead of me in school," Palmer said, "but we knew each other pretty well. He was a good guy." His mother—or maybe it was his grandmother—knitted those cardigan sweaters he would become famous for. Because they owned a piano, Arnie marked them down as wealthy. But they probably weren't. "Fred took a couple of golf lessons from Pap," he said.

Rogers was hardly athletic, but he traveled in the sporting circle because of a typical good turn he paid the star high school quarterback, Jim Stumbaugh, when Jim was hospitalized with an injury. Fred took notes for him in class and shuttled his homework back and forth. After Stumbaugh recovered, he persuaded the other jocks to give Fred a chance. "But Arnie was always friendly," Rogers said, "even during my fat phase, when I was pretty lonely. He and I had airplanes in common, the love of them. With another friend, Rudy Melichar, we were forever assembling balsa wood and plywood and construction paper and lacquer model kits. Some that you could throw—and crash—others that just sat there. The more intricate and authentic, the better. Painting them green, silver, or gray and carefully applying the decals and so forth. Arnie and I smelled faintly of paint, glue, or varnish most of the time."

Whenever they could, they'd race down the country club road to Latrobe Airport, formerly the Longview Flying Field, a gaping stretch of open land with a grass runway, no control tower, no instrument landing, no radio direction. They passed their hands over the few biplanes parked there and imagined themselves aviators like Wiley Post. They sat in the flight room by a potbelly stove and listened to the grizzled pilots dramatizing their closest calls. Arnie would become a pilot in time. ("Did Fred?" I asked him at the desk. "No, he didn't," Palmer said, "but you know the tremendous success Fred made of himself, so he had occasion to log lots of flying time in private planes. Both of us just loved the sky.")

Arnie's thickest confederate was an adult, Charlie Arch, a pro shop worker born without elbow joints and with only four fingers on each hand. But his heart was perfect. Throughout Palmer's boyhood, Arch served as cheerleader and occasional angel, furnishing the compliments Pap withheld and tiding the boy over with small loans for cowboy movies and model airplane parts, the mounting sums of which Arnie kept meticulous track. "During the Depression," he said, "Pap was making a meager salary and sometimes had to go to a friend to borrow money just to make ends meet. I remember how intent he was on repaying that debt. It became a part of my early life that you must pay back. It's been with me all my life." Almost the first check Palmer wrote as a professional golfer was for $1,000 to settle (over-settle) his long-standing tab with Charlie.

Twelve-year-old Palmer was with Arch in the pro shop when the bulletin came over the radio that the Japanese had bombed Pearl Harbor. "I just wish I was older," he told his friend bitterly. "I just wish I could fly."

Arch's brother, Tony, who would become a glider pilot in the war, took Arnie up in a Piper Cub, a two-seater, for his first flight. Palmer said, "I should have been scared to death, especially the way Tony flew the airplane, damned near stalling it a couple of times, but I wasn't. I liked it. It thrilled me more than anything ever had. After that, I didn't just *want* to fly. I *had* to fly." He recounted for Rogers every second of the experience. "It felt as real to me," Fred said, "as if I had been up there with him."

They did not have religion in common. Rogers attended First Presbyterian and was devout. (He would become an ordained Presbyterian minister.) Arnold dutifully accompanied Cheech to Youngstown's Lutheran Church, but his faith was informal. Like golf, he practiced it outdoors. Milfred's nickname, "Deacon," a family mystery never fully explained, had something to do with religion. But characteristically Pap wouldn't talk about it. Arnie believed it referred to some service his father had performed for a black minister. ("That was the story, anyway," Doc Giffin said.) "Pap did favors for everyone in town," Palmer said. "But the simple fact is, he wasn't a Milfred, and he wasn't a Jerome. He was a Deacon." A deacon of his own secular church. "I prayed for compliments from my father, but they never came, which was good in a way. Because I never got satisfied. I never stopped trying to please him. I think he knew that."

Player said, "Arnold and I were waging a series of exhibition matches against each other in South Africa, and his father was along. We were driving back to the hotel in Cape Town, after I shot sixty-eight to his eighty, when he said, 'I've had a terrible head cold all day.' To which Deacon said, 'Yeah, if I shot eighty and got whipped like that, I'd have a terrible head cold, too. Don't give me that bullshit. You just played lousy.' I got such a shock. I think Arnold wanted nothing so much in life as his father's approval, and, for all that Arnie accomplished, I don't believe he ever completely got it."

In 1992, I was on the phone with Palmer. I had called to ask about a young South African comer named Ernie Els, who in his first American major had been paired with Arnold for the Thursday and Friday rounds of the PGA Championship at Bellerive in St. Louis. Neither man scored his best; both missed the cut. But the 22-year-old impressed the 62-year-old. "Right on the spot I extended an invitation for him to play in my tournament at Bay Hill," Palmer said. "I don't remember ever doing that before."

"I can't tell you how much it meant to me," Els said. "It was like he opened the door to golf and invited me in. Arnold Palmer. I felt so glad and so lucky when I came to win his tournament eventually." Twice.

What did Arnold see in Els?

"This kid has a real confidence in himself," he told me, "and, as someone once said, he doesn't have to talk about it. He's one of those 'I'll show you' types. I guess I kind of like that."

By any chance was the "someone who once said" that a tough guy on a tractor?

Palmer didn't answer. He just laughed.

3

1950

WINNER:

Southern Intercollegiate

West Penn Amateur

Greensburg Invitational

Medalist, National Collegiate Athletic Association (NCAA)

"Then I'd remember he was gone."

Palmer's first golfing hero was golf's first television star, Lew Worsham, whose time in the light at two events lasted only seconds but stayed in Arnold's memory permanently (for a reason). Worsham was the head professional at historic Oakmont Country Club in suburban Pittsburgh, just down the road from Latrobe, back when most tour players were club pros somewhere.

In the 1947 U.S. Open at St. Louis Country Club, the first televised Open (just locally, on KSD-TV), Worsham and Sam Snead played off over 18 holes. Still tied on the 90th green, both players had tap-in second putts under three feet for pars. A measurement was called for to see who was "away." Lew was 29 inches from the hole, Sam 30½. Snead missed; Worsham made. Lew was the National Champion.

And the klieg lights weren't through with him yet.

In the first golf tournament televised across the entire nation (by ABC), the Tam O'Shanter of 1953, he won again, even more abruptly. Standing in the final fairway, trailing clubhouse leader Chandler Harper by a stroke, Worsham struck a 110-yard pitching wedge that landed 40 feet from the hole, tumbled, skidded, reared back, wriggled, ran, and rolled straight into the cup for an eagle 2 and victory. It was the first golf shot that ever lifted anybody off a couch.

Bud Worsham, Lew's kid brother, graciously shared him with Arnie, who met "Bubby" Worsham ("I couldn't handle 'Bubby,' so I renamed him 'Bud'") at a Hearst newspapers tournament in Michigan, the biggest week on the junior calendar. Twelve months later, they rode a train together to and from the same event in California, 48-hour rides that solidified their alliance. Through an open hotel window in Hollywood they chipped golf balls to the crown of the Brown Derby restaurant and on a tour of Metro-Goldwyn-Mayer met the bugle-nosed comedian Jimmy Durante and jointly fell in love with the aquatic movie star Esther Williams. "Bud had a game leg, like Pap," Palmer said. "In a lot of ways, he reminded me of Pap. Bud could stand on just his good leg and hit the ball almost as far as I could on two. He was an indomitable character, a little dangerous but in an innocent way—fun. By the end of that trip, we were best friends."

That was the summer after Palmer's senior year in high school, and his plans were murky. Pitt and Penn State offered partial golf scholarships, tuition without room and board. But he couldn't think of any way to swing the rest. So he was looking into business colleges or maybe the Army.

"Riding the train, Bud told me he had just accepted tuition, board, and books at a little Southern school called Wake Forest College, which of course I had never heard of. 'It's in Wake Forest, North Carolina,' he said. 'You can play there all winter long and barely need a sweater. You wouldn't be interested in coming with me, would you? I'll bet I could get you a full ride, too.' And I'll be darned if he didn't."

Arriving that autumn, they went straight to the Carolina Country Club in Raleigh, where Palmer shot 67 and Worsham 68, the first time either of them ever saw the course. For three years they were inseparable, rooming together and lateraling Wake's number one and number two playing positions back and forth without rancor. Even though each lived to beat the other, neither ever rooted against his friend. For supplemental recreation, they wrestled in the dormitory. It took two men at a time, like Bud and Coach Johnny Johnston, to give Palmer a respectable match. "He still never lost," said another team member, Dick Tiddy, who someday would be the head pro at Arnold's Bay Hill Club in Orlando.

There haven't been many better generations of collegiate golfers, counting Mike Souchak and Art Wall Jr. at Duke, Harvie Ward at North Carolina, Ken Venturi at San Jose State, Gene Littler at San Diego State, Don January and Billy Maxwell at North Texas State, and Dow Finsterwald at Ohio University.

"I'm four days older than Arnie," Dow said. "Can't you tell? Four days wiser, too, as I tell him all the time. When he and I were freshmen, our schools played a series of games all around the Carolinas. The first time out against me, he shot twenty-nine on the front. That was my introduction to the son of a gun."

As sophomores, Bud and Arnie persuaded the athletic director, Big Jim Weaver, to let them convert the sand greens on Wake's nine-hole course to grass. Weaver gave them a dollar an hour (to split), a wheelbarrow, two shovels, and access to a landscaping manual. Now Arnie was Pap at Latrobe in the 20s. These may have been his happiest days.

At the time, the Wake Forest campus was some 65 miles closer to Duke than it is now, only about 20 miles away then. On a Homecoming weekend, Bud urged Arnie to accompany him and basketball player Gene Scheer to a dance in Durham, a "mixer." Worsham had a 1939 Buick. It wasn't like Palmer to pass up a dance anywhere (as it combined two of his favorite things, pretty girls and discreetly palmed bourbon-and-Cokes). But instead he and Jim Flick, Scheer's roommate, went to a movie. Flick was an athletic hybrid, part basketball player and part golfer, who would eventually achieve renown as a swing doctor for the likes of British Open champion Tom Lehman.

The following morning, Arnold looked over at Bud's bed and saw it hadn't been slept in. Neither had Scheer's, across the hall. Palmer sat on his own bed for over an hour, full of dread. When Flick and Coach Johnston came to his door, the looks on their faces only confirmed what he already knew. "Heading to Durham in Johnny's car," Arnie said, "I think he told me they were dead. I'm not sure." They passed the bridge where the car had run off the road and flipped over in a stream.

Then they started going to funeral parlors in Raleigh, a dull buzzing blur of funeral parlors. "Finally, we walked into one where a highway patrolman asked me, 'Are you family? Can you make an identification?' I said, 'Best friend,' and he took me into a back room [where both broken bodies were laid out together on one table. The shock of it, like a bomb going off, left him deaf and floating]. For some insane reason, we went looking for the Buick next." They found it in a junkyard, crushed.

That night, undoubtedly with the best intentions, Flick moved Bud's stuff out and his own stuff in with Arnie.

"You knew Flick, right?" Palmer asked me, sitting at his desk.

"Yes, I first met him in Cincinnati," I said. "He was a teaching pro at the Losantiville club. Billed himself as the inventor of the 'square-to-square' method."

"Square-to-square was old," Arnold said, "when my father was young. I'm not proud of this, but I could never be close to Jim after he moved Bud out so soon. It's not his fault, it's mine. We were in the same business, but I just couldn't know him. We'd say hello through the years, but I wasn't able to say much more than that. He telephoned me now and then; I'm not sure I ever called him. We spoke on the phone just before he died [of pancreatic cancer in 2012, at 82], and you know something? He didn't say a word about his illness. We just talked about golf. Some things, you never get over."

Flick worked with Nicklaus late, after Jack turned 50.

"Oh, I *know*," Palmer said, "I was there at the Tradition, Jack's first senior event, when he turned to Jim on the practice tee and asked, 'What do you see?' Jim replied, 'I see a feel player who's become too technical.' Jack won that tournament and thanked him afterward. Flick knew his stuff."

Arnie came home from Bud's funeral outside Washington, D.C., and, in a heartbroken fog, ghost-walking to classes, learning nothing, finished the semester at Wake, whose very name seemed to stand now for the vigil he was keeping. Then, essentially, he ran away. He didn't want to go to college anymore. It's not true, as people later said, that he didn't want to play golf anymore. He longed to play golf, just not there.

"I was going crazy," he said. "I kept turning around to tell Bud something, then I'd remember he was gone. If I'd have been with him that night, maybe I would have been at the wheel on the way home. I probably would have been. Everything might have been all right."

To the puzzlement of Pap and with the understanding of Doris, Arnie joined the Coast Guard. As a yeoman.

He spent three years guarding coasts, first in Cape May, New Jersey (slipping over to Wildwood occasionally for nine holes of golf); later in Cleveland, playing a lakeside course where the flag sticks were sometimes frozen solid into the cups. In his dress whites, Palmer must have been presentable, because he was selected to be part of an honor guard at the Washington premiere of the movie *Fighting Coast Guard,* starring Brian Donlevy, attended by President Truman. But air-sea rescue intrigued Arnold more than Hollywood glamour. He still had a photograph of himself with Esther Williams, but flying beguiled him more.

The move to Cleveland was facilitated by an arm he broke (not his own) in a jujitsu class where his steel hands, powerful upper body, and wrestling experience from Wake Forest held him in better stead than his opponents. He was summoned to a captain's mast— for punishment, he presumed—but instead was offered a transfer to whatever station in the country had an opening. For its proximity to Pennsylvania and for its golf courses, he chose Cleveland.

Hitchhiking home from Cleveland, wearing his uniform, carrying his golf clubs (a foolproof prop for hitchhiking), he was picked up by a large man heading to Harrisburg in a Cadillac. "You drive," said the man, who immediately put his hand on Palmer's leg after they settled into the front seat. "I knew about women," Arnold said, "but I didn't know about men."

After being set straight (so to speak), the man decided he wasn't going to Harrisburg after all. "The *hell* you aren't," Palmer said. "You said Harrisburg and we're going to Harrisburg." At the first

Harrisburg exit, Arnie pulled over, grabbed his clubs and duffel, and said, "Thanks for the lift."

An officer who was a keen golfer set Palmer to ramrodding the construction of a driving range and tried to talk him into applying for officer candidate school, with an additional two years' commitment. Arnie was flattered but not tempted. Still, he wondered what he would do after his discharge. He wound up selling paint supplies in the morning and playing what he called "salesman's golf" with potential customers in the afternoon. Palmer's employer campaigned for him to return to Wake Forest to complete a business administration degree, and he did go back for a semester, taking over as interim coach (player-coach) from Johnny Johnston, who had inherited the A.D. job from Big Jim Weaver, now the commissioner of the new Atlantic Coast Conference.

Playing majestically, Palmer won the ACC individual championship but fell a few credits shy of a diploma and never did graduate. ("I must say," he told a graduating class many years later, "that I was not a budding Rhodes Scholar during my undergraduate years—and you don't need to giggle at that—but, thanks to some of my professors and the young man who quickly became my best friend when we entered Wake Forest together, I acquired my education—an education that has played an important part in the success I have had in life. Bud Worsham was that friend. Many of you do not know who he was. Let me tell you about him. He was more than a brother, closer than any brother could be . . .")

Palmer resumed selling paint in Cleveland.

The choice between turning pro and remaining an amateur wasn't as automatic then as it is now. Bobby Jones had proved a bigger fortune could be made serving on boards and with banks than on tour, and Jones hoped Jack Nicklaus, in particular, would follow his example. At the bottom of a last-ditch letter, Jones wrote Nicklaus, "But if you're bound and determined to turn pro, I have had a very fine relationship over the years with the Spalding company. . . ."

There weren't really any amateurs.

"I think of Palmer," Finsterwald said, "as the greatest amateur-professional who ever lived. By that I mean he never stopped playing the game for the love of it, like an amateur. Sure, he liked making a nice living. But he loved to play. Arnie and I enjoyed a lot of the same things, like cowboy movies. Remember Bob Steele? Ken Maynard? Sunset Carson? Arnie will watch anything with manure in it. I can't prove it, but I think Arnie dreamed of riding horses, strumming guitars, and shooting bad men. Except for Roy Rogers pictures, I know his favorite film of all time was *Northwest Passage*, starring Spencer Tracy, because Tracy reminded him of his dad.

"But the thing we truly had in common, the thing both of us cared about most of all, was playing golf. That may sound funny, but you'd be surprised how many good players, how many pros, weren't able to enjoy it nearly as much as Arnie and I did. To us, it was more an avocation than a vocation. Check out his face after he pulls off a tough shot. The look of pure joy that comes over him. He's alive."

(Lee Trevino once said, "Arnold and I are the same. We have to slap rubber every day. Slap rubber. Nicklaus also likes to fish, ski, play tennis, and go to his kids' football games. Player also likes to ranch and breed thoroughbreds. I've heard Gary say he'd rather win a Derby than a Masters. But Palmer and I have to hit golf balls every day. Slap rubber. It's the only thing we really care about.")

Finsterwald paused for a second, and then laughed.

"You know that PGA Tour slogan?" he said. "'These guys are good.' Well, I wish they'd make a new commercial showing Retief Goosen missing the little putt at Southern Hills and then winning the U.S. Open playoff the next day. 'These guys are human.' That's Arnie more than anything. Human."

4

1954

WINNER:

U. S. Amateur

Ohio Amateur

All-American Amateur

Atlantic Coast Conference Championship

Waite Memorial (with Tommy Sheehan)

"Are you ever going to stop screwing around and be a man?"

IN HIS *New Yorker* profiles of major golf championships, Herbert Warren Wind opened with the rocks; moved on to the snakes, the Indians, the settlers, and the architects; detailed a half dozen or so Walker Cups contested on the premises; then recapped one by one every previous major conducted there until finally coming to the tournament at hand. The *New Yorker* paid by the word.

But Herb could get to it quicker if he had to. At a previous post, with *Sports Illustrated* in the magazine's rookie year of 1954, he used the opening paragraph to compare the finalists in that summer's U.S. Amateur at the Country Club of Detroit: one, "a graying millionaire playboy who is a celebrity on two continents," and the other, "a tanned muscular young salesman from Cleveland who literally grew up on a golf course."

Wind was an officious-looking chap in a light-brown suit (picture a homicide inspector viewing the body), nowhere near as sour and severe as his countenance. He loved words and he loved golf. (Early one Masters week, he walked up to me in Augusta's toy airport and inquired anxiously, "The golf course, is it firm?" "Hell, Herb," I said, "I just got here.") "There was no need to exaggerate the personalities of the two finalists or the nature of their duel," he wrote, "for the contrast was a highly dramatic one without gilding one blade of grass."

The graying millionaire playboy was 43-year-old Robert Sweeny, a California-born investment banker from London, Oxford University, and the Royal Air Force's Eagle Squadron (Yanks piloting RAF bombers before America entered World War II), who won the British Amateur 17 summers earlier and spent six months of his year making financial killings in the States while playing golf with (and occasionally beating) Ben Hogan at Hogan's winter retreat, Seminole Golf Club in West Palm Beach, Florida.

To get to Sweeny, the tanned muscular, 24-year-old salesman had to win seven matches. He defeated Frank Strafaci, 1-up; John Veghte, 1-up; Richard Whiting, two extra holes; Walter Andzel, 5 and 3; Frank Stranahan, 3 and 1 (Stranahan, 32, a bodybuilder, once mauled him, 11 and 10, at a North and South Amateur); Don Cherry, 1-up; and Edward Meister Jr., three extra holes. Cherry was the Mafia singer who wasn't yet married to Miss America of 1956, Sharon Ritchie, who eventually put him on the waiver wire in favor of Kyle Rote. Sweeny's road to the finals included a 3 and 1 victory over Eddie Merrins, who would become Bel-Air Country Club's fabled "Little Pro."

The night before his semifinal match, the first of two 36-holers, Palmer telephoned Pap and Doris, who jumped in the car and drove from Latrobe to Grosse Pointe Farms, pausing for three hours in Ohio to nod off by the side of the road. Just before they arrived, Arnold kissed the Chicago model he had been squiring all week, patted her on the bottom, and sent her home.

His parents pulled up just as he was about to tee off against Meister, a 38-year-old publisher of trade papers for the fruit industry and a former captain of the golf team at Yale. It was an especially stifling August day in Michigan, and the match was as static as the breeze for all of the morning and much of the afternoon, until Meister seemed ready to assert himself down the stretch. He could have won their match with a 10-footer at the 35th hole, a 14-footer at the 36th, a five-footer at the 37th, or a 16-footer at the 38th, but missed them all. A slick five-foot putt Palmer had to make to send the match to extra holes was the putt that stayed with him forever. On the third extra hole, a 510-yard par 5, Palmer reached the green with a driver and 2-iron, anticlimactically two-putting for birdie to end the longest semifinal in Amateur history. It was Sweeny versus Palmer the next day for the title.

"He looked like a movie star" in pressed linen pants and an expensive haircut, Arnold said. "He was as thin as a reed" (and as high-waisted as the New York Giants shortstop Alvin Dark). Sweeny could make a blank white visor look important, and feel jaunty. He had a female companion in the gallery who was just about the most decorative young woman Palmer had seen since Esther Williams. "Let's put it this way," he said, "she was more than amply endowed." At the fourth hole she squirmed through the ropes to toss her arms around Sweeny and give him a substantial kiss. He made a 45-footer at two, an 18-footer at three, and, to pay her back for the smacker, a

20-footer at four. "I was already three down," Palmer said. "It's not enough that he's rich, handsome, a bomber pilot, and gets the girl, he also makes every damn putt he looks at."

As they walked off the fourth green together, Sweeny pinched the back of Palmer's neck (on top of everything else, Bob was six feet three, four or five inches taller than his opponent) and whispered something that was missed by Wind and the other reporters tramping behind. Smiling at the memory, Palmer said, "What he told me was, 'Don't worry, Arnie, you know I can't keep this up forever.' Bob was a real sportsman, a real gentleman. I appreciated that. Even during the nip and tuck of our match, I knew I would always have a good feeling about him." And, true to his word, Sweeny three-putted the fifth.

But their game wasn't squared until the 27th hole. "At lunch," Palmer said, "I told myself, *Stop playing him, start playing the golf course,* which became my match-play strategy for the rest of my life. Bob made another long putt at the twenty-eighth hole to go one-up again, but I caught him at the thirtieth and went ahead for the first time all day at the thirty-second. I'd been outdriving him by thirty to forty yards, and finally my irons were kicking in."

One hole in front going to the last, Palmer hit a particularly deep drive, absolutely on a string, and an iron shot hole-high that sounded like a tuning fork. It's a myth that, if you lined up every great golfer on the same range without knowing who any of them were, you wouldn't be able to tell the best players at a glance. The truth is, if you can get close enough, you can hear it: the crystal sound of silver on glass. Playing with Tom Kite and Payne Stewart in a practice round before the AT&T at Pebble Beach, I never had to turn to see who had just hit. Kite's contact was only solid; Stewart's was musical.

Sweeny hit his final drive into the wilderness, and after an extended search actually shanked his second shot. He wasn't yet on the green in the hole he had to win. His subsequent concession was given wholeheartedly, and Palmer was the U.S Amateur Champion, 2-up. For some reason fathomable only to a USGA potentate, Sweeny was rewarded for his gracefulness with an arbitrary halve on the last hole. "Is that OK with you?" referee Joe Dey asked Arnold, who didn't care. So it went on the board and in the books as 1-up. After a moment's confusion, a brass band on the clubhouse terrace struck up "Hail to the Chief" and, this being Wolverine country, "Hail! to the victors valiant / Hail! to the conqu'ring heroes . . ."

Breaking out of a clinch with his mom, Arnie said, "Where's my father? Let's get Pap in here! He's the one who really won the U.S. Amateur!" Just then Deacon broke through the crowd. He wasn't smiling exactly, but Arnie could tell he was happy. "You did pretty good, boy," he told his son, whose eyes filled with tears. It came over Palmer like a sunrise that he had just received a compliment from his dad.

Three months later, on November 17, Palmer wrote a letter to Dey, stating, "It is with mixed emotions that I advise you of my decision to turn professional. I feel the deepest appreciation to all USGA officers for the fine relationship I have enjoyed. Yet, I cannot overlook my life's ambition to follow in the footsteps of my father and become a PGA pro. [Technically, despicably, his father was not a PGA pro. By the PGA's rules, "cripples" were required to make special application, and Pap's was denied.] We both have counted on this since I first started playing golf. My good fortune in competition this year indicates it is time to turn to my chosen profession."

Leaning back in his office chair, he said, "Only the players seem to understand how meaningful the U.S. Amateur is. You can't know how much it matters to us, how much it matters to me. Winning that tournament was, and still is, my proudest achievement in golf. I spent three hours one night with Tiger Woods when he was still at Stanford. More than three hours, four hours. At *his* request, too. It

was good. I was playing at Silverado [in the Transamerica Seniors].
Among the many things we talked about at dinner were what he
called [in that shorthand way young Woods had of speaking] the
'U.S. Am.' Winning three U.S. Amateurs in a row, and three consecutive USGA juniors before that, is absolutely incredible—all together, six straight years of match play. I think it's his most amazing
feat of all, and I think he'd say so, too. That dinner was the one the
NCAA made a federal case out of just because I picked up the check.
Fifty bucks. It almost cost Tiger the remainder of his college eligi-
bility, and maybe helped nudge him into the pros."

Nineteen fifty-four was also the year Palmer and Nicklaus first
brushed, at Sylvania Country Club near Toledo. Arnold was a
24-year-old amateur defending his Ohio Amateur championship
(successfully), and Jack was a 14-year-old dreamer a year away from
qualifying for a U.S. Amateur, six and seven years away from winning it twice. In the clattering rain, Palmer was the lone player practicing on the range, drilling iron shots under the storm. "About
quail high," Nicklaus said, tracing the trajectory with the flat of his
hand. Of course, Arnold didn't know who the boy was who was
watching from a hillside, but then, Jack didn't know who the man
was he was watching. The metronome kept clicking back and forth
in the rain, and Nicklaus thought he could hear the sound of a pick-
axe against the earth.

"I just saw this unbelievably strong guy," he said, speaking in
his Florida office, "beating the ball to death—he was a beater more
than a swinger in those days. Knocking down nine-irons, lower and
harder than you could believe. Later, someone told me who it was,
and I said, 'Oh, *that's* Arnold Palmer.'"

They would end up hyphenated like Dempsey-Tunney. Nobody
wanted Dempsey beaten, either.

Young Nicklaus had just come through a touch of polio, Pap's disease. "I had polio when I was thirteen," Jack said nonchalantly, as if this weren't surprising. His body ached, his joints stiffened, he lost his coordination and 25 pounds. Kid sister Marilyn, three years younger, was afflicted at the same time. It took her a full year to walk again, Jack only a few weeks. But the fiery joints that accompanied post–polio syndrome stayed with him from then on. Arnold probably never knew how much Jack and Pap had in common. It mightn't have made much difference anyway, in Palmer and Nicklaus's complicated relationship.

───────

In 1997, 21-year-old Masters champion Tiger Woods was sitting on the single bed in his former room at Cypress, California, surrounded by the posters (Alec Guinness as Obi-Wan Kenobi), football cards (Chargers Hall of Fame wide receiver Charlie Joiner), and bumper stickers ("I'm with *That's Incredible!*") of his childhood. "For *That's Incredible!*," he said, "I sat on Fran Tarkenton's lap, and at the end of the show hit Wiffle balls over the heads of the audience. I beaned a cameraman. Everyone thought it was hilarious, but I was mortified."

Taped to the wall above the bed's headboard was the famous newspaper clipping of Nicklaus's milestones by age, yellowed from all the years Woods spent checking them off one by one.

"Age 13, shot a 69 . . .

"Age 15, played in U.S. Amateur . . .

"Age . . ."

"That top one," I said, "was actually a day–night doubleheader."

"How do you mean?" he asked.

I repeated for him what Nicklaus told me:

"My dad and I went out late on a summer afternoon to play just the front nine at Scioto [the Columbus course where Bobby Jones won the second of his four U.S. Opens]. We did that a lot. This time

I shot thirty-five and begged Dad to play the back nine. But he said, 'Nope. Mom and Marilyn are waiting dinner.'"

. After a silent, sullen ride home, Charlie Nicklaus pulled up to the house, turned off the engine, and said, "But you know something, Jack? If we're mindful of your mother's feelings and still manage to eat quickly, we can be on the tenth tee in thirty-five minutes.".

When they reached the par-5 18th hole, it wasn't just dusk, it was dark, and the sprinklers were out. Jack said, "I hit a driver off the tee and I don't know what club second. But something on the green. In those days there were heavy hoses attached to the sprinklers, and I remember Dad and I had to pull hard to clear a path so I could putt. I had about a thirty-five-footer for eagle and sixty-nine. It went right in the center. That was the first time I ever broke seventy. I was thirteen."

"I was twelve," Tiger said.

———

Over the Labor Day weekend of 1954, the newly minted National Amateur Champion traveled to Shawnee on Delaware, Pennsylvania, to play in Fred Waring's two-man Bill Waite Memorial Tournament at the personal invitation of the famed orchestra leader (Fred Waring and the Pennsylvanians) and patent holder on the Waring blender. One of the junior hostesses was a freckled brunette college student with an upturned nose, Winifred Walzer, whose father Shube owned a canned goods company. Palmer was introduced to Winifred and Waring's daughter Dixie on a Tuesday. He and Winnie held hands for five days, after which he asked her to marry him. As the first-place trophy was being presented to Palmer and partner Tommy Sheehan, "Uncle Fred" (as Miss Walzer called Waring) all but announced the engagement.

Arnold started to win her, she told Bob Drum years later, when he let her in on a proposition he just that second received from a dancing partner, an older golfer's older wife (the mother of four children, by the way). "Let's you and me run away together," the woman whispered, nibbling his ear. In a subsequent movie about Philadelphia's Main Line, *The Young Philadelphians*, Alexis Smith portrayed an equally desperate older woman, and Paul Newman played an equally petrified younger man.

"When he included me that way," Winnie told Drum, "I got a wonderful feeling of confidence that, if I did marry him, he'd always tell me everything." She was probably too young then to understand that whispering women might be part of the deal.

Winnie had studied at Brown University and its distaff branch, Pembroke, and she certainly seemed like a Philly Main Liner— aristocratic families in Tudor homes with old money and plenty of it. But while her parents were prosperous enough, they were far from grand. Shube was emphatically a down-to-earth character, and he didn't consider a blue-collar golf bum, no matter how good-looking, to be a catch for his only daughter.

Out of a golf bet at the storied Pine Valley club in southern New Jersey, near Philly, Palmer promoted a diamond ring. Then or now, almost nobody playing Pine Valley for the first time broke 80. A quarter of a century after the scrub-and-sand course appeared like Brigadoon in 1913, someone finally shot a par 70 the first time out, but it took Masters and U.S. Open champion Craig Wood to do it. Pine Valley wasn't a place usually associated with romance, either. "Barbara and I stopped off there on our honeymoon," Nicklaus said. "We came from Hershey," where Jack Grout, his boyhood teacher, had once been an assistant pro. "I always wanted to play Pine Valley and wasn't smart enough to call ahead. In the pro shop I started to tell them, 'My wife and I . . .' 'Your *what*!?' they said. 'Where is she now?' 'In the car right out front.' 'Oh, my dear Lord!'"

While Jack played the course, Barbara circled the property, being

careful not to contaminate the male-only grounds with woman-
hood, occasionally catching glimpses of her new husband through
the greenery. He shot 74.

By the terms of Palmer's wager, for every stroke under 72 he
would receive $200; for every one over 80, he would have to pay
$100. So no winnings for the likeliest score (72 to 80), but with a
definite potential for ruin. He opened with a bogey but closed with
a 67. Winnie had her rock.

A couple of months went by.

Palmer said, "Pap and I drove to Miami, to my first tournament
as a pro, staying together in the same motel room. I missed the cut
and didn't even go back to the room Friday, completely ducking
him. I went out on the town with that model from Chicago [who
had rematerialized]. When I eventually got back to the motel, Pap
was waiting up. He read me the riot act. 'You're too lovesick to play
golf,' he said, 'but not too lovesick to go out with another woman
when you're engaged? Are you ever going to stop screwing around
and be a man?'"

Arnie had no answer for that.

"Where's your fiancée right now?" Deacon demanded.

"Coopersburg [just outside Bethlehem, Pennsylvania]."

"Get your ass to Coopersburg!"

"I dropped Pap at the airport and drove all night, showing up at
Winnie's door needing a shave. No wonder her father hated me."

They ended up eloping ("I took her out the window, as a matter
of fact"), but, as elopements go, it was fairly crowded. Deacon and
Doris were there, with both sets of Arnold's grandparents, and little
brother Jerry. Shube gave it a pass. Palmer said, "The hardest thing
I ever had to do in my life was ask Shube Walzer for five hundred
bucks to stake me on tour. Pap gave us five hundred, too. We put
most of it into an old trailer shaped like a loaf of bread," the first
of two trailers (containing a toilet, a shower, a kitchen, and a bed).

Towed by a weary pink Ford. Sometimes pushed up hills by Winnie.

Before the caravan pulled out of Latrobe, Pap brought Arnie to a living room window and said, "Do you see that tractor [their vintage tractor] out there? If you listen to all of the other pros on the practice tee and take their advice about your swing and your game, that tractor will be waiting for you when you get back."

5

1955

"You could see it, you could smell it. It was golf."

IN 1955 THE PGA was still enforcing a six-month probation period for touring pros, before they were eligible to collect any prize money at sanctioned events. This was to thwart the hit-and-run artists who might drop by the circuit, grab a bit of cash, and leave. After Palmer's apprenticeship was up, on May 29, 1955, he tied for 25th place in the Fort Wayne Invitational. For $5,000 a year over three years, he had signed an endorsement deal with Wilson clubs, but the $145 he cashed in Fort Wayne represented his first real paycheck. In 10 previous tour-operated events, he made nine cuts and was denied $1,144.86 in "winnings."

Soon after becoming official, Palmer took third place in Minneapolis–St. Paul, good for another $1,300, and kept going. Finally, in August, he won the Canadian Open (and $2,400) by four strokes over Jackie Burke, one year to the day since winning the Amateur.

He also gleaned as much pro-am money as he could, "four hundred here, six hundred there, so we could hold our heads above water," and looked for non-PGA events as far away as Panama (where second place behind the respected Argentine Tony Cerda brought him $900). "I guess I racked up seven or eight grand that year. Winnie used to keep the books for Shube; now she kept them for me."

She did everything she could for him—and his game. George Low, the Scottish putting guru, golf hustler, card sharp, horse plunger, and fairway philosopher, said, "Leave it to Arnie to marry the first girl who would shag golf balls for him." Low spoke like that, in epigrams. "I never bet against Ky Laffoon on the putting green because he was part Indian. He could see in the dark."

As a cook, Winnie was unsuccessful. But as a wife, in every important way, she was a champion. Any 20-year-old woman who cheerfully spends her wedding night inside a jukebox at a trucker's motel off the Breezewood exit of the Pennsylvania Turnpike is entitled not to wait for the first year to play out before telling her husband she loved him, she'd always love him, and she'd follow him to the ends of the earth, but the trailers had to go. And, by the way, she was pregnant.

The Masters not being a PGA-sanctioned event, Palmer was allowed in 1955 to keep the $696 he won at his inaugural Masters for finishing equal 10th (alongside Byron Nelson and Dick Mayer) behind winner Dr. Cary Middlecoff, Ben Hogan, Sam Snead, Julius Boros, Bob Rosburg, Mike Souchak, Lloyd Mangrum, Stan Leonard, and Harvie Ward.

"Going to Augusta that first time," Palmer said, "was the greatest thrill of my life. The atmosphere was just so nice there. Everything about it turned me on. Being on the golf course was fantastic. [One day he was paired with 53-year-old Gene Sarazen.] To me, it was like playing all those tournaments where I wasn't eligible to make a dime." Pure, like that.

"I still tried my damnedest to win those events, or to finish sixth, or twentieth, or fortieth, whatever." There was something almost noble in the trying. "I've always liked the hardest courses the best. When I get on a hard, exacting golf course, I feel like I'm wrestling a bear."

From the moment he turned the Ford into the Augusta property and rolled onto Magnolia Lane, "you could see it," he said, "you could smell it. It was golf. Ed Dudley [three times a Ryder Cup player] was the head pro back then. It was a thrill meeting him, too." In his gut, Palmer knew he wasn't going to win the tournament that year, because he was too busy staring at everything and everybody. But he was equally certain he was going to win it eventually and that this was going to be his home.

"Why do I want to win the Masters?" Palmer would later say. "Why do I want to breathe?"

"There's a stillness, a silence, about the Masters," said Snead, the least sentimental of the great champions. "The players all tiptoe around like we're in church. If we came back a week later to play the Screen Door Open, the winner would probably have to shoot two sixty-nine [nineteeen under par] and then play off with two or three others."

The U.S. Open has a singular atmosphere, too: less lovely and clammier. Two months after that first Masters, Palmer came to his first Open as a professional (following two missed cuts as an amateur), playing four rounds this time and tying for 21st place ($180). On the way to the recommended "cheap motel" nearest San Francisco's Olympic Club, Arnie and Winnie encountered Tom and Mary Lou Bolt.

"They were checking in just ahead of us," Palmer said. "Tommy was already notorious for his temper, for whipping clubs into water hazards and the rest, but he should have been famous for kindness, too, and for generosity shown a newcomer. [Also for his satin swing, almost the equal of Snead's.] Tommy was a dozen years older than I, but we became fast friends as he went about showing me the ins and outs of the trade. Before long we started traveling together with our wives."

At the age of two and a half, Thomas Henry Bolt crossed the Red River in a covered wagon, moving from Haworth, Oklahoma, to Paris, Texas. Tommy had the face of a Choctaw Indian and a shanty Irishman having themselves a hell of a fight. His nose looked like the thumb on a boxing glove. Bolt's specialties were long irons hit too solidly to be long irons and woods hit too straight to be woods. Unfortunately, he was never better than an ordinary putter (even at Southern Hills in Tulsa, where he won his U.S. Open in 1958). Bolt didn't step out on tour until he was 34. Some life had to be lived first, including in Italy with the U.S. Army. He had a carpenter's knuckles and a sergeant's command. His stories resounded with thunderclaps.

"I could listen to him all day," Palmer said. "You probably know about that shouting match in the press tent when he was forty-two years old but the morning paper had him at forty-nine. The reporter apologized profusely, swearing, 'It must have been a typographical error.' 'Typographical error my ass!' Tommy said. 'It was a perfect four and a perfect nine!'"

But Bolt had a quieter side. He tried to get Arnie to remember things, little seemingly inconsequential things, like what it feels like to take the ball out of the last cup after a victory. "Hold on to those feelings," he advised Palmer. "You're going to need them someday."

"And, standing behind you, watching you swing," Arnold said, "Tommy could see more than almost anybody."

Standing behind 17-year-old Tiger Woods at Riviera in 1993, Bolt saw "kind of a Mule Train swing—you know, a bullwhip flip at the top. I put his left hand on the top of the club, like Ben [Hogan] showed me. Then I stood and watched him for a while, marveled at him. But I thought to myself, 'As hard as this kid goes at it, how long can he last? Man. Seventeen years old.'"

Still wearing his flat white Hogan cap, Bolt was sitting in a cart one morning in 2001, an overcast morning, at Black Diamond Ranch in Florida, a dramatic course carved, like Tommy, out of a quarry. The members regarded him as a statue that moved. "When you throw a club," he advised them all only half kiddingly, "always make sure you throw it down the fairway."

"Tommy was the best ball striker I ever saw," Billy Casper said, "but his temper was every bit as ferocious as you've heard. I was playing with Tommy in Michigan one year when he flubbed a four-wood shot from the rough. Then he wheeled and threw the four-wood as hard as he could where nobody was standing. A skinny post was sticking out of the ground about thirty yards from Tommy. The club wrapped around that post as neatly as if you were tying a bow. It stuck there, and that, combined with Tommy's rage, made me laugh so hard I couldn't play anymore. A hole would go by, I would picture the club around the post, I'd look over at Tommy, and I'd almost go to my knees. Whenever I saw Tommy after that, I'd still get tears in my eyes."

The memory of young Palmer delighted Bolt. "In those days Arnie seemed to own only two pairs of pants," he said, "the pair he was wearing and the pair at the dry cleaners, and they were both too big for him. I think that's the real reason why he hitched at his trousers all the time. I showed him a few tricks, but never the meat and potatoes of the game. His dad gave him all that. What Arnold had that was absolutely his own was emotion. I'm not talking about temper, either. I mean the emotion he carried in his heart and on his sleeve. He was different from other golfers that way. He showed up different."

Don January, who first encountered Palmer in collegiate golf and followed him by a year to the profession, said, "Most of the good pros back then were purposely stoic. They wanted to hide their feelings. Arnold threw his out there for everybody to see. He'd hitch up his pants with his elbows. He'd hit and have that finish with everything twirling, and his nose would be snorting like a bull in heat. He was always a player with a great set of nerves. He'd get in that funny, knock-kneed stance, putting on a green that was half-grass and half-dirt, and run a thirty-footer six feet by and just climb on the other side and pour it back in there."

"You'd have to ask Arnie," Bolt said, "but I believe I helped him with his temperament, just a little, if only by bad example. The top of Arnie's head used to come off, too, you know, now and again."

"It's true," Palmer said. "When Bolt won the Open, he harnessed his anger. He went into Tulsa with a feeling of peace and serenity that, he told me, he wished he always had. I don't think Tommy knew where it came from that week—not really. He said it came from the television preacher, Bishop Fulton J. Sheen. But wherever it came from, he birdied the first hole of the tournament and calmly asked himself, 'I wonder who's going to finish second.' [The answer: 22-year-old Gary Player.] It helped me get control of my own temper, which wasn't in *his* class but was still considerable."

Bolt said, "One time, during Palmer's first pro season, a guy in his threesome was nettling him, sort of hazing the rookie, if you know what I mean. And if you knew the guy I'm talking about, you'd understand *exactly* what I mean. When he wouldn't lay off, Arnold dragged him into the trees and kicked his ass. I won't tell you the player's name."

"It was Marty Furgol," Palmer said, referring to a New Yorker 16 years his senior, a Ryder Cup player who won five PGA tournaments in the '50s and posted top 10s in the U.S. Open and PGA plus an 11th at the Masters. "But Tommy's exaggerating. I didn't kick Furgol's ass, though I sure as hell wanted to. It was in Portland. I don't know whether he was just giving a newcomer the business, but he kept placing himself in my line of sight. Addressing the ball, I'd look up and see him standing there in the fairway directly between me and the green. I asked him to move. He moved a few feet. I asked him again. He moved a few more feet. I ended up going over the green, chipping back and missing the putt. On the way to the next tee—in front of more than a few spectators, too—I grabbed him by the collar.

"'Listen Marty,' I said, 'if you ever do that to me again, I'm going to beat the hell out of you, if not with my fists, with a golf club.' My hands were shaking."

At dinner that night Winnie told him, "So Marty Furgol's the reason you shot seventy-six today?"

"No, you're right," he admitted after a moment. "I'm the reason I shot seventy-six. I lost my composure and learned a lesson." The next day he shot 66. Doug Ford, the third member of their group, whispered to him, "You're growing up, aren't you?"

Traveling with the Bolts in 1955, Palmer scored his first top five in Vancouver, finishing third as Tommy won. By Toronto in the Canadian swing, it was Arnold's turn. After shooting 64, 67, and 64 again, he entered the final round with a six-stroke lead, paired with Burke and Bolt.

"I duck-hooked my drive on the sixth hole," he said, "and found the ball in the woods beside a fallen tree. I was entitled to remove a broken limb without penalty as long as the ball didn't move, and I was delicately doing just that, looking for a window to the green, when Tommy came up behind and said, 'For Christ's sake, Arnie, you're leading by six shots!' He wanted me to chip out sideways into the fairway. 'Shut up!' I said. I know Tommy cared about me, but under the rules only your caddie can give you advice."

With a 6-iron, Palmer sent the ball veering through a latticework of upper branches onto the green and into the path of his inaugural pro victory. "I'm shutting up," Bolt said humbly. Tommy didn't do much winning after his National Open in Tulsa, for which he received $8,000. (Twenty-third place at Southern Hills earned Palmer $200.) "I guess I had got to where I was going," Bolt said. Still, he would finish third alone behind Jack Nicklaus and Billy Casper in the 1971 PGA Championship, at the advanced age of 54. A perfect 5 and a perfect 4.

Palmer brightened at his desk. Then he smiled. Then he chuckled. "Tommy and Mary Lou were 'The Bickersons,'" he said. "You know, the battling couple on the radio, Don Ameche [and Frances Langford]. The night of my first win, at a fishing camp where we were staying in adjoining cabins, the pots and pans started flying out their screen door shortly after dinner, followed by the dishes, the glasses, and eventually the steak knives. 'Winnie,' I said. 'I think our time with the Bolts has come to an end.' She and I headed on to Montreal alone. Tommy and I stayed pals, though. I loved him."

As Palmer was winning his U.S. Open at Cherry Hills in 1960, Bolt was depositing two balls and finally the driver itself into a lake at 18. Herbert Warren Wind wrote, "Considering the size, beauty and beckoning nature of the water hazard, there was something classic about Bolt's performance, like Hillary scaling Everest or Stanley finding Livingston."

6

1958

"For some reason he was at his meanest with Arnold."

"ARNIE AND I FIRST met at George S. May's old Tam O'Shanter in Chicago," Gary Player said. "Jimmy Demaret introduced us."

May was a snake oil impresario and door-to-door Bible salesman with the accumulating paunch of a sportswriter and the entrepreneurial instincts of Phineas T. Barnum. He paid an unheard-of $50,000 to the winner of his self-proclaimed "World Championship" that carried an additional guarantee of 50 paydays, $1,000 a toss, for exhibitions spaced out over the year at obscure locations throughout the globe, which helps explain why many of May's champions were never heard from again. Almost every pro golfer, young and old (except of course Hogan, too dignified for carnivals), was drawn to the song of the calliope and the smell of the midway.

"I'm a young guy from South Africa," Player said, "and Demaret, a Texan, three-time Masters champion, and a wonderful, wonderful man, always smiling, always laughing, always joking, said, 'C'mon, there's another young fellow here you have to meet.' Today's players might not have even heard of Demaret, but he was a hell of a player, a *hell* of a player. Would more than hold his own with anybody now. And he was the most colorful performer, dresser, and talker in the game."

Palmer was slamming drivers on the practice tee, spinning those helicopter blades over his head. But the uniqueness of Arnie's swing wasn't what jumped out at Player. "It was those forearms," he said. "I thought, 'Man, this guy is strong.'" The balls were rocketing down the range.

"It was quite a breezy day, and he bent down, yanked out a few bits of grass, and tossed them up in the air. But he didn't look to see which way the wind took them. I asked him, 'Why do you do that?' 'I don't know,' he said. 'All the good players do it, so I do it, too.' Jimmy stood there, in his purple socks, laughing like crazy."

Player was born in 1935, six years after Palmer, but as Arnold got his start in the profession relatively late, at 25, Gary's came astonishingly early, at 17. His mother, Muriel, from whom he inherited his miniature features, died when he was eight following the cruelest siege of cancer. "She never saw me hit a golf ball," he said with a sadness that could still call him to the edge of childhood. Unlike a lot of tough guys, Player was utterly unafraid of sentiment.

If he didn't look like a tough guy at five feet six, consider the experience of a six-three Ohioan who during a round with Player replied to a sincere compliment by saying, "I'm not having any of that gamesmanship today, Gary." Player stopped in his tracks. "If you say so much as one more word to me the rest of this round," he told the man, "I'm going to *fuck* you up."

His father, Harry, was a gold miner with corrugated hands but a smooth disposition. "'The best friend I have in the world,' my dad used to say, 'is a rat.' Down in the hole, he would break off little pieces of his sandwich and feed them to the rat. You see, that rat knew when the cave-ins were coming. Never in his life did my father make more than two hundred dollars a month. We lived in a crummy little house. One day in nineteen fifty-two, Dad rolled up with a set of Turfrider clubs from Wilson. He shrugged and said, 'I had a bit of money.' Eight years later the bank manager told me how an overdraft had to be taken to buy those clubs. When I began to win golf tournaments, my dad would put his arms around me and just cry."

At one of Player's earliest competitions, nobody could understand why the grim boy in the oversize sweater hadn't jettisoned his heavy wool as a chilly morning turned into a scorching afternoon. The reason was, under Harry's old sweater, Gary was wearing Harry's old trousers, and the belt line washed up practically to his armpits.

Player said, "When I told my father I was turning pro at seventeen, he said, 'That's crazy, son. You can't. You just can't. I promised your mother you'd get an education.' 'Dad,' I said, 'I'm *going* to get an education, a *world* education. See these hands? They're going to hit more golf balls, and I'm going to travel more miles to do it, than any man who ever lived.'"

What Harry didn't know was that his son had been practicing signing his autograph for two years, since a teacher inquired, "What do you intend to do with your life?" "That was my art teacher, Mr. Miller, an Englishman," Player said. "'Professional golfer,' I replied. 'Well, I don't know what that will get you, my boy, but if you're any good, you're going to be signing a lot of autographs. Always keep this in mind: beauty of curvature. It's important. Here, cup your hand. No, a little more. There, there, there, there, and there. Now go practice that.'"

Player said, "Take a look at my autograph, and then set it down next to Palmer's and Nicklaus's, and Hogan's as well, for that matter. Every letter perfectly legible. Now, don't tell me those guys didn't practice, too." (Palmer did; the one who set him to practicing was his first-grade teacher, Rita Taylor. She taught him the Palmer Method. No relation.)

Before the spring of 1957, Harry Player wrote Augusta National autocrat Clifford Roberts to ask if 21-year-old Gary might be included in the field at the Masters. The young South African tied for 24th that year. He would be the first international golfer to win the Masters (1961) and to win it (1974) and to win it (1978).

Like everyone else on tour, he was mesmerized by Hogan. "They called him 'the Hawk,'" Player said, "because of those piercing eyes that looked straight through you. He came over to me once in a locker room, wanting to know how much I practiced. ["Hogan invented practice," Demaret said.] I answered him at some length. And the fact was, with the possible exception of Hogan himself, I practiced more than anybody. 'Double it,' he said gruffly, and walked away."

At an exceptionally weak moment—in Brazil, actually—Player put a call in to Fort Worth to solicit Hogan's help. He was *that* lost. Gary was suffering from just the sort of hook Ben had cured. In his follow-through Player was actually crossing his right foot over his left to try to head off the hook. "I hate a hook," Hogan had said. "It nauseates me. I could vomit when I see one. It's like a rattlesnake in your pocket."

Player got right to the point: "Mr. Hogan, I've been fighting this awful hook, and if I could just talk with you for a few minutes about my swing. Next to you, nobody has worked harder than I have. But I'm in trouble. I just don't know what to do."

"I'm going to be very curt with you," Hogan replied.

("I didn't know what that word meant," Gary said. "'Curt'?")

"Are you affiliated with a club manufacturer?"

"Dunlop."

"Call Mr. Dunlop," Hogan said, and hung up.

"I suppose he was a little like that with everybody," Player said. "You know, 'The secret's in the dirt. Dig it out of the dirt, like I did.' But for some reason he was at his meanest with Arnold. At a Ryder Cup, when Hogan was the U.S. captain, Palmer started to go over with him what he thought might be a favorable pairing that afternoon, and Hogan responded, 'What makes you think you're playing this afternoon?' Talk about mean, man. That's mean as crap." As a matter of fact, Arnold didn't play that afternoon.

In 1958, some weeks before the Masters, Palmer, Player, and Hogan were at dinner together with a gang of other tour pros in New York City. Bill Fugazy, the limousine mogul, was their host: "I'm surprised Hogan went," Player said. "He didn't go to many functions like that. During dinner, Ben was very, very rude to Arnold. We were all talking about swings, and Arnold was in the middle of saying something when Hogan cut him off. 'What do *you* know about the goddamned swing,' he said, 'with that swing *you've* got?' The whole table went quiet."

"Ben had to be joking," Dan Jenkins said, "and was probably a little over-served. In those days, everybody joked about Palmer's swing."

But Player and Palmer didn't think he was joking.

"Arnold just swallowed it," Gary said. "He could have reached over and snapped Hogan in half. I admired him for not doing so. Not retaliating when he so obviously could. I respected that immensely. It became my model later on, when I was blamed in America for supporting South Africa's system of apartheid, and blamed in my own country for *not* supporting it."

To loud criticism in the States, Player accepted an invitation to play golf with South African prime minister (and president-to-be) John Vorster (a white supremacist with bushy eyebrows), but Player had an ulterior motive. "Once I had established a relationship with Vorster, I was able to go to him later and say, 'I'd like to invite the black American golfer Lee Elder to come to South Africa and play.' He stared at me under those stupid eyebrows like I was a crazy man. But then he said just two words: 'Go ahead.' Activists in America pressured Lee not to come, but he came. It took a lot of balls. He did it to change lives. How I admired him."

Player paused a moment to look at the sky.

Then he said, "Whenever I got picketed on a golf course in the U.S., whenever a cup of ice was thrown in my face, whenever a telephone book slammed me in the back, I thought of Palmer at that dinner in New York, and I took it."

At the Masters a few weeks later, Palmer and Dow Finsterwald played a Tuesday practice match against Jackie Burke and Hogan. Weary and disappointed from an 18-hole playoff loss (78 to 77!) to Howie Johnson at the Azalea Open the day before, Palmer was still searching for his game against Burke and Hogan. But Dow carried him, and they won their bet, $35 apiece. "Afterward," Player said, "Arnie and Finsty got to the lunchroom first. The other two came in, and Hogan went to a different table. Arnie heard him say to Jackie, 'How the hell did *he* get in the Masters?'"

("Just loud enough to make sure I heard it," Palmer said, seated at his desk.)

"Well," Player said, "you know what happened next, don't you? That was the first year Arnold *won* the Masters."

"There was a tremendous rainstorm Saturday night," Palmer said. "I reached the twelfth tee Sunday with a one-stroke lead over Ken Venturi, my playing partner. That's when everything hit the fan."

The 12th hole, a par 3, represented the middle of "Amen Corner" on the far end of the course. The expression was coined at that tournament, maybe at that instant, by Herbert Warren Wind, borrowing from a 45-rpm jazz recording ("Shouting at the Amen Corner") by Chicago clarinetist Mezz Mezzrow. As Wind reckoned it, the corner began with the approach to the par-4 11th and ended after the drive at the par-5 13th.

Only players, caddies, and officials were permitted inside the ropes surrounding the 12th tee. From their tee shots at 12 until their second shots at 13, the golfers broke off from the crowd for a quiet interlude of relative privacy.

"My tee shot at twelve [155 yards, six-iron] flew the green," Palmer said, "and embedded itself in the mud between the fringe and back bunker. To me, an obvious drop without penalty. But the official standing there, Arthur Lacey, said, 'It's only half-plugged.' I said, 'That's like being half-pregnant.' Because of the heavy rain, just for the Sunday round, we were playing wet-weather rules 'through the green' [taking in all parts of the course except the tees, greens, sand bunkers, and water hazards]. I knew I was right. 'I'm going to play two balls,' I told Lacey. He said, 'You don't do that here.'

"'Huh?'"

Palmer barely moved the indented ball, into a puddle of casual water, from where he received an uncontested free drop. But he required a chip and a couple of putts from there for a double bogey 5. Returning to the embedded scratch, he dropped another ball over his shoulder. Rolling nearer the hole twice, it was eventually placed, and this time he got up and down for 3. "We'll let the rules committee sort it all out when we get in," he told Venturi.

"I *agreed* with Palmer on the original call," Venturi said. "That ball was absolutely embedded. But he didn't declare he was playing a provisional until after he made the double bogey. To me, that was wrong. Dead wrong."

Arnold said, "I *did* declare the second ball, to Lacey, before I played the first. Ken didn't hear me."

The killer for Venturi came in the 13th fairway as Palmer was in the go-or-layup position, weighing the considerable risk of a 230-yard second shot over water to the par 5. Had he known the score, he might not have gambled. He looked across the fairway at Ken, who was either one behind or one ahead and had already laid up with his own second.

"They're going to give me a five back there, aren't they?" Palmer said.

"You're goddamned right they are," Venturi told him. So Arnold went for it with a 3-wood, and got it. "He met the ball squarely," Wind wrote, "and it rose in a low parabola. There was some draw on the shot, and it curved from right to left as it crossed the creek and landed comfortably on the green." Eighteen feet from the hole. Straight in the cup for eagle.

Sitting nearby in his green combination wheel chair/golf cart, Bobby Jones experienced a flashback. That night, he would say, "Today I was watching Palmer at thirteen and once more Gene Sarazen was hitting from that mound at fifteen [in 1935]. As Gene followed through, I remember thinking to myself, 'It's the perfect golf swing.' Of course, I had no way of knowing it was going in the cup for a double eagle. When Palmer hit his, I turned to Cliff [Augusta National chairman Cliff Roberts] and said, 'He really got that one.' It gave me the exact same feeling of exhilaration I felt all those years before. And this time I was surprised it *didn't* go in the cup."

Shortly, Jones and Roberts came riding up like the cavalry. They heard Palmer out, and after conferring with several other green jackets behind the 15th green, ruled that Arnold had made a 3 at 12. In exasperation, Venturi began three-putting his head off. And when the head comes off, the turnip goes on. Playing together, both Doug Ford and Fred Hawkins had reasonable putts at

18 to tie, but each finished a stroke behind Palmer. As the defending champion, Ford helped Arnie into the green jacket, making him at 28 the youngest Masters winner since 25-year-old Byron Nelson in 1937. Palmer had his first major title.

"The rules of golf are very touchy and troublous things to administer," Wind wrote (*troublous* being a typical Herb word; he liked fillip, too, as in "an arm of Rae's Creek, four or five feet wide, adds a nice fillip of menace"), "and my own feeling on the subject is that if a man is notified he has been appointed to serve on the rules committee for a certain tournament he should instantly remember that he must attend an important business meeting in Khartoum and tender his exquisite regrets to the tournament committee."

"Two years later," Venturi said, "Palmer finished three-three-three to beat me by a shot, and I was forced to sit there at the green jacket ceremony as the runner-up. He turned to me and whispered, 'I'm sorry it had to be you, Ken.' I looked away and said, 'Two years too late.'"

Player said, "Venturi started to tell me once how Arnold had cheated him at the twelfth hole, but I stopped him right there. They always yell 'cheater' at the end. 'That's crap with a capital *C*,' I told him. More than once, I've said to Palmer, 'The reason I'm proud to have you as my friend is because you always do the right thing.' Always doing the right thing was what made him Palmer."

Many years after the incident, sitting in a locker room at Eagle Creek in Naples, Florida, Venturi was reflecting on his interesting life. "I played baseball with DiMaggio," he told me. "I roomed with Sinatra. I knew Dean Martin, Sammy Davis Jr., the whole Rat Pack." He also knew disappointment. "I had *three* heartbreaks at the Masters," he said.

The first and worst was in 1956, when he was a 24-year-old amateur and opened the tournament with a 66, the best score by an amateur still. That Saturday night, leading the tournament by four strokes, he was summoned to an audience with Roberts. In those days Masters tradition paired the Sunday leader with Byron Nelson, but Venturi's close connections to Nelson and Hogan ("I was taught by Michelangelo and shown by Da Vinci") worried the chairman.

Roberts invited Venturi to pick any other playing companion for the final round. In a typical show of bravado, he chose Sam Snead, with whom he had never been paired before. "Snead's a tough man to play with," Roberts warned. "So am I," Ken said.

Sam was known for intentionally pulling the wrong club, making sure his playing partner saw the number on the back, then hooding it slightly to change the loft. If he wanted to, he could hit all of his irons the same distance. So could Hogan. So could Bobby Locke, the South African. So could Christy O'Connor Sr., the Irishman. So could a lot of the great ones.

Venturi shot 80 and lost to Burke by a stroke. A measly stroke.

His father was a San Francisco ship chandler who, when he wasn't supplying twine and other supplies for the wharf, collected green fees at Harding Park, a public golf course. Ken liked baseball and was good at it, "but golf was easier for me," he said, "because it was easier to be alone." He was a stutterer who became a national communicator, for CBS. "I knew I was going to win the U.S. Open [which he did at sweltering Congressional Country Club in 1964 in a double round so delirious it ended the double rounds], but I never thought I'd be able to speak a whole sentence." With a sheepish smile he said, "I guess I'm the fellow who lost the Arnold Palmer sweepstakes. But then, I was always more of a Ben Hogan guy anyway." (Isn't it funny how only the Hogan acolytes—Venturi, Bolt, Gardner Dickinson—were ever able to pull off those flat white linen caps?)

Venturi won his final PGA tournament in 1966, in the Lucky International at Harding Park, where his father had collected green fees and where Ken played his first round of golf. "I guarantee you," he said, "I wrote that acceptance speech when I was fourteen years old." By two strokes, he beat Palmer.

After Arnold won the '58 Masters, did he throw his victory back in Hogan's face?

"What would have been the point of that?" he said. "I admit, though, I felt an extra touch of personal satisfaction, and maybe he could see it the next time he looked at me. When I first came to Augusta, peeking through all those magnificent trees, it was such a thrill. Seeing Bobby Jones there, and Gene Sarazen, and Byron Nelson, and Ben Hogan—those were the guys my dad and I used to talk about. I read Byron's book, and Jones's book. I remember things that happened to them. To actually know them, to see them play, to play with them, to eat with them, to have them call me by name, meant so much to me. I wanted to hear my name on Hogan's lips, too, I'll admit it. I ached for that. But, to the day he died, he never pronounced 'Arnold' and he never pronounced 'Palmer'—it was always 'Fella,' or 'Hey, you.' I resented the hell out of it. But there was nothing I could do about it. Also, I didn't want to spend my life being bitter, especially with all the good fortune coming my way."

Hadn't Palmer always been a great one himself for momentarily misplacing names and addressing old friends as "pard" or "pro"? He once propped his arms up on the shoulders of the lovable Brit writer Peter Dobereiner, saying, "I'm worried about our friend, Peter." "Yes, so am I," Dobers said, "because I'm he."

"It's not the same thing, trust me," Palmer said. "Hogan had a purpose for everything he did, and he had a purpose for this. I was just never quite sure what it was. I think he wanted me to know that, as far as he was concerned, I wasn't an 'entity.' I was just another player. He and Byron and Snead and I played an exhibition once at Preston Trail [in Dallas]. I played my best that day, and I got the impression it bothered him."

There's a photograph of them on the tee, Palmer with his L&M, Hogan with his Chesterfield, looking everywhere but at each other.

"I talked easily with Nelson and Snead," Palmer said, "but Hogan? Zero. I had more conversation with Valerie [Ben's wife]. She was a terrific lady. The whole thing between us embarrassed her. He was a great player. He proved he was a great player. But he wasn't a great guy."

To try to understand, it might help to know Hogan had a brother named Royal and a sister named Princess and he was just Ben. He was born in Stephenville, Texas, raised by a seamstress (Clara) and a blacksmith (Chester), who shot himself to death in 1922 in their home. If it's true that Ben was present at his father's suicide, he was nine.

At the age of 15, playing in the annual caddie tournament at Fort Worth's Glen Garden Country Club, he lost the finals match (normally a nine-hole game) to Nelson after Byron made a 30-footer on the ninth to tie. Hogan thought he had won a sudden-death playoff at the next hole, but the terms of the match had been redrawn in midstream, to a full 18 holes, and another long putt ultimately beat him. One junior membership was at stake. Nelson got it.

In 2002, Byron was sitting on a park bench at Las Colinas in Dallas at 90 years old, the first born and last survivor of the class of 1912. "I never knew there was a game of golf until I was thirteen," he told me. "I didn't know the name, even. Do you know what it says on my birth certificate? 'Rural Area, Ellis County, Texas.' By fifteen I was caddying at Glen Garden. Contrary to all the stories that have been written, I never once caddied in a group with Ben. He worked mainly for a man named Ed Stewart. I had a regular, too, a judge. At the time I thought he was old. He was probably fifty. The first time I was ever conscious of Ben was at the Christmas party Glen Garden threw the caddies—turkey with all the trimmings—followed by the big caddie tournament where all our regulars caddied for us.

"Ben quit high school to turn pro. He would go off to a few tournaments, run out of money, and come back. Go off again, run out of money again, and come back again. [Before breaking through, Hogan rammed his head against that brick wall for more than a decade, in one tournament finishing 38th and winning $8.50.] He was more determined to be great than any man I ever saw."

In 1949, Hogan and Valerie crashed head-on into a Greyhound bus on a foggy road near Van Horn, Texas, leaving Ben broken like china from pelvis to collarbone, ankle to rib. He limped his way to U.S. Open titles in 1950, 1951, and 1953. In 1952, two 69s gave him a two-stroke lead in the Open at Dallas's Northwood Club, but on a 36-hole final Saturday in murderous 98-degree heat, he shot a pair of 74s for third place by himself behind Julius Boros and Porky Oliver. In 1953, Hogan played in six tournaments total, winning five of them (including the Masters, U.S. Open, and Open Championship), finishing third in the sixth. (You might want to reread that sentence.) Logistically, the British and PGA—at match play then—essentially overlapped. Everyone in the Open field at Carnoustie in Scotland was obliged to play in a qualifier, not that Hogan's legs were up to trudging 36-hole PGA matches anyway.

"He played his best golf," Nelson said, "after his automobile accident, after he learned to walk again. Whatever Hogan did to Arnold that hurt Arnie so, I can't believe he truly meant it. You know, Ben knew that people as a group didn't like him. Ben had some friends, but most people didn't like him. He was so driven and he was so good. I think he had, I don't know, kind of a fear of being close to people. Ben told me finally, 'Byron, I didn't realize that so many people liked me.' You could almost cry."

Sam Snead did cry. He was kicking back at the Greenbrier with his feet up in front of the television, pleased with his round that morning on the White Course. He had taken $300 off a sportswriter who said, "Don't think I don't know you could beat me playing left-handed. I'm going to put it on my expense account." He laughed and said, "Amateurs still ask me to read their putts. What they don't realize is I have to walk all the way to the hole just to tell if it's uphill or down."

A 1953 clip of Hogan and Snead was replaying on the TV, from the awards ceremony following the U.S. Open at Oakmont. It was Hogan's fourth and last Open victory, Snead's fourth and last second-place finish in the only major tournament he never won. In 1937, Sam's first U.S. Open, he needed just a bogey-6 on the final hole at the Philadelphia Country Club to tie Ralph Guldahl. He made an 8. In the clip with Hogan—Snead had seen it a hundred times—he reaches over wanly to touch the elusive trophy in Ben's arms. Holding out the large silver pot, Hogan rubs it up and down Sam's stomach. Rubbing it in, Sam always thought.

"The three things in golf I feared most," Snead said, "were lightning, downhill-sidehill putts, and Ben Hogan."

That was one of his stock lines. Another couple were: "If you ever received a blood transfusion from Hogan, you'd die of pneumonia." And, by the end of Ben's career: "He had the yips so bad, you could smoke a whole cigarette waiting for him to take the putter back." But then, in a whisper, Sam said earnestly, "If Hogan had been guaranteed another National Open putting 'side-saddle,' like I do, he still wouldn't have done it. It looks so god-awful."

Snead's victim on the course that day said, "You know what he's doing with the trophy, don't you?"

"What?"

"You want to touch *it*. *It* wants to touch you."

And Sam began to weep.

Hogan's final Masters, at the age of 54, was writer Dave Kindred's first, at 26, in 1967. In Saturday's third round, Hogan shot a course record 30 on the back nine, birdieing 10, 11, 12, 13, 15, and 18 for a score of 66 that brought him within two strokes of the leader, Bobby Nichols. "I've had standing ovations before," Hogan said in the Bartlett Lounge, "but not on nine consecutive holes." His left knee and his left shoulder throbbed like toothaches, from the new cortisone shots as much as the old injuries. He said, "I left blood out there in every cup."

After Hogan's birdies-and-bogeys session, Kindred and a few others trailed him back to the locker room, where Ben said, "There's a lot of fellas [there's that word, 'fellas'] who have got to fall dead for me to win tomorrow. But, I don't mind telling you, I'll play just as hard as I've ever played in my life."

"Palmer sat off in a corner," Kindred said, "changing his shoes and listening."

Of course, nobody fell dead Sunday. Hogan shot 77 to tie Snead for 10th place, a full 10 strokes behind the winner, Gay Brewer. That morning Bob Drum and Dan Jenkins set the over/under on Ben's score at 75, and even Jenkins took the over. Palmer shot 69 to finish solo 4th.

Among the writers, maybe only Dan knew Hogan well. They played numerous rounds together, usually just the two of them in Fort Worth, where Jenkins was the beat writer at the old *Press*. "I'd be watching him practice," Jenkins said, "and he'd say, 'Let's go.'

"In nineteen fifty-six, Ben called me up and said, 'I want you in a foursome for an exhibition at Colonial benefiting the Olympic Games.' I said, 'OK, I guess, but there must be somebody better than me.' 'No, I want you,' he said. I worked half a day at the paper, came out, didn't even have a golf shirt, wore a dress shirt, rolled up the sleeves, changed my shoes, didn't hit a practice ball, got to the first tee, and five thousand people were waiting. Now, what do you do?

"Somehow I got off a decent drive into the fairway, and proceeded to top a three-wood fifty yards—it was a par five—then topped another three wood, then topped a five iron. All I wanted to do was dig a hole and bury myself in the ground forever. As I was walking to the next shot, still a hundred yards from the green, Hogan came up beside me and said, 'You could probably swing faster if you tried hard enough.' I slowed it down, got calm, and shot seventy-six. He shot his usual sixty-seven. That's the Hogan I knew."

In 1993, Kindred and I went to Shady Oaks Country Club in Fort Worth to ambush Hogan, who had just turned 81. Most days he sat alone in a long-sleeved white shirt and a tie knotted to his neck looking out a grill room window at the 18th green, sipping white wine and smoking. Shady Oaks's young pro, Mike Wright, told us, "I'll introduce you, but I'm not making any promises."

Ted Williams once shook Hogan's hand and said, "I just shook a hand that felt like five bands of steel." When I shook his hand, it still did. British broadcaster Henry Longhurst's old description of Hogan was holding up fairly well, too. "A small man," said Longhurst, "normal weight, no more than a hundred and forty pounds, height about five feet nine inches, with smooth black hair [now gray and largely gone], wide head, wide eyes, and a wide mouth which tends, when the pressure is on, to contract into a thin, straight pencil line. You could see him sitting at a poker table, saying, expressionless, 'Your thousand and another five.' He might have four aces or a pair of twos."

Rising with a bounce, Hogan said, "Welcome, welcome, it's good to see you," but he didn't sit back down because he didn't want us to sit down. He intended for this to take 10 minutes, not the entire afternoon. It was only the second time I ever saw him. At the Masters in 1977, Hogan came back to Augusta just for the Champions' Dinner that he had started in 1952 with a letter to Cliff Roberts:

Dear Cliff:

I wish to invite you to attend a stag dinner at the Augusta
National on Friday evening, April 4th, at 7:15 p.m. It's my
wish to invite all the Masters Champions who are going to be
here, plus Bob Jones and Cliff Roberts. The latter has agreed
to make available his room for the dinner party and I hope
you can be on hand promptly at 7:15 p.m. My only stipulation
is that you wear your green coat.

Cordially yours,

Ben Hogan

Because sponsors of the upcoming Liberty Mutual Insurance
Legends of Golf tournament (precursor to the 50-and-over senior
tour) were tossing his name around loosely to advertisers and writers, Hogan dropped by the press barn to straighten everybody out.
"I don't know what these people have been telling you," he said,
"but I want you gentlemen to know that I will not be putting my
game on public display under any circumstance."

"But we heard you just shot your age [64] at Shady Oaks," someone said.

"Ah, well," he mumbled.

Someone else wanted to know, "Have you ever had a perfect
round of golf?"

"No," he said, "but I almost dreamt it once. I made seventeen
straight holes in one and lipped out at the eighteenth. I was mad as
hell."

Kindred and I came to Fort Worth from Scotland, where we
played Carnoustie. The highlights of Hogan's victory there (in his
only Open Championship appearance) were four 4s he made at the

par-5 sixth, known as "Hogan's Alley," one of many holes at Riviera, Colonial, and other places so designated. Even for me, I played woefully at Carnoustie, but I had an eight-footer at the sixth for eagle. Missed it, of course.

"Tom nearly made a three at the sixth hole," Kindred told Hogan, who said, "I can't remember individual holes anymore."

"That's all right, Mr. Hogan," I said, "they all remember you."

In 1997, when 21-year-old Tiger Woods was running away with the Masters, Kindred, Jenkins, and a bunch of us wrote down our top ten golfers of all time and threw the lists unsigned into the center of the table. Dan might as well have signed his:

Ben Hogan, Ben Hogan, Ben Hogan, Ben Hogan, Ben Hogan, Ben Hogan, Ben Hogan, Jack Nicklaus, Tiger Woods, Doak Walker.

Before 1958 ended, the reigning Masters champion, Palmer, and the recent PGA champion, Finsterwald, came together at storied Athens Country Club in southeastern Ohio for "Dow Finsterwald Day." Arnie's old friend had won his major just weeks before by two strokes over Billy Casper in the first PGA since the format was switched from match play to medal. (In 1957, Dow had lost the last match of the match-play era to Lionel Hebert.) Two amateurs were along in Athens: 37-year-old Ohio State Hall of Famer Howard Baker Saunders, and 18-year-old Jack Nicklaus.

"Jack was included," Dow said, "because he had won the Ohio Open at Marietta and, not just throughout the state but all across the country, was sort of recognized as the coming guy. There wasn't any doubt about this kid's talent. The only question was: What did he have between his ears and inside his chest? Well, we found out, didn't we? I can't say I knew then the historic significance of Jack's and Arnie's first round of golf together, but time did kind of stop there for a second when they shook hands. I can still see them."

A nine-hole course with two sets of tees, Athens Country Club was designed in 1921 by Scioto pro George Sargent, then renovated in 1928 by the saintly Scottish architect Donald Ross. "Someone proposed a driving contest," Dow said, at the 338-yard par-4 first hole. "Arnold led off, knocking it right on the green. Then Jack stepped up on those tree trunks of his and drove his ball thirty yards *over* the green. It's true the ground dropped off pretty steeply back there, but still."

Jack made four, Arnie three. Nicklaus went out in 35, Palmer 30. Thinking back, Arnold said, "I shot sixty-two that day, and I *tried* to shoot sixty-two [to sixty-eight for Jack]. I wanted to impress him. I was certainly impressed *by* him. I never was surprised by anything Jack did, only in some cases by how soon he did it."

By the way, the date was September 25.

7

1959

WINNER:

Thunderbird Invitational

Oklahoma City Open

West Palm Beach Open

"Agent of the big shoulders."

PALMER AND MARK MCCORMACK first crossed paths in 1950, in Raleigh, North Carolina, at a collegiate golf match where Arnold was playing number two for Wake Forest (behind Bud Worsham) and Mark number five for William & Mary. They literally crossed paths, as McCormack saw Doug Weiland, Bill & Mary's number two, walking alongside "this tan, well-built guy hitching at his pants." Mark signaled to Doug, *How's it going?* Weiland responded by dragging an expressive forefinger across his throat.

They didn't actually meet until six years later, and didn't have their initial conversation until two years after that. In 1959, with a handshake, Palmer and McCormack combined forces to start making conglomerates of each other.

Mark was a Chicagoan, godson to the poet Carl Sandburg ("*Hog Butcher for the World . . . Stormy, husky, brawling*"), with whom he played more than a few rounds of golf. McCormack was competent enough to compete in four U.S. and three British Amateur championships. In 1958 he was a regional medalist while qualifying for his only U.S. Open, the Tommy Bolt Open in Tulsa, where Mark missed the cut.

"I was good, but I wasn't good enough," he said. "If you want to beat Bobby Fischer, don't play him at chess." When he came out of Yale Law School, he went to work for a firm in Cleveland. "But I had my own game," he said, and his own game plan.

"Mark and another guy started a little agency," Palmer said, "booking exhibitions for golfers. Dow Finsterwald and I signed up along with just a few others. Gene Littler. Bob Toski. You know, modest payoffs, two-hundred-fifty-, three-hundred-dollar outings—spendable money, as I liked to call it. But pretty soon I knew my man and went to him with a proposal. I needed a full-time business manager to handle everything I had been piling on poor Winnie: taxes, travel, accounting, fielding the extraneous offers that had started coming in. Seeing what was appropriate to do and what wasn't." The door was left open for McCormack to add other clients later, but, for the time being, Palmer wanted him exclusively. They shook on it. Through the years McCormack and Palmer signed and cosigned a thousand contracts, but they never had one of their own. "Just that handshake," Arnold said. It was enough.

McCormack's immediate chore was to extricate Palmer from bad deals he had made on the fly in that era when golfers gratefully signed away their images for free balls and shirts. Arnold fought him all the way. "You put everything on a dollars-and-cents basis," he said to Mark. "I can't do that. I like these people. Improve the terms if you can, but let's not lose them. They're my friends."

Among the friendliest was the Wilson Sporting Goods Company's glad-handing player rep, Joe Wolfe—or, as McCormack referred to him sarcastically, "*good old* Joe Wolfe." Studying the Wilson paperwork, Mark was flabbergasted to find that his client, the 1958 Masters champion, had re-upped through 1960 under pretty much the same pauper's terms as the original three-year agreement of 1954.

And it was a "worldwide" deal, meaning Palmer couldn't make a nickel anywhere at anything without Wilson's involvement and consent. In even smaller print, a rider actually tied Palmer down, at the company's option, until 1963. "Of course, nothing tied them to him if they wanted out," McCormack said. "What a contract."

Hamstrung by the value Palmer placed on friendship and trust ("Wait and see, Mark, these are nice people; in the end I'm sure they'll do what's fair"), McCormack under protest hammered out the long-term agreement Arnold thought he wanted. After Mark insisted on several minor clauses involving increased royalties, deferred income, and insurance, the tentative agreement was sent to James D. Cooney, Wilson's elderly chairman (a former district judge from Iowa) for his signature.

Wilson had been a meatpacking company originally, and still was, primarily. The relatively small sporting goods offshoot came about when somebody wondered if any money could be made from the other parts of the animals—goods like baseball gloves, footballs, and tennis racket strings. Canny in most things, but knowing little about sports (let alone golf), Judge Cooney didn't recognize a sweetheart deal when it was handed to him. "'Deferred income'?" he exclaimed. "'Split-dollar insurance'? Don't we already have a contract with this Palmer fellow?"

Cooney's loud "No!" hurt Arnold and wised him up, but Mark

was beyond ecstatic. "Palmer's going to have to become a million-aire," he said, "whether he likes it or not." On November 1, 1963, the Wilson contract expired and the world changed. The first set of new clubs (serial number 00001) rolled off the production line of the Arnold Palmer Golf Company in Chattanooga, Tennessee, and went directly to Pap, who told Arnie, "I guess this makes up for all the clubs I gave you when you were a kid."

From then on, McCormack's basic function was saying "Hell no" for a man who couldn't even say "Heck no." Mark knew he had a terrific product to sell, a bold style coupled with a natural warmth. Not just a greatness—a goodness, too. With Arnold Palmer's name on your laundry, you knew it would come back clean. Together, they rethought the business of sports.

McCormack's archetypal golfing hero was Frank Stranahan, of all people, the fitness enthusiast with the barbells in his suitcase who was Palmer's fifth-round victim at the 1954 U.S. Amateur. "I'll never forget," Mark said, "in the forties my dad and I went to a Kansas City Open at the Hillcrest Country Club. There was this player doing well, Frank Stranahan. I was just a kid, but he was only eight or ten years older. I had my Brownie camera. Walking from the putting green to the tee, he saw me and stopped, smiled, and let me take his picture. I never forgot that. He had a red shirt on, and I never forgot that shirt, either. My goal was to get one of those red shirts."

On the other hand, there was Henry Picard, who refused Mark's request for an autograph. "You know, I never liked Picard after that," he said, "and actually rooted against him. You hear things about kids and autographs and the way players treat the public. They're true."

McCormack had a sensational long game. With amazing vision and foresight, he could see all the way to Australia and Japan. He pictured Arnold Palmer teashops on the Ginza, and made plans for the private airplane he knew was coming before Arnold did (the one with the initials *AP* on the fuselage), not to mention the streams of jets that followed. Then, with Palmer's permission, he brought Player and Nicklaus into the fold, if not technically creating "the Big Three" (and a TV show of the same name), then promoting them to a tee.

"He was a genius," Player said. "After us, the pope. It was Twiggy. It was Pelé. It was everything and everybody. When I went to see him the first time, he had this little apartment in Cleveland, and the kids are on the table and the wife is changing the diapers, and he ends up building an empire, an empire."

Golf Digest named McCormack the most powerful man in golf. *Tennis* magazine named him the most powerful man in tennis. *Sports Illustrated* named him the most powerful man in sports. His International Management Group stretched out into 80-some offices in 30-some countries, but Palmer stayed the primary client, even after Margaret Thatcher and Mikhail Gorbachev came aboard. In his mid-80s, without hitting a single golf shot that counted, Arnold was still earning $40 million a year under his perfect logo, an umbrella.

McCormack and I were sitting outdoors in the strawberries-and-cream section at Wimbledon. He had just signed on as the pope's flack for a papal tour of Europe ("Give us this day our daily Wonderbread," prayed one of London's fishier fish wraps), and though he wanted to talk about the ball-kid costumes he had personally designed for the tournament, I kept steering the conversation back to the pontiff.

"So what'll it be," I asked him, "Cinzano on the altar cloth and Amana on the miter?"

"Strictly piety items," he said humorlessly. Mark said a lot of funny things without knowing it.

He complained about the column I wrote, taking particular offense at the headline "A Pope and a Smile." "Well, you know, Mark," I said, "I don't write the headlines, but I wish I'd written that one."

We weren't pals. He was a chilly character, and I guess I enjoyed winding him up too much.

"You're more than entitled to your cut from the dresses and shoes," I'd say, "but where do you get off taking fifteen percent of Chris Evert's winnings on the court? I've never seen you out there with her."

"We [meaning IMG] give her peace of mind so she can concentrate on her game," he said.

McCormack had contracts down cold, emphasis on the word *cold*. In his first attempt at recruiting Muhammad Ali—whom he came to represent eventually—he asked, "How much does Rahman get?" (Rahman was Muhammad's little brother.) "Fifty grand," the champ said, "which isn't bad for drivin' and jivin'." "And what does Bundini do exactly?" "Mostly he holds the spit bucket." "You're going to have to get rid of all of these guys, Muhammad." For the time being, Ali got rid of McCormack instead.

Mark couldn't fathom why Spanish golfer José María Olazábal refused to ditch hometown manager Sergio Gomez, a "small-timer" in McCormack's estimation, in favor of big-time IMG. "Strange guy, Ollie," McCormack said. "I don't understand him at all. He doesn't seem the slightest bit interested in all the money he could be making." One year, Olazábal returned his stipend from Titleist with a note that read, "I haven't played all season long [due to a foot injury] and I cannot accept your money when I haven't earned it." What about that couldn't McCormack understand?

In the middle week of the Olympic Games in Los Angeles, *Time* managing editor Ray Cave, the author of that *Sports Illustrated* Sportsman of the Year piece on Palmer in 1960, called from New York to sound me out on a cover idea. "What would you think of

Zola Budd?" he asked. Ray, who was a great guy, knew a lot about sports, but he didn't know Zola Budd, the barefoot South African runner, from Billy Budd. I thought to myself, *McCormack*.

I talked Ray out of Zola, who clipped heels with Mary Decker a week later. Decker fell like Phaintin' Phil Scott. As it turned out, Budd would have been a hell of a prescient *Time* cover, proving I wasn't always right about McCormack.

Mark kept score by dollar signs. The worst insult he could impart about anyone was "I feel kind of sorry for [so-and-so]. He's had a difficult career, which is waning. He's a very bright guy who has just not been very successful in life."

But give McCormack this: as devoutly as he cherished cash, he loved Palmer, too. There's no doubt about that. You could hear it in his voice. His favorite description of Arnold was a scene he witnessed on the golf course in 1962 and retold constantly.

"It was at Colonial," he said. "Arnold was in a playoff with Johnny Pott and was looking at a delicate little chip from just off the green. Behind him, a small boy was chattering to his mother. Arnold turned around with a scowl but then, looking at the kid, laughed. The gallery laughed, too. All of the tension in the atmosphere drained away. As Arnold retook his stance, the boy started to cry. His mother was beside herself with embarrassment. Arnold turned again and laughed again. In the next instant he heard a muffled sound and stopped a third time. She had a hand over her son's mouth now and the child was turning blue. Arnold knelt down and took the kid in his arms. 'Hey, don't choke him,' he told her. 'This is just a golf tournament. It's not that important.' Almost holing the chip, he won the playoff."

There were many similar stories. A 10-year-old boy named Roger panicked when he became separated from his parents in the multitudes following Palmer at Pebble Beach. Arnold went into the gallery, reassured him, took him by the hand, and walked him down the middle of the fairway, knowing Roger's parents would see him there. Sure enough, a mother's voice immediately called out, "Roger!" Roger Maltbie went on to win back-to-back tournaments his rookie year on the PGA Tour, finish fourth at a Masters, lead an Open Championship after 36 holes, beat Hale Irwin in a playoff at Nicklaus's inaugural Memorial Tournament, and make a long living on television walking fairways beside players.

"The greatest thing about Palmer," McCormack said, "is that his instinct for kindness, even at the most critical moments, overtakes his tremendous desire to win. I've been around a lot of great athletes, and I believe he's the only great athlete who ever lived whom you can say that about."

No lawyer/agent ever worked harder or longer than McCormack. In 1994, via cruise ship, he set a record for working vacations that will never be broken. "It was for eleven weeks," he said. "I started out in Buenos Aires in January and ended up in Japan in April. I went around Cape Horn up to Chile and across to Easter Island and the Pitcairn Islands, Tahiti, then down to Auckland, Christchurch, Dunedin, then over to Tasmania, up to Sydney, then up to Cairns, and around the corner to Bali, Singapore, and Thailand and then to Hong Kong and Shanghai and Kobe, where I got off. [So, when I had asked him, "Where do you get off . . . ?" it turned out the answer was Kobe.] I visited eight of our offices during the trip. I had a penthouse suite for [wife] Betsy and myself. I had two outside double cabins for family and business associates and friends. And I had a single cabin for secretaries. We would work in the mornings."

Betsy Nagelsen, the former touring tennis pro and client, was his second wife, 26 years his junior. "I'm going to die first, probably," he said. "To find the ideal age for a man and woman, someone said you should divide the man's age by two and add seven. So when you're forty, she should be twenty-seven. We would be just about right according to that formula."

They had a daughter in 1997. The day before Maggie was born, Mark referred to himself as "a youngish sixty-seven" but aspired to be younger still. McCormack died in 2003, of vanity. He went in for a face-lift and didn't come out, leaving an estate said to be upwards of $750 million.

"After I won the Open Championship in nineteen sixty-nine," said Englishman Tony Jacklin, who also won the U.S. Open in 1970, "I signed with McCormack. That day I turned into a kind of hamster, stepping into a cage, running my ass off for the next fifteen years. The animal I least associate myself with is a bloody hamster.

"When Mark said things like 'Tony, I think you ought to go to Nigeria to do this exhibition match, then stop off in Paris to play the European Tour, then hop the red-eye to America to catch up with the U.S. Tour,' well, you tend to do it, don't you? At least I did. I shouldn't have. Chasing every dollar was a disastrous thing to do, for me. And, I think, for Arnie, too. McCormack ran him ragged as well. Him most of all."

Arnie and Tony were friendly rivals through the years. "He beat me in a Ryder Cup singles," Jacklin said. "In a UBS singles, I got my revenge. We had some lovely times. The fans didn't know the golfer, don't know the golfer, as well as they knew and know the man. I'm talking about on the course. He was a tough guy on the course, an unbelievable competitor. Gave no quarter. Just as selfish as golfers are selfish. The ill will he had for your shots radiated off of him like squiggly lines. You could feel it. Don't get me wrong, he was the first one to shake your hand when the game was over, to look you in the eye and say, 'Well played.' But, until then, he was the last one to do anything of the kind. There were no mid-round compliments from Palmer, just as it should be."

Jacklin believed McCormack settled on what Arnold's legacy should be long before he had to, selling him thereafter as something better and more important than *just* a winner, *merely* a winner, which was true enough. "Premeditatedly," Jacklin said, "Mark took the emphasis *off* winning, knowing winning is always temporary. And, as a new business model—the most money for the longest time—he was proved right, wasn't he? But the campaign cheated the competitor, maybe the all-time competitor. I think it's completely understandable that Arnold stopped winning so soon—too soon. After all, what he was, who he was, didn't depend on winning. It didn't really matter if he won, except to him. Desperately. I blame McCormack for that."

By the '60s, McCormack was already telling the *Wall Street Journal* haughtily, "Arnold has reached the point where his on-course successes aren't terribly important to his enterprises anymore." Which was where McCormack had been going all along. Of those enterprises, *Sports Illustrated* said, "The way he has been expanding, everyone may soon be flying to the moon in an Arnold Palmer rocket and staying in an Arnold Palmer motel overlooking the Arnold Palmer crater."

The depiction of McCormack in Jacklin's autobiography was unsparing. "I got a note from his first wife, Nancy," Tony said, "who read my book. She wrote, 'I don't think Mark gave either one of us his best shot.'"

Palmer wanted to quit smoking in the early 1960s, "not because he hated the taste or smell of tobacco," McCormack said, "though he did come to feel that way, I think. What he really hated was the idea that there was something he couldn't control. He hated that on the golf course and he hated that in life." Naturally, Mark encouraged him to hold off until the contract with Liggett & Myers was up.

Most pro golfers smoked then. Hogan represented Chesterfield on beaming subway billboards that, absent the flat white linen cap and the dour expression, looked only faintly like him. Sometimes the Hogan ads were posted near a grinning Beau Jack, the two-time lightweight boxing champion and onetime Augusta National bootblack and caddie, saying, "I read Red Smith's column every day in the *Herald Tribune*." ("Everybody," Red said with an affectionate sigh, "knew poor Beau was illiterate.")

Because Jack Nicklaus was self-conscious about his squeaky voice (when Nicklaus yelled "Fore!" in Columbus, dogs as far away as Cincinnati jumped), he took dulcet-toned ABC broadcaster Chris Schenkel's facetious advice on how to lower his register, and began puffing chains of Marlboro Reds. "I'd had a few smokes at Ohio State," Jack admitted, but his fingers didn't turn yellow until he was a rookie on tour. "Looking at a highlight film, I saw myself with a cigarette dangling from my lip, tossing it to the ground so I could putt, then picking it up and jamming it right back in my mouth. *Ugh*. Then and there, I quit smoking on the golf course, but I'd still mooch a cigarette from Jim Murray or some other writer in the interview room, until I stopped for good when I was forty."

For Palmer, quitting smoking was a tedious, miserable, on-and-off process. The cigarette was part of his equipment and image, a workingman's emblem and prop, and he at least had to consider the possibility that its tranquilizing effect in the heat of competition was a factor in his success. "I smoked pretty heavily from about the age of fourteen or fifteen," he said, "on the sly, of course, out of Pap's view. He knew I smoked, but he didn't know how much."

At the Crosby Clambake early in 1964, the weather on the Monterey Peninsula was atrocious even for a Crosby week, and Arnie's sinuses were screaming. "Bob Hope liked to call Bing's tournament 'The Pneumonia Open,'" he said. "Crosby didn't even smile at that. I went to San Francisco straight from there to see a sinus specialist, who knew I was a smoker. Who didn't? I'd flick my cigarette and then hit my shot. I don't think I ever had one that lasted two holes."

(English Ryder Cupper and raconteur Peter Alliss said, "Palmer didn't smoke a cigarette so much as burn it to the ground. One long drag and a five-inch ash appeared.")

"With a sinus condition like yours," said the doctor, "you should think about quitting." Also, warnings from the surgeon general were increasing in volume. "'OK,' I told Winnie, 'that's it. Cold turkey.' 'Well, if you're really serious,' she said, 'I'll stop with you.'" It was a pact.

But she had misgivings:

"What about in the mornings? What about after a good dinner? What about at a party? When your hands have nothing to do and the room is full of smoke?" Then, finally, the clincher: "And what about three-foot putts?"

As he stopped, restarted, and stopped again, his weight, mood, and golf fluctuated accordingly. McCormack, a nonsmoker, inevitably argued for his client's return to what Arnold hatefully called "those coffin nails."

At a London tournament run by the Piccadilly Tobacco Company free samples showed up in Palmer's hotel suite, and Mark said, "I think I'll have a cigarette," the first of his life. Soon Palmer was puffing along. "Only in England," he resolved. Later, "Only in Australia." "Only out of the United States." "Only off the golf course." "Only when the cameras aren't watching."

In 1969, just before the PGA Championship in Dayton, Ohio, Palmer tossed his L&Ms into the trash once more and went straight out and shot 82. "Arnold," Dave Marr told him, "you're the only guy I ever knew who gave up smoking and golf the same week." Two years later, on New Year's Eve, motivated by a betting pool pitting a dozen or so friends (including Dow Finsterwald), he quit again and made it stick. Palmer said, "When I see some of the old film clips and how silly I am with that thing hanging out of my mouth, how obnoxious I looked, I could just cringe. My dad tried to convince me of that when I was younger, but, like all kids, I knew more than he did."

In the 1959 Masters, Palmer had a decent chance of repeating. But at the 12th hole, where he had played two balls in 1958, he played two again, the first one into the water. The next was just starting to rise as it roared like a 707 over the green. Unable to get it up and down, he barely got it up, up, and down, making a triple bogey 6 and losing by two strokes to Art Wall Jr. "My first *majors* catastrophe," Palmer called it, with more to come.

On the back nine that Sunday, he looked up at a scoreboard and saw this message:

GO ARNIE
ARNIE'S ARMY

Since the early '40s, khaki-clad soldiers from nearby Camp Gordon (now Fort Gordon) had been admitted to the National free of charge (provided they wore their uniforms) and eventually were given parts in the play. German POWs incarcerated at the camp, engineers from Erwin Rommel's Afrika Korps, were put to work constructing a wooden bridge over Rae's Creek that preceded a stone one ultimately named for Byron Nelson. By the '50s, swarms of GIs covered the grounds, posting the birdies, bogeys, and pars. "I never got picked for that duty," said Doc Giffin, who in an exquisite coincidence was a corporal stationed there at the time. As was McCormack, an officer. Arnie's Army could have been a PR brainchild of Doc's or a marketing ploy of Mark's, but wasn't. It was a spontaneous expression of love.

"Among Palmer's other assets," wrote Herbert Warren Wind, "Arnie's Army should not be discounted. Some golf actuaries [McCormack?] estimate that the support of this faithful legion is worth five shots a tournament to him—at least two of them in the last round—but whatever the validity of such metaphysical computations, Palmer unquestionably derives enormous sustenance from the knowledge that thousands of people are pulling for him and will not suddenly desert him to chase off after some other player who, according to the grapevine, is really pouring it on."

It shocked Palmer to say it, but the advent of Arnie's Army was his overpowering memory of 1959, "even more than the triple bogey," he said.

8

1961

WINNER:

San Diego Open

Phoenix Open

Baton Rouge Open

Texas Open

Open Championship

Western Open

"We just call him Dent."

Palmer, Dwight Eisenhower, Bobby Jones, and Bob Hope made up the first foursome of American golf. This quartet sold the U.S. game in the middle of the 20th century. "Ike doesn't get nearly as much credit as he should," Palmer said, "but the World Golf Hall of Fame is about to take care of that." Just then Doc Giffin coughed, and Arnold asked, "Am I speaking out of turn?" A little. "Well, wait until Doc gives you the go-ahead to say so, but the president is being inducted into the Hall this year, and it's about time."

On September 10, 1966, Palmer's 37th birthday, he looked up into the Latrobe sun and saw a Jet Commander just like the one he owned. But because Arnold's airplane had never ventured anywhere without him, he took the one in the sky for a look-alike. A few minutes later, when Winnie asked him to get the door—"It's the TV repairman," she lied—there stood Eisenhower with a suitcase and a question: "You wouldn't have room to put an old man up for the night, would you?" Along with a weekend's kit, the former president carried an oil canvas of a barn, a horse, and a corral he had painted on his farm as a birthday present for Arnie, initialed in the lower right-hand corner "D.D.E." ("You won't believe this," Palmer said, "but I had a teacher once who thought *I* could become a painter. Not a housepainter, either.")

To set up the birthday surprise, Winnie had dispatched the plane to Gettysburg and made the many necessary Secret Service arrangements. Mamie Eisenhower, who was terrorized enough by large aircraft, followed overland. "It was my gas; I paid for the gas," Palmer said, "but what an unbelievable gift. We didn't play golf. He couldn't play anymore. We just hung out. Talked about everything, watched a football game together in the back while Winnie and Mamie watched the Miss America Pageant. We played bridge the next night. He always laughed and teased me, saying I bid a little too much like I play golf. He was the greatest."

They took a short drive to Laurel Valley in Ligonier and resumed where they left off in their dangling conversations on generals: George S. Patton, Douglas MacArthur, George Marshall, Omar Bradley, Bernard Montgomery, and Fox Conner (you'll have to look him up). Flying and the space program were on the docket, too, as Eisenhower told Palmer: "I insisted on test pilots for astronauts. NASA said they didn't need them and didn't want them. Too temperamental. But I was adamant. I wanted men like you."

"He was just being nice," Palmer said, but Arnie was dancing inside.

Eisenhower once said of Palmer, "How I admired that man. He lived the kind of life everyone dreams of. It always stirred me to play in his group, and those days always will rank among my fondest memories." Imagine the commanding general of the Allied Forces in World War II and a president of the United States looking at someone else's life as the one "everyone dreams of."

"Who's a bigger winner than I am?" Pete Rose asked before his fall. "I played in more winning games than Joe DiMaggio played games."

"Eisenhower," I replied. "He never lost any of those wars or elections."

Pete thought it over for a moment.

"OK, besides Eisenhower, who's a bigger winner than I am?"

Arnold and Ike first bumped in Augusta the day after Palmer was measured for his original green jacket. (Arnie had been led to believe they would play golf then, but they didn't until a later time at Augusta.) Though Eisenhower was a member at the National, it was his habit to stay out of the way tournament week and arrive on Monday. A letter he wrote to Palmer kicked off their association:

Dear Mr. Palmer,

Because of the general confusion the other day, I failed to realize when Ben Fairless [a steel mogul from Pittsburgh] introduced us that you were Arnold Palmer of 1958 Masters fame. I hope you will forgive my lack of reaction and accept, even this belatedly, my warm congratulations on your splendid victory.

Ben suggests that sometime we might have an opportunity to play at Augusta. This I should like very much though, judging from the brand of golf I have recently been displaying, I would be more than embarrassed.

Sincerely,

Dwight D. Eisenhower

The popular '50s and '60s assertion that "Arnold Palmer sold golf to the American public, and his number one customer was Eisenhower," was only half-true. Eisenhower was sold on golf before Palmer was born. In her book *"Don't Ask What I Shot": How Eisenhower's Love of Golf Helped Shape 1950's America,* Catherine M. Lewis illustrated Ike's dedication to the sport by quoting from a letter written by his wartime caddie, Lieutenant Jimmy Preston, to a sister in 1943. At the time, Eisenhower and Preston were serving together in Italy:

When I rolled out the map of the golf course, the general got that slight frown on his face and walked around the table two or three times. This [course] was designed by the Special Corps and yours truly; he hadn't seen any of it. Then he said we had a problem. He and General Marshall were going to play on Friday, teeing-off at 0900 hours. I said we'd be ready. He said, "No, you're not reading me. This is a shot General Marshall can easily make. There has to be one helluva bunker right here." He called in an Army Air Force general and asked him who was the best low-altitude pilot in Italy? I don't know who the pilot was or if he ever wondered what he was doing, but the bunker his bomb made was as near to perfect as any I ever saw in the States. General Marshall just about wore out his sand iron and General Eisenhower won.

So Ike was calling in air strikes to win golf matches long before he knew Palmer. But, in league with television, they were certainly coconspirators in the promulgation and popularization of American golf. During his eight years in the White House, President Eisenhower openly and unapologetically played no fewer than 61 rounds a year and as many as 122, largely at Augusta, Cherry Hills near Denver (Mamie's hometown), and Burning Tree in Bethesda, Maryland. When he wasn't playing, he was practicing on the White House lawn and leaving spike marks on the Oval Office floor. (President Kennedy told *60 Minutes* creator Don Hewitt, "Look what that son of a bitch did with his golf cleats.") Democrats tried to make something of it, dispensing campaign buttons that read: "BEN HOGAN FOR PRESIDENT! IF WE'RE GOING TO HAVE A GOLFER, LET'S HAVE A GOOD ONE!" But the people sided with Ike.

During that period, Herbert Warren Wind quoted a man from New York City as saying, "Before Ike came in, every time I carried my golf bag down to Grand Central and boarded a train for a golfing weekend, I could count on running into disapproving faces and at least one slur carefully delivered so I could hear it—you know, something like, 'Don't strain yourself, Reginald.' Now it's all changed. Strangers look at me as if I were a member of the 4-H Club. And when they speak to me, they give me a warm smile and a cheery word: 'Looks like a grand weekend to get out of doors.' All of a sudden, I'm on the same level with the Fourth of July and Mom's apple pie, and I like it."

Looking up at Eisenhower's picture on his wall, Palmer said, "The president and I eventually did play at Augusta," where the local caddies all seemed to have been christened by Damon Runyon. For example, Burnt Biscuits Bennett served amateur Tiger Woods. Eisenhower's regular bearer was Cemetery Perteet, whose heart rate was said to be so faint that he was forever waking up in the morgue. Ironman Avery trailed along after Palmer, wondering incredulously, "Are you chokin', boss? Tell me somethin', are you chokin'?" Dave

Marr, runner-up to Palmer in the 1964 Masters, said, "I'd be thinking to myself, 'Shut up, Ironman!'. Because Arnie would invariably grit his teeth, hitch at his pants, and go make a birdie."

Palmer's most memorable game of many with Eisenhower took place in 1964 at the stately Merion Golf Club outside Philadelphia, where Hogan won the 1950 Open. Ike wanted to be introduced on the first tee (and he was) as "a dirt farmer from Gettysburg, Pennsylvania."

"I had been trying to cure his flying right elbow," Palmer said, "which wasn't working for him as well as it was for Nicklaus. So intent was the president on keeping that wing tucked in, he rubbed it raw. His shirt was all bloody. But when I said, 'You're bleeding, Mr. President,' he shrugged and said, 'It's only a scratch.' He was so determined to play his best game, which meant eighty-one or eighty-three with a birdie or two. Damn, I respected that. And at seventeen he holed a cross-country putt for our side, taking all the money from Jimmy Demaret and actor Ray Bolger [the Scarecrow in *The Wizard of Oz*]."

Because of a stiff knee left over from the football fields at West Point, Eisenhower had no choice but to overuse his upper body—not unlike Pap, which was appropriate. "I loved him like a second father," Arnold said.

Palmer knew many presidents and kings (or ex-kings, like Mrs. Simpson's husband, Edward, a particular chum), and played golf with most of them. But he was close with only one. From Palm Springs, site of the Bob Hope Desert Classic (which Palmer won five times), President Nixon had Hope and Palmer flown by Marine helicopter to San Clemente to join Vice President Gerald Ford, Secretary of State Henry Kissinger, and a roomful of top advisors for what was labeled a "mini-summit" on the Vietnam War.

When the matter was put to Palmer last, he proposed, "Why not go for the green?"

"Everybody laughed," he said, "but I was dead serious. Stop laying up."

("Here lies Arnold Palmer," Bob Drum once proposed for his friend's tombstone. "He went for the green.")

According to Palmer, "Nixon liked golf more than he let on, but pretended otherwise because he thought that was the smart political call." President Kennedy, with whom Palmer was scheduled to play for the first time in December of 1963, made the same call. At Pine Valley's short 10th hole, Vice President Dan Quayle, an accomplished golfer, tried rooting his hole in one out of the cup to avoid making the evening news. He failed miserably.

"That was the difference between Eisenhower and Nixon," Palmer said. "Ike never pretended to be anything but what he was."

On March 27, 1990, the 100th anniversary of Eisenhower's birth, Palmer was asked to join Walter Cronkite and others addressing a joint session of Congress:

"Mr. Speaker, members of Congress, ladies and gentlemen, I am pleased to be here. I feel a lot better over that three-foot putt for Nicklaus, Trevino, and Player than I feel here right now, though I'm extremely proud to be here."

He talked about the 1958 Masters and making his first contact with Eisenhower:

I told my wife we were going to play golf with the president. And, in the same sentence, I said, "Winnie, I want you to write Ironman"—who was my caddie—"a check." It was normal to do a sizeable check for the caddie working for you when you won the Masters. I made fourteen thousand dollars in that tournament, a lot of money in nineteen fifty-eight. I told her, "Make it for fourteen hundred." Later that evening, you could tell Winnie wasn't very excited about my playing golf with the president, because she wrote the check for fourteen *thousand* dollars. [When Ironman tried cashing it at the club, the mistake was caught.]

A number of years ago, on my thirty-seventh birthday . . .

Finishing up that story, he declared:

I must say, not many people in America have this opportunity. But it sort of tells you about America. We spent a weekend together. We talked about things that were important to him. His interest in America, and in history, and in people all over the world. A general who all of us lived in awe of. A president who none of us could imagine sitting down at the breakfast table in pajamas and robe just talking about his life and his doings for so many years, and feeling that he wanted you to know what it was all about.

I suppose one of the greatest things I remember about Ike—and I say Ike with great reverence because, the morning he arrived for my birthday, I asked him what I should call him. Mr. President? General? He said, "Arnie, when we're alone, you call me whatever you want. I like just plain Ike. But when we're in company, if you want to be more formal, it's perfectly all right with me." That's another privilege that someone like Arnold Palmer—born and raised in Latrobe, Pennsylvania, son of a golf pro who raised chickens and pigs to eat—who would ever believe it?

He and Winnie were called to Walter Reed Hospital near the end.

We walked into his hospital room, and it's very difficult to imagine—he was very ill—but his first words were, "By gosh, it's great to see you kids." Think about it. It's something that, today, makes chills run up and down my back. . . . On behalf of all the athletes whom I think I have some right to represent here, for what he has done for the world, for America, and for what he gave us in his lifetime, thanks.

One of the last things Eisenhower said to Arnie at Walter Reed was, "Have you quit smoking *off* the golf course yet?" Both Ike and Mamie had been dedicated smokers.

The third member of America's first foursome was Robert Tyre Jones Jr., Bobby Jones. Had there been no Jones, there'd have been no Latrobe Country Club. Had there been no Latrobe Country Club, there'd have been no Arnold Palmer. Heroically and humbly, Jones brought *two* ticker-tape parades to Broadway and golf, and then, with nobody left to beat, retired from tournament competition at the age of 28. Slickered down and knickered up, he was a full partner with Babe Ruth, Jack Dempsey, Red Grange, and Bill Tilden in the Golden Age of Sport, a gentlemanly figure of widespread admiration and respect. Wind wrote, "Golf without Jones would be like France without Paris—leaderless, lightless, and lonely."

With the immense help of Wall Street financier Clifford Roberts (who became Eisenhower's moneyman), Jones built the loveliest golf course in the world at Augusta, Georgia, and started a small competition in 1934 called the Augusta National Invitation Tournament. Spring and sportswriters had a lot to do with the event's rise to a major championship. Traveling with baseball teams barnstorming their ways north from the Florida training camps, newspaper columnists including the syndicated star Grantland Rice, a member at the National, only naturally stopped off at Jones's Invitational to tip their skimmers to Bobby.

"There were Opens and there were Invitationals," explained Tiger Woods, who was born in 1975, the year a black golfer first played in the tournament that, in a melancholy irony, had come to be called the Masters. "Invitationals were the ways around the Opens," Woods said tartly.

Jones and Roberts might not have been any more racially bigoted than the average American born in 1902 or 1894, but neither of them was a champion of affirmative action. Mr. Cliff's cackling affection for phrases like "our dark-complected friends"—and his insistence on including in the club's official biography drawings of bug-eyed "darkies" with thick white lips spouting dialogue like "Yes, suh," and "No, suh," and "We is doin' jus' fine, suh"—fell right in with the game of golf at the time (and 30 years later, for that matter).

In 1961, Palmer's sixth full season on tour, the constitution and bylaws of the Professional Golfers' Association of America still stip-ulated in Article III, under the heading "Members, Section I": "Pro-fessional golfers of the Caucasian Race, over the age of eighteen (18) years, residing in North or South America, who can qualify under the conditions herein specified, shall be eligible to apply for mem-bership." *Los Angeles Times* sports columnist Jim Murray referred to the PGA of America as "the recreational arm of the Ku Klux Klan."

Perhaps the biggest casualty of golf's Caucasian clause was a short, cigar-smoking (since age 12) North Carolinian named Char-lie Sifford, winner of the Greater Hartford Open in 1967, when he was 45, and the Los Angeles Open in 1969. He still holds the record for the saddest line in a press guide: "Turned professional—1948; joined PGA Tour—1961."

In 1974 the National Golf Association (the black USGA) pre-sented Sifford a faux green jacket at a banquet in Cleveland and declared him an authentic master. Cornered by two young newspa-per reporters, one from Cleveland and the other from Cincinnati, Charlie was drinking a Scotch and milk.

"You know something," he said, "I led the first pro tournament Arnold Palmer ever won, the Canadian Open of nineteen fifty-five. Canadians didn't have any problems with blacks trying to qualify for golf tournaments. The first time I ever saw Arnie—obviously, I'd heard of him—he was staring at the leaderboard outside the clubhouse on Thursday afternoon, muttering to himself, 'How on earth did Charlie Sifford shoot sixty-three?'

"'Same way you shot sixty-four, Chief,' I replied, 'except I did you one better.'

"He stuck out his hand and said, 'Well done, Mr. Sifford.'

"'I'm Charlie,' I said.

"'Great playing, Charlie.'

"And we were friends. Paired with Arnie once—it might have been in Dallas—we got up to the third green, and my ball wasn't on it. It was behind the green, in the rough. 'That's not where you went,' he told me. 'I know,' I said, and then I played it as it lie. All I ever asked of Palmer, Player, and Nicklaus was to be treated with respect, and all three treated me with the utmost respect. I didn't want them going to bat for me. I went to bat for myself. Oh, I asked one other thing of them: Play hard against me. Play your hardest. And they did, too, just the way they always had against each other. That's the way we all wanted it."

"Was it Dallas?" Palmer asked at his desk. "Or Greensboro? The story is, a marshal saw somebody in the gallery move Charlie's ball but kept quiet about it. For years, then, that marshal followed Charlie to make sure it never happened again. I'm not certain if that's a true story, but I hope it is."

Also in 1974, during his annual greeting to the Masters press corps, Roberts brought up the inevitable subject before anyone else could. Flanked by two other committeemen in green jackets, he held court in front of the big board on the stage of the Quonset hut, knowing the interview room was far too small to contain this much controversy.

"One of our former caddies, Jim Dent," Roberts began, "is hitting the ball so far that Jack Nicklaus told me he's outdriving Jack twenty to sixty yards. And I'm told Jim has been improving his short game. He might win a tournament and be eligible to play here. [A criterion established in 1972.] If he does, you'll find a lot of people around here very happy about it."

Asked if he remembered Dent as a caddie, Roberts said, "Very indistinctly," but added, "I think I'd recognize him if I saw him." Jim stood six feet two and weighed 230 pounds.

"He's got a brother who was a caddie here, a cousin who was a caddie, and another cousin who's a maître d' here still."

Dave Anderson of the *New York Times* inquired, "May we have the maître d's full name, please?"

After rocking left and right, consulting in whispers with the two green jackets, Mr. Cliff cleared his throat and said, "We just call him Dent."

A year later Lee Elder broke the color line.

Despite his blue-collar background, despite being the son of a Roosevelt Democrat, despite growing up anti–country club in a distinctly Democratic enclave, Palmer was a Republican. Maybe this had to do with Eisenhower, but more likely it had to do with golf.

Though Arnold described himself as "a middle-of-the-road Republican," *middle-of-the-road* and *moderate* are softeners used on both ends of the spectrum by people who might not realize how far left or right they truly are. Pro golfers don't just *tend* to be conservative. When the U.S. team wins the Ryder Cup—admittedly a rare occurrence in modern times—a quorum isn't guaranteed at the White House if a Democrat is in office. (Intermittently Palmer was approached about running for office himself. He enjoyed the dance but never seriously considered it.)

Masters champions were empowered as a group to vote Sifford, or anyone else, into the field. They controlled one tournament berth. In 1969 the '59 Masters winner and '59 PGA Player of the

Year, Pennsylvanian Art Wall Jr., tried to marshal support for Charlie, who had just won his L.A. Open. Sifford received only a solitary vote: Wall's. Old-shoe Bob Murphy was elected. Pro golfers weren't revolutionaries.

"What would you have had us do?" Palmer asked. "Call press conferences? Scream at the top of our lungs? I wasn't a crusader, and neither was Jack. I wanted things to change, but I couldn't change them."

Was he sure about that?

"I think you have an exaggerated opinion of just how much influence I had."

I don't think so.

Nineteen seventy-six Masters champion Raymond Floyd said, "You have to understand, Arnold loved and respected the *best* of the Masters Tournament, and there was a lot of best." Palmer wasn't about to challenge Jones publicly, not there. That wouldn't have been good manners, and nobody ever cared more about manners than Palmer.

Floyd's first year at Augusta, 1965, he sported a particularly obnoxious pair of flashy multicolored golf pants on Thursday. "'C'mere a minute,' Arnold called me over in the locker room. 'Son, this isn't just another golf tournament,' he said. 'This is different, special. Wear a more respectful pair of pants tomorrow.' And I did, the next day and from then on."

Jones died in December of 1971, heroically and humbly, in a wheelchair and hideous pain from syringomyelia, a virulently progressive spinal disease. In late September 1977, Roberts had his hair cut in the club barbershop and sent an employee into town to buy him a new pair of pajamas. Somehow during the night, probably with help, he made his way out onto the property to the lower end of Ike's Pond near the par-3 course (Ike had a cabin, a tree, and a pond), where he shot himself in the head with a pistol. His new pajamas peeked out from under his trouser legs. His slippers were on the wrong feet. He was 83.

"I'll tell you the honest truth," Palmer said, leaning forward at his desk. "For years and years, I was scared to death of Clifford Roberts."

Twirling a 4-wood on the aircraft carrier *Ticonderoga* in the China Sea, war-touring comedian Bob Hope was the fourth great ambassador of American golf. Like Eisenhower and Jones, he also had a direct connection to Arnie.

"After Eisenhower," Palmer said, "Bob did more for golf, not to mention golfing charities, than anybody who wasn't officially involved with the game. He was a devoted player [and a better one than his comedy implied]. Bing Crosby was, too. It's a little-known fact that both of them played in the British Amateur, a major championship. Bob's was at Royal Porthcawl [in Wales]. Somebody named Fox beat him. Don't ask me how I remember that."

Hope took up the game in 1930, the year after Palmer was born, while traveling vaudeville's "northern circuit" of Winnipeg, Calgary, Minneapolis, Seattle, and Tacoma. One morning a comedy troupe, the Diamond Brothers, jingled through the hotel lobby with golf clubs on their shoulders, and Hope followed them to the course. In celebrity pro-ams, his pro partner was often Jimmy Demaret. "Demaret knew Bob's swing inside and out," Palmer said—that slow, liquid, bent-elbowed, multihinged Bob Hope swing. "Jimmy would reposition Bob's hands for him, which was perfectly legal for your playing partner to do, and then, using his regular action, Bob could hit it under one tree and over another. At his best, with Demaret along, I'd say he was a pretty strong three or four handicap."

Hope did his share to help make Palmer the world's definitive golfer, casting him in the 1963 movie *Call Me Bwana* with Anita Ekberg. Portraying himself, Palmer shouted "Fore!" from off-camera.

"Fore?" repeated Hope's character, a big-game hunter on safari. "Pardon me," Palmer said, entering the tent, "have you seen my ball? Oh, here it is [in an egg cup on the table, about to be peeled by Hope]. Pretty tough lie."

"You look familiar," Hope said.

"I'm Arnold Palmer."

Only eight takes.

Speaking at an exhibition in Mason, Ohio, Hope said, "I sounded Arnie out on the idea of the movie in nineteen sixty-one. I just wanted him on the set, so we could hit balls together during all the waiting-around time. We did, as a matter of fact. He gave all the grips new grips."

By 1964, Palmer knew he had fallen down a rabbit hole when, seated in a movie theater watching Auric Goldfinger and iron-brimmed Korean caddie Odd Job cheating James Bond at golf, he heard Bond's caddie say, "If that's his original ball, I'm Arnold Palmer."

"'Tisn't," Bond said.

"How do you know?"

"I'm standing on it."

Grand-marshaling everything from the Tournament of Roses in Pasadena to the Miss America Parade in Atlantic City, Palmer became an omnipresent celebrity, even guest-hosting *The Tonight Show* for Johnny Carson. It was the most wooden performance since Charlie McCarthy. Comedian Buddy Hackett said, "He made Spiro Agnew [one of his guests] look like Shecky Greene." For *Bonanza* star Lorne Greene and Lakers owner Jack Kent Cooke, Hackett performed a parody of Palmer, the talk show monologuist, at an NBA All-Star banquet in Los Angeles. But he wound up by saying, "The funny thing is, the audience liked him."

"For a one-night stand," Palmer said, "I wasn't that bad. I started with a few lines, not really a monologue. I'm not funny in that way.

Not a stand-up comedian. I was nervous, though. I could do it now a lot easier, because I'm more confident, more relaxed."

In rapid-fire riffs on TV specials, Hope played straight man to Palmer for corny exchanges that made viewers cringe and Arnold perspire. "Bob could miss a line," he said, "but I couldn't. Talk about pressure."

BH: Arnie, you've probably picked up as much money at golf as any man in history.

AP: Don't you believe it, Bob. Sam Snead's got more buried underground than I ever made up top.

BH: I wondered why he liked to play barefoot. I thought that was just a story.

AP: No, sir, he's got gophers in his backyard that subscribe to *Fortune* magazine. He's packed more coffee cans than Brazil.

BH: Where does he get all that loot?

AP: Pigeons. Amateurs who think they can beat him.

BH: Why is everyone staring at me?

AP: Ever play Snead, Bob?

BH: Sure. I almost beat him. I was even with him until the last hole when we doubled the bet. Hey, wait a minute! You don't mean he . . .

AP: Welcome to the flock.

"I first laid eyes on Palmer," Hope said, "in the mid-fifties at a pro-am in Los Angeles. He was on the adjacent fairway. My partner, Gene Littler, pointed him out to me.

"'See that guy?' Gene said.

"'You mean the one with the muscles?'

"'Yeah. He's going to win everything. He makes the ground shake.'

"He made the world shake. When I first met Arnie, I could tell he was just one of those guys you wanted to know and be around. That's how the public felt, too. Not that I had so much of it myself, but I knew a little something about star power. And he had it. Without trying, he made you smile. I knew about smiles, too."

Like most clowns, Hope knew about tears as well. Have you ever listened to the original lyrics from "Thanks for the Memory"? They're excruciatingly sad.

Hope told Palmer a wistful story, one that Bob left out of his routines and books, like his golf memoir, *Confessions of a Hooker.*

"Heading off on another Christmas tour for the USO," Palmer said, "Bob was rushing through the house, kissing his children good-bye. Finally, when he reached the door, the youngest child shouted, 'Good-bye, Bob Hope!'

"'That broke my heart,' he told me."

9

1962

"Why don't you just sashay your ass back out there and play them over?"

IT WAS AS IF God said to Nicklaus, "You will have skills like no other," then whispered to Palmer, "but they will love you more."

Through many seasons of frosts and thaws, at times golf's most problematic relationship included a measure of true warmth and authentic affection. But it never strayed very far from the principle on which it was founded: mutual jealousy. Arnie envied Jack's ability; Jack envied Arnie's lovability. Grace came easily to Palmer; golf came easily to Nicklaus.

In November of 1961, the younger man, ten years younger, turned pro. As December was running out, Nicklaus participated in an exhibition at Florida's Country Club of Miami with Palmer, Player, and Snead, using the exercise to measure his game, stroke for stroke, against theirs. "I hit my opening drive into a lake, I was so nervous," he said in his office, "but by the end of the round I felt like I belonged. I think Gary won. Arnold and I scored about the same, but he played better than I did and I putted better than he did. He was pulling for me to play well, which wasn't the usual vibe Palmer gave off. But I could feel it."

Nicklaus's first PGA paycheck, in 1962, was for $33.33, one-third of last-place money (less a penny) in the Los Angeles Open at the inner-city municipal course Rancho Park. The winner, San Diegan Phil Rodgers—"Philamander" to Nicklaus, his old amateur cohort and roommate in the Crow's Nest dormitory at Augusta National—later said, "And he's been making threes ever since."

Early in Jack's rookie season, on the last day of the Phoenix Open, he and Palmer played their original round together as fellow pros. Nicklaus said, "I needed a birdie at eighteen to finish second to him—I was only thirteen shots behind. He had won the week before and now he was spread-eagling the field. I guess you could say I was looking a little down. I'll never forget our walk from the seventeenth green to the eighteenth tee. 'Relax,' he whispered, 'you can birdie this hole. C'mon, it's important.'

"I *did* birdie it, to finish second alone and lose by just twelve. I made twenty-three hundred bucks."

The '62 Masters a couple of months later amounted to a do-over for Palmer. The April before, he looked certain to repeat his '60 glory as he strode up the 18th fairway (in the company of amateur Charlie Coe) needing only a par to beat Player, the leader in the clubhouse. In fact, when Arnold shot 68 and 69 Thursday and Friday, that made six rounds in a row and 24 months since he had been out of the Masters' lead. Augusta had become his home all right.

Steady Sunday rain bumped the final round to Monday. "Which made it kind of a strange day that got stranger," Player said. "The only ones pulling for me that Monday were my wife and my dog."

"Of all the things Pap tried to drum into me," Palmer said, "the biggest was never to celebrate until the task at hand is accomplished completely. No matter the situation, think only of swinging the club, staying down through impact, and finishing the job. 'Or you'll be sorry,' he said."

With his drive at 18 safely in the fairway and a 7-iron securely in his fist, Palmer heard a friend's voice in the gallery and walked over to the ropes. For years he wouldn't say who it was, but it was George Low, the Scottish wit and putting specialist (early-day Dave Stockton). "Way to go," Low said, clapping him on the back. "You've won it."

"And at that moment," Palmer said, "I lost my mind." For the first time all day he noticed the hue of the sky and everything else around him. "Coming out of" the 7-iron, he shoved a dreaded knee-high fizzler off to the right, landing in the greenside bunker. Instead of taking a restorative moment, he took hardly any time at all to hoist his third shot too high out of the sand, sending the ball hopping across the green and bounding down a hill into the gallery. His fourth shot, with a putter, ran away in the opposite direction. Then he missed the 15-foot bogey putt that would have salvaged a place in a playoff. As the defending champion, he helped 25-year-old Player into his first green jacket.

"It was my fault, no one else's—entirely my fault," Palmer said, looking out his office window. "Golf is a game where you keep learning the same things, forgetting them, learning them again, forgetting them again, learning them again, forgetting them again, over and over and over. I wasn't finished with this lesson, either."

Billy Casper, who tied three others (including Nicklaus) for seventh place, said that night, "I think you're destined to win or lose these things. Sure, you have to play good, but I think there's something else, too."

A year later, 72 holes into the '62 Masters, Palmer, Player, and Dow Finsterwald were tied at the top with 8-under-par 280s. A 66 in the second round brought Palmer a two-stroke lead that he kept until a wretched Sunday front nine (39) appeared to knock him out of the running. He had to birdie 16 (with a chip-in) and 17 (with a 10-footer) just to shoot 75 and join an 18-hole playoff, the first three-man playoff in Masters history. "I didn't have any zip today," he told the writers. "Does anybody know where I can get some zip?"

Palmer wasn't much zippier on the front side the following day. "But the back nine, I think, was just about the best of Arnie ever," Finsterwald said. "I played terrible in the playoff [77]—I was suffering from a bad case of 'the lefts'—but, as I said at the green jacket ceremony, I had a good ticket for watching him, and he was something to see."

Trailing Player by three strokes at the turn, Palmer made a 25-foot putt for birdie at 10, while Gary was bogeying. "Now the game was on," Arnold told Bob Drum later. At the par-3 12th, his old Waterloo (1959) and near Waterloo (1958), he hit an 8-iron inside four feet and cashed in another two-shot swing. Birdie at 13, birdie at 14, birdie at 16. He shot 31 coming home for a 68 to beat Player by three and join Snead and Demaret as the only men with three green jackets.

"This could have been five jackets in a row, I guess you know," Drum sneered typically as he and Palmer passed each other entering the press barn.

Palmer whispered, "Don't remind me."

Looking back, Player said, "When you have a love affair with Arnold Palmer, you don't worry about when he beat you or you beat him. You're just so grateful to have been in his time, and to know him. One year Arnie should have won the Masters and I should have lost. The next year I should have won and he should have lost. But we don't look at it that way. At least not most of the time. Do you judge your friends by when they beat you or you beat them? Not that Arnold and I haven't had our moments. Moment, I should say."

In the middle of a round once, they had a significant disagreement. "A confrontation," Player called it, "not worth going into now, but pretty intense at the time. You know golfers. We were about to slam off in silence when he caught me by the arm. 'Let's go get something to eat,' he said. We sat down together and brought it all out. We had tears in our eyes, both of us. Usually only one guy does the crying. We clasped each other's hands with our elbows on the table like arm wrestlers. 'I love you, my friend,' I said. It's too bad Jack and Arnie couldn't have sat down like that in the early years."

At the height of Nicklaus's powers (four days before a tournament victory that included a 62), I drew him for a partner in a pro-am at the Ohio Kings Island Open. Ostensibly, it was a blind draw. Of course, the fix was in. He told me so before we teed off. These things are always fixed.

"Don't tell Charlie and Burch [the organizers] that I told you," he said, "but when you wrote this was an attractive golf course for a blind date, they thought they better try to warm you up." With

Desmond Muirhead, Jack had codesigned the Kings Island layout, his first foray into golf course architecture.

In a bathroom after nine, a fan walked up to Nicklaus at the urinal and started talking to him. Jack turned to me and said, "Welcome to life in the fishbowl."

Walking five hours with him—just talking, not interviewing—was interesting. "Look over there," he said, pointing out Associated Press golf writer Bob Green in the gallery. "I really respect Bob," he said. Nicklaus knew that the majority of golf writers clung to the press tent like Tibetans to Shangri-La, as if venturing even a few feet outside the portal might oxidize them like the lady in *Lost Horizon*. "Bob has a deadline every minute," Jack said, "and yet there he is, out on the golf course."

"He comes out to smoke," I said.

"You *are* like that, aren't you?" Nicklaus said.

He told me, "My dad and I visited the AP offices to ask them to stop calling me 'Fat Jack,' but they wouldn't. At the time, Will Grimsley [the wire's lead sportswriter] was in love with Palmer." Characteristically, Nicklaus resolved the issue by slimming himself into a model for clothes and a mold for golfers, towheads shaped like fly rods.

I asked, "Did you ever take it out on the AP?"

"No," he said, "but I've never forgotten it, either."

———

The 1962 U.S. Open, where Palmer-Nicklaus broke in their hyphen, was set at Oakmont in Palmer country, 42 miles from Latrobe. Demonstrating a sense of theater, the USGA paired Arnold and Jack for the first two days. Fearing overlong rounds on what still might be the most difficult golf course in America, the blazer brigade with their armbands, briar pipes, shooting sticks, Croix de Guerres, and dandruff sent the players out in twosomes all three days, including Saturday's double round.

"From our opening tee shots Thursday," Nicklaus said, "the galleries were extremely loud and extremely partisan, but I didn't notice. I was playing golf. My father told me about it afterward." (Charlie Nicklaus was furious.) The ground actually quaked from foot stamping in greenside grandstands as Nicklaus prepared to putt. He didn't feel the tremors. Still in his "Fat Jack" phase, he didn't hear anyone shout "Miss it, Fat Guts!" either.

"Someone standing in the deep rough," Player said, "held up a sign that said, 'Hit it here, Ohio Fats!' It was shameful."

The truth is, when Nicklaus's concentration was dialed up to full beam, he was only faintly aware of other people on the moor. Out of decency he had trained himself, every half hour or so (like baseball broadcaster Red Barber turning over his egg timer as a reminder to repeat the score), to acknowledge the spectators with a wink, an incredibly synthetic wink, like a love letter marked "Occupant."

This was the essential difference between Palmer and Nicklaus. Second-timers in Palmer's gallery imagined he recognized them and had missed them and wondered where the hell they'd been. Leaning on his club, waiting for his turn to play, he cast his eyes about for feminine inspiration. "On the golf course," said Raymond Floyd, "all I ever saw was a mass of people. I saw, but I didn't see. Palmer was able to focus in on everybody in the gallery individually. It wasn't fake."

Meanwhile, Nicklaus only pretended to see anyone. He had a Marine haircut in 1962 and a rifleman's thousand-yard stare. He was ruthlessly thought-out, shrewdly calculated, nearly calibrated. On the golf course, in talent and in other ways, he was alone.

Jack started the tournament with three straight birdies, including a chip-in at the third hole after driving into Oakmont's signature "Church Pews" bunker. He faltered a little then, double-bogeying the ninth, but righted himself for a 1-over-par 72, three shots and eight players (including Palmer and Player, with matching 71s) behind first-round leader Gene Littler.

"I shot sixty-eight in round two," Palmer said (to 70 for Nicklaus), "but I seemed to be the only one [except maybe Jack] who noticed I wasn't making anything on the greens." He took 31 putts Friday after 35 Thursday and would need 38 in the early Saturday round (missing three tiddlers). "I was leading the tournament," he said, "and putting like an idiot." ("I feel like I'm putting with a wet noodle," he said at the time.)

Beginning Saturday's late round two strokes behind and two groups ahead of Palmer, Nicklaus three-putted the first hole to fall three shots back. But it was his first three-putt of the week, and his last. For 90 holes, Palmer would out-three-putt him either 10 to 1 (according to the USGA) or 13 to 1 (by Palmer's own calculations). If Arnie made either of two makeable birdie putts on the 71st or 72nd hole, there wouldn't have been an 18-hole playoff the next day.

"Before the playoff," Nicklaus said, "Arnold came up to me in the locker room and asked, 'Would you like to split the prize money [$15,000 for first, $8,000 for second] and play for the trophy?'"

"I did?" asked Palmer, sitting next to him.

"*Yes*, he did," said Nicklaus firmly. "I took it as a gesture made to a young kid. I will never forget it. *He* obviously has."

Pooling purses was a common but secret practice then. Finsterwald said, "Gary and I had agreed to split our winnings in that Masters playoff [as it turned out, $12,000 for second, $8,000 for third] and did, ten grand apiece."

Jack and Arnie didn't. However, they did consent to divide the players' bonus share of the extra day's gate receipts into equal portions, $2,500 each, rather than the customary winner-take-all.

That extra day was the most raucous and unsportsmanlike yet.

"Arnie didn't like that at all," Winnie said. "He felt terrible about it for Jack. They were both embarrassed." "It wasn't easy for me," Nicklaus said, "but it wasn't easy for him, either." "Of course," Palmer said, "I was sorry that his father was so hurt by the fans' behavior. But I think it might have actually worked to Jack's benefit, especially in the playoff. Because it didn't affect his concentration one little bit, and just knowing it was going on probably stoked his competitive fire. Nicklaus had the ability to just close himself off from everything. It's a great attribute. He could just shut himself off and go play. I'm not sure I ever wanted to do that. And I don't think you can just show up one week and do it. You can't just say, 'Oh, this is the U.S. Open, I'm going to do it now.' Especially me."

Anyway, their playoff wasn't close. Jack went four-up after six holes and with an even-par score won by three, 71 to 74. It was his first PGA Tour victory and his third consecutive top-five finish in the U.S. Open. At 22, still the holder of the U.S. Amateur title, Nicklaus was a major champion. "I've always believed," Palmer said, "if I could have just held him off that day, I might have been able to hold him off for a while. But not forever."

In 1962, for the second time in three years, Palmer missed by just a single stroke in a fourth round of being live in the Grand Slam after three legs. But he wasn't alone at the top of the game anymore.

Bundling Palmer, Player, and Nicklaus, McCormack booked them for exhibitions all around the country and the world, often with Arnold at the controls of his own plane. "Arnie, Jack, and I lived in each other's pockets," Player said, "like brothers, including brotherly fights. We were the fiercest competitors."

Flying out of Seagraves, Texas, Nicklaus and Player had to hold on to each other to keep off the ceiling. They were all over the sky. "I think FAA regulations must have been a little laxer in those days,"

Player said. "I can tell you, Arnie was a great one for buzzing golf courses. That was another thing that pissed off Hogan. I vividly remember Arnold banking the plane over Firestone [in Akron] when the tail seemed actually to scrape the ground. Wow." Palmer said, "I'd have Gary crouching under his seat. 'Whoa, whoa, whoa!' he'd shout. I shouldn't laugh, but it wasn't always hard-nosed stuff, was it? We had some fun."

"In Canada, where the three of us shared a suite," Player said, "I got even. Arnold was on the phone with Winnie and I took a big bottle of ginger ale and shook it like this with my thumb on the top, let it go, and just drowned him. 'Winnie,' he said, 'I have to call you back. I'm sopping wet.'"

When the Great Ginger Ale War was over, the three drenched combatants went to the hotel manager, "like penitent schoolboys," Player said, offering to have the drapes cleaned or replaced. Gary said, "We told him we had not behaved in the most exemplary fashion, but he just laughed and said, 'Don't worry about it.'"

"In Zambia, on the ride from the airport to the hotel, our driver told us he had just seen a gaboon viper, the most venomous snake in the bush, with the longest fangs. What a miserable sod that snake is. So, a few minutes later I'm standing on the hotel balcony, three stories up—and, crikey, I don't like heights! I climbed over the railing onto a narrow ledge [Player stood up and pantomimed the scene] making my way inch by inch over to Palmer's room. Pressing my lips to his window, crossing my eyes and doing my best impression of a gaboon viper, I went tap-tap-tap and he jumped out of his skin, falling right on his ass. Then he got a golf club and, waving it above his head, ran straight at me. I nearly went over. It's hard to believe, isn't it? Grown men."

Laughing in his office, Nicklaus said, "I can remember one night when Arnold and I got to kicking each other's shins under the table. I don't know why. I kicked him. He kicked me. Neither would give.

We ended up with the biggest damned bruises. We used to do the stupidest stuff."

They did some thoughtful stuff, too. "In South Africa," Player said, "Jack and Arnie stayed with my family at our ranch—McCormack, too. Mark was afraid to go with us down a gold mine, but Arnold grabbed him at the last second and yanked him into the iron cage. They slowly lowered us eight thousand feet. I stopped laughing. To think my father worked there for forty years. It's a dog's life. I could tell that Jack and Arnie knew exactly what I was thinking as we went down and down. When the guide told us how many tons had to be dug to get just one ounce of gold, the two of them simultaneously tried to cover up their Rolex watches with their sleeves. I smiled, and they did, too.

"We saw the men mining the gold and then went into a room filled with gold bars. The guy giving the lecture on how they melted the gold down and poured it said, 'These bars are very heavy. Nobody in the world can pick one up. In fact, anyone who can pick one up can have it.' Arnold wrapped his huge hand around one bar—his pinky finger was bigger than my index finger—and lifted it straightaway. Well, this guy nearly crapped himself. 'No, no, no,' he said, 'I only work here!' 'You *used* to work here,' Arnold said. 'Your ass is out of here now.' But then he let him off the hook. Our laughter echoed through the caverns. That was one of the great moments of my life. Because laughter is happiness."

McCormack paired Palmer and Player in a black-and-white TV series called Challenge Golf, pitting them against the likes of Nicklaus and Phil Rodgers. "Those matches took eight hours to film," Player said, "and inevitably we'd have to go back and do retakes, because I was a giggler. My schoolteachers used to say, 'If you don't compose yourself, Mr. Player, you'll have to leave the room.' Arnie would look at me a certain way, and I'd start to laugh, and then he'd laugh, and the director would remind us how much money we were wasting. Arnie and I played thirty-three Challenge Golf matches, losing three of them."

In the 1962 (Palmer), 1963 (Nicklaus), 1964 (Palmer), 1965 (Nicklaus), and 1966 (Nicklaus) Masters, Jack and Arnie monopolized the green jacket unequally. When Nicklaus became the better player but Palmer remained the more salable product, Jack quit McCormack in a huff. A pettiness developed between the two golfers (exacerbated by business clashes) that wasn't worthy of either man. A sportswriter wearing a Golden Bear–brand golf shirt in Palmer's presence was liable to have what Arnold called that "yellow pig" logo and the skin beneath it pinched by his strong hand. Quietly, Nicklaus had the bear redrawn into a less-ambiguous shape.

As rival golf course architects carving their initials into mountainsides, each damned the other's creations with the faintest praise, still savaging shins under the table. Nicklaus sent his regrets to Arnold's Bay Hill tournament in Orlando, explaining that one of his sons had a basketball game that weekend. Palmer responded that he wouldn't be able to play in Jack's Muirfield Village event near Columbus, either, because Riley had something going on that week. Riley was Arnie's golden retriever.

In the 1967 U.S. Open at Baltusrol, where Palmer and Nicklaus were tied after 54 holes, Arnold shot 69 to Jack's 65 in the final round to finish second alone. They were 1–3 at the Pebble Beach U.S. Open in 1972. On Sunday afternoon, each had 10- or 11-footers at almost the same instant, Palmer for birdie at 14, Nicklaus for par at 12. Had Arnold made and Jack missed, Palmer likely would have won. The opposite happened.

During this time, Nicklaus's regular gun bearer was a sorrowful-looking Greek with a mushroom cloud of gray hair, Angelo Argea, whose motley mustache was an amalgam of hair and nicotine. "He never read a putt in his life," Jack told me. "He never got a yardage in his life." What did he do then? At just the right moment, when his boss was looking a little forlorn, Angelo would say, "Isn't it about time for a song?" Under his breath, Jack would start to sing. "He was a con man," Nicklaus said fondly, "but a genuine one." And once in a while, for no particular reason, he'd say, "Fuck Arnold Palmer."

"I think of Baltusrol as the place where the torch started to be passed," Palmer said, "or the putter—'White Fang.' Nicklaus birdied three, four, five, and six with that thing. Do you remember White Fang?"

White Fang was a Bulls Eye putter that belonged to a friend of Deane Beman, the future commissioner. The brass blade had been painted white to minimize glare. In a putting funk for weeks leading up to the Baltusrol Open, Nicklaus was trying everybody else's putters and for some reason just liked the look of the center-shafted one with the snowy head. Practicing with it on the Tuesday before the tournament, Jack shortened his long and languid stroke into a brisk pop. "Orchestras began to play," he said, "and angels to sing."

"I was at Baltusrol the other day," I told Nicklaus quite a long time later, "and I saw White Fang. It's on display there in a glass cabinet."

"That's a replica," he said. "I have White Fang at home."

Then he told a father's story:

One of his boys had flung a rock through a neighbor's window, and Jack had to go next door to apologize. He was still shaking when, looking out the kitchen window, drinking a cup of coffee and trying to calm down, he saw little Mike, his youngest, digging happily in the backyard. *OK. Relax. Everything's all right. Hmm, what's that he's digging with?*

WHITE FANG!

The vinegar between Palmer and Nicklaus didn't spill out publicly until the 1975 U.S. Open at Medinah in Illinois, where both were in contention. Playing as a twosome in the fourth round, each became preoccupied with the other and lost track of Lou Graham, John Mahaffey, and the rest of the field. "That happened a lot," Nicklaus said. "When two guys spend as much time together as Arnie and I did, their competitive juices flow. They just want to whip each other." "There were times," Palmer said, "when Jack and I took ourselves completely out of the tournament, because he tried so hard against me and I tried so hard against him."

In the Medinah press tent, during a rare joint postmortem, Nicklaus was bemoaning his three closing holes so pitifully that Palmer finally had enough. "Why don't you just sashay your ass back out there," he said, "and play them over."

Jack looked stunned, as if he'd been slapped. Palmer tossed a muscular forearm across Nicklaus's scalded neck, and Jack tried to smile. But the friction between them was now plain to see.

———————

Dan Rostenkowski, the former U.S. congressman from Illinois, said, "I was shocked to see the level of discomfort between Arnie and Jack. They were like a couple of high-tension wires. I knew Arnie fairly well. We had been pro-am partners at the Kemper Open. I was like a sixteen handicap and, watching me hit balls before our round, his eyes opened wide and he said, 'Oh boy, we're going to do some good here!' He called me once on the Hill. The guys in the cloakroom were thrilled. 'It's Arnie Palmer!' they kept saying. 'Arnie Palmer!' He was about the only thing Democrats and Republicans had in common."

The former chairman of the House Ways and Means Committee was speaking on a telephone in the warden's office at a federal correctional institution in Wisconsin, where he was serving 17 months for mail fraud.

"'Congressman,' Arnie said, 'we've got to do something about the tax code,'" the chairman recalled. "'What do you mean *we*,' I told him. 'We've got to fix it,' he said. 'It's ridiculous!' '*I'll* fix it when you get me on the golf course and give me a free lesson.' He laughed like a son of a gun. 'So that's how Washington works,' he said. 'Don't you know it?' I told him.

"It was Arnie who said to me, whenever he met a man on a golf course, he knew that man's character by the third hole. He was so right. I followed Arnie every step of the way at Medinah. Do you remember the terrific storm that came up Saturday night, all those lightning crashes on the seventeenth hole?"

"Not really," I said, "but I remember the lead story in Sunday's *Trib* was Sam Giancana getting whacked in his basement."

"Yeah, Tommy," the chairman said, "maybe we better not go into that on a tie-line to a penitentiary."

In the 1980 Masters, Nicklaus and Palmer were so far out of the hunt, they found themselves paired together at the back of the field. The night before, Winnie telephoned the club to check on Arnie's tee time and came skipping into the kitchen, singing, "Guess whom you're playing with tomorrow?"

"I'll beat his ass," Palmer said, and did, 69 to 73.

Not until Palmer was 60 and Nicklaus 50 would the tension start to ease. Arnold made the first move. At a senior event, the Tradition, he knocked Nicklaus over by asking him to have a look at his swing. "Can you imagine?" Jack said in his office. "Me? We'd played thirty years and that's the first time he ever asked me."

They began having meals together again and playing practice rounds. At Augusta in 1996, Tiger Woods's last Masters as an amateur, the three of them went out together Wednesday morning. On the par-5 13th, Woods popped up his drive and for once was away. Nicklaus had his back turned to Tiger. Peeking over Jack's shoulder, Palmer saw the 20-year-old pull out an iron for his second shot and whispered, *"He's laying up."*

"Oh, Arnie," Jack said affectionately. "He's not."

Woods slammed a blue darter over the creek and onto the green.

"I love that story," I told Nicklaus in his office. "I think of that as the moment Arnold realized his class had graduated."

Jack laughed and said, "My class has graduated, too."

Nicklaus named Palmer the honoree of his Memorial Tournament, the playing honoree, and Jack returned to Orlando that year to participate in Arnold's tournament as well. Palmer made the cut at Muirfield Village; Nicklaus missed it at Bay Hill. "We didn't always see eye to eye," Jack said, "but there's one thing I'll always be proud of. In the important matters, when it came to the tour and the game of golf, we always stood together."

Such as when touring players in 1968 broke away from the Professional Golfers' Association of America, run mostly for and by club pros, to take control of their own show. They called themselves the Association of Professional Golfers at first, then the Tournament Players Division of the PGA, and finally just the PGA Tour. McCormack favored something short of the complete rupture Nicklaus advocated. Palmer argued Mark's position for a while but ultimately sided and voted with Jack.

"We didn't do everything perfectly," Nicklaus said. "You try for perfection in golf, but you never get there. Not even close."

"My nature is to compete," Palmer said, sitting beside Jack at the Memorial press center in Dublin, Ohio. "It always has been and it always will be. Jack had nothing to do with that except he was there a lot." He turned to Nicklaus and said, "For ten years in a row, I had a chance to win the U.S. Open. You won them, but I had a chance."

("At the end of the day," Player said, "the three of us played not for money, not for trophies, not for history, but for each other.")

"Jack and I were just different," Palmer said. "He was always slow, but he didn't do it because of his opponent. He did it for himself. That's just the way he played. Me, I'm the other way. I like to move, in golf and in every other thing. I like to go fast, particularly in my plane. I got where I got—wherever that is—by doing it my way. I was maybe too aggressive in certain instances, and maybe it cost me some tournaments. Jack was maybe too conservative, and maybe it cost him a few. But you are what you are. I never mimicked anybody. That was the real me."

Nicklaus said, "Arnold and I have had differences of opinion on some golf matters, which is only natural. When he was thirty, I was twenty, and that's a difference. So is fifty and forty, because he went to the senior tour while I was on the regular tour. There's not a whole lot of difference, though, between sixty and fifty or seventy and sixty. We play a lot of golf together now, and we still try to beat each other's brains in."

"We continue to have the needle out," Palmer said, "but we know now that we love each other, and we always did."

The needle was still glistening when a Canadian writer approached the two of them as the session broke up to ask Nicklaus if he would be returning to Glen Abbey for the Canadian Open, Arnold's first professional victory, just about the only blue ribbon to elude Jack.

"Barbara says she's going to keep sending me back there until I get it right," Nicklaus said.

To which Palmer inquired innocently, "Are you sure she's talking about golf?"

10

1963

WINNER:

Los Angeles Open

Phoenix Open

Pensacola Open

Thunderbird Classic

Cleveland Open

Western Open

Whitemarsh Open

Australian Masters

Canada Cup (with Jack Nicklaus)

"Hell, I could have kicked that one in."

IN 1963, FOR THE second consecutive year, Palmer found himself on a 73rd tee with 18 holes yet to play, merely tied for the lead in the U.S. Open. With two others this time: old Julius Boros (the U.S.

Open champion from 11 summers earlier) and young Jacky Cupit, at the Country Club in Brookline, Massachusetts. Forty-three isn't old for most work, but only one man more seasoned than Boros (Ted Ray, by 82 days) had ever won a National Open.

Julius was a Hungarian American with a gentle way and an easy swing who didn't leave the accounting profession for tournament golf until he was nearly 30. "Moose," as the players called him (for the same reason they would call Craig Stadler "Walrus"), never stopped seeming like a CPA. He was as burnt brown as a tobacco leaf and unfailingly considerate to caddies. His bag wasn't the one I was carrying at the 1961 Eastern Open in Baltimore, when I was a high school sophomore. I was working for an amateur paired with Boros the first two rounds. After my man missed the cut, I stayed in the caddie T-shirt, "Eastern Open" on the front, "Mr. Boh" (National Bohemian beer) on the back, because it was my only ticket in.

Palmer told me, "I won the Eastern Open in nineteen fifty-six. I'd been playing so much golf leading up to that tournament, I was exhausted before I even got to the first tee. Paired with Doug Ford, I hit my opening drive so far out of bounds that the ball went bouncing down a highway in the general direction of downtown Baltimore. 'I think I'll withdraw,' I told Ford, who said, 'I don't blame you, nobody can make up two strokes in just seventy-one holes.' At one point I led by twelve."

Doug Sanders won the '61 tournament by a stroke over Ken Venturi. As play was winding down, I bumped into Boros near the scorer's tent, we shook hands, and he said, "Walk with me a minute, son, I want to show you something."

We went over to the practice putting green, where, sweating out Venturi's finish, Sanders was putting with his foot. That is, he was rolling 10-footers with the left side of his rainbow-colored right shoe straight into the cup.

"What's he doing?" I asked Boros.

"'Dougie,' he said, 'my friend wants to know what you're doing.'"

"When I play in pro-ams," Sanders said like a proud child, "sooner or later one of the amateurs will miss a ten-footer and I'll say, 'Hell, I could have kicked that one in.' Before long the wallets come out, and let's just say I've made a hell of a lot of money over the years with this foot."

Boros laughed and we walked away. But halfway to the clubhouse, he stopped, put his hand on my shoulder, and said, "Dougie's a great player and a unique talent, but he'll never win a major. Do you get the message?"

Twice Sanders finished second to Nicklaus in the British Open, both times by a single stroke, including that devastating 30-inch putt missed at St. Andrews in 1970. Gene Littler beat him by a stroke at the U.S. Open. Bob Rosburg beat him by a stroke at the PGA. By two strokes, Sanders missed a playoff at a Masters won by Nicklaus. When golfers and golf fans talk about the mythical "best player never to have won a major," don't they know it's Sanders?

Growing up a Georgia field hand, he had been the kind of boy who slipped stones or melons into his cotton sack to improve the payoff ($2 per 100 pounds). As a caddie, he specialized in restoring desolate golf balls salvaged from hawking the course, filling in their nicks and cuts with soap, covering them over with white shoe polish, and selling them as gamers. Sleeping through most of his schooldays, he unconsciously majored in metaphors.

"I have always taken care of my cover," he said with breathtaking honesty, "better than my core."

His closetful of old golf shoes, as shiny and bright as hard Christmas candy, represented no mystery. Sanders didn't have shoes of his own until he was 8. "One left," he said, "and one right."

To the barefoot boy tramping two and a half miles home from the golf course, the lightning bugs looked like ghosts. They would go with him to all the big cities of the world. "I never got tired of walking up that road," he said. "I just got tired of walking up that road broke."

In 1999, behind the home in Houston where Sanders lived with a white cat, I stayed in his guesthouse, a tired place with old bedding where at different times Frank Sinatra, Dean Martin. and Spiro Agnew slept. In Doug's living room, I told him my Julius Boros story. Setting a record for non sequiturs, he immediately launched into an account of how he and a girl from the seventh grade made love standing up behind a Hammond Map of the World after the teacher left the classroom. He didn't get the message.

"I arrived at the Country Club at Brookline in nineteen sixty-three," Palmer said, "imbued with all things Francis Ouimet, just as the USGA intended." Fifty years earlier, Ouimet, a 20-year-old amateur (and commoner) who resided on Clyde Street across the way from the 17th hole, defeated the British aristocracy, Harry Vardon and Ted Ray, in an 18-hole playoff that redrew the economic image of golf and redefined amateurism. Ouimet and his 10-year-old caddie, Eddie Lowery, became the new image of the sport and, eventually, a postage stamp. "Then, wouldn't you know it?" Palmer said. "For the first time in the history of the U.S. Open, not one amateur made the cut."

The defending champion, Nicklaus, missed it, too. Invited into the press tent Thursday, Jack opened the questioning by asking a question of his own: "What do you guys want to know from a seventy-six shooter?"

"Nicklaus or myself might have been the Las Vegas favorite," Palmer said, "but the players saw Boros coming from a great distance that spring. He had won at Colonial with an amazing score for Colonial—what was it? [279]—and the Buick at Grand Blanc [Mich.] with an even more impressive total [274]. There were some in the locker room who thought those four rounds of golf could well have been the best ever played. But I liked Brookline and my chances. Old-style driving course. Small greens. And I had just won a playoff with Paul Harney in the Thunderbird Classic at another old-style, tree-lined course, Westchester."

The wind and the scores at Brookline were up. Palmer shot 73, 69, 77 (missing three putts under 3 feet), 74; Jacky Cupit, a 25-year-old Houstonian, 70, 72, 76, 75; and Boros, 71, 74, 76, 72. Among the three men, they had exactly zero birdies in the third round, and nobody in the entire field managed to shoot par on the last double day. Boros said, "Saturday morning, when Cupit and I shot seventy-six and Palmer seventy-seven, I pretty much despaired of all of our chances in the afternoon. I was already packed up, ready to go, when news of the triple tie reached me. Cupit gave back a two-stroke lead with a six at seventeen, then missed a very makable birdie putt at eighteen that would have won. I lost track of Palmer, who had been fighting an intestinal bug all week, but I could hear the roar when Arnie's last putt went in for a par. Three to play off, just like Ouimet, Vardon, and Ray. But who was who?"

"In the playoff I bogeyed the first," Palmer said, "Boros bogeyed the second, and Cupit double-bogeyed the third, but then Ol' Man River [as Arnold rechristened Julius] put a couple of birdies together and said, 'See ya.' On the tee at the eleventh hole, I reached back for a little something extra and found my ball perched in the middle of a rotting tree stump. Remember those honeybees outside this window? Already four shots behind, I couldn't afford either to take a drop or go back to the tee, so I had to lash at the ball as hard as I could with a four-iron." Three lashes later, like a bite of steak following a Heimlich maneuver, the stump spat the ball out. "I made a seven and a seventy-six," he said, "losing by a million [Boros 71, Cupit 73, Palmer 76]. I had dropped a second U.S. Open playoff in a row [with one to come]."

By the way, if it seems like he's losing a lot of playoffs, consider that he still holds the PGA Tour record for playoffs won, 14, tied with Nicklaus.

"Arnold birdied three of the last four holes in our playoff," Boros said, "and I thought to myself, 'He just doesn't quit, does he?' For a while then, I called him 'pigeon,' but I shouldn't have. I didn't mean it. It wasn't true."

Herbert Warren Wind wrote, "Boros moves his cigarette and his phrases around in a way that recalls Humphrey Bogart," but Palmer said, "He reminded me more of Boris Karloff."

By 11 strokes, Doug Sanders missed the Brookline playoff, but he picked up $525, or 26.25 tons of cotton. Cupit, who went on to win tournaments but didn't come close in a major again, never could shake quite loose of that 12-footer he had at the 72nd hole to win the U.S. Open. Hell, he could have kicked that one in.

11

1964

WINNER:

Masters

Oklahoma City Open

Piccadilly Match Play

Canada Cup (with Jack Nicklaus)

"How many of them could I have won?"

THE LEAST PUBLICIZED MADDENING thing about golf is the doubt that attends winning, not losing. When he was a boy in Latrobe, the tournament Palmer always dreamed of, fantasized about, pretended to be leading, was the U.S. Open. Winning it was the obsession. "What if I hadn't won at Cherry Hills in nineteen sixty?" he asked. Won so soon. "Might I have won four others, or five? How do you ever know?" Did he lose his edge? Did he spend too much of his edge too early? "The only thing harder than trying to keep your edge," he said, "is trying to get it back once you've lost it." (Ask Tiger Woods.)

The 1964 Masters, a practically perfect week for Palmer, left in its wash a similar kind of doubt.

Wednesday's rainstorm softened and lengthened the National course; Arnold didn't mind. As a result, only the longest drivers had much of a chance. What annoyed him, when the skies cleared, was a peppy little airplane chugging over the property Thursday towing a banner that read, "Go Arnie Go." Had he not been a flier, he'd still have been the principal suspect. "If I knew it was someone working for me," he assured the writers, "I'd fire his ass."

On the subject of decorum, Palmer lectured five-foot-seven, 116-pound Puerto Rican playing partner Juan "Chi Chi" Rodriguez to keep the Panama hat on his head, stop using it to sweep the crowd into frenzies, and, for God's sake, quit dropping it on the cup. "I love Chi Chi," he said that night, "but at times I want to kill him." Rodriguez said, "I thought when you hit it inside the other guy, the claps were for you. I was too naïve to realize it was his stage."

Sitting at his desk, Palmer said, "After any tournament, a player can always look back and count up the wasted shots. But that week, except maybe for one at four (par 3), one at twelve (par 3), and one at fifteen (par 5), I honestly felt like I didn't waste any shots. Every day I started off the exact same way. Steady as you go. [Four 4s at the first, four 5s at the second, four 4s at the third.] I was never exactly Gene 'the Machine' Littler, you know. But I was pretty close to it that week. I couldn't have walked around and placed my ball any better."

"I played with him the first day," said Labron Harris Jr., a 22-year-old amateur at the time. "I couldn't believe how precise he was. That wasn't his reputation, you know. He was very protective of me, which *was* his reputation. He always marked the short second putts, knowing the crowd wouldn't be waiting for Harris to putt out before running to the next hole. I was just a punk kid from Oklahoma who could play some. Golf was Arnold Palmer's kingdom, but he knew how to make you feel a part of that kingdom. People don't realize now how big he was then. He was it."

Opening with a 69, Palmer was tied with Player (who, for some reason, had lost his voice) and three others for the lead, two strokes ahead of Nicklaus. In that crowd of first-round leaders was Davis Love Jr., whose wife would give birth to Davis Love III the Monday after the tournament. Palmer shot 68 Friday (now seven ahead of Nicklaus) and 69 Saturday (a full nine up on Jack).

"Sunday morning on the range," Arnie said, "I was warming up between Dave Marr and Bruce Devlin [the Australian], six strokes ahead of both of them. I looked over at Devlin's driver and chuckled." Overnight, a new silver weight strip had been taped to the back of its head. "I recognized the fingerprints on the Band-Aid," said Palmer, a proponent of lead adjustments himself. "I thought, 'Von Nida must be around.'"

Norman Von Nida, whose absence from the World Golf Hall of Fame is a mortal sin, dominated the Australian game during the '40s and had a benevolent hand in the success of countless young Aussies to come. For three consecutive years (once he got out of World War II alive, a considerable upset), Von Nida finished top six at the Open Championship. On the European Tour, he won 13 times in a 17-month stretch, 70 or so tournaments in all, just about everywhere in the world. But he came over for only one U.S. Open, and the biggest noise he ever made in America was in 1948 when a Texas Ranger had to pry five-foot-six, 120-pound Von Nida off a much larger Houston and Ryder Cup pro named Henry Ransom after Ransom allegedly cheated. "Sure enough," Palmer said, "I looked up at one point Sunday and there was old Von Nida smiling at me in the gallery."

That sputtery little plane buzzed the course again. This time the banner read, "GO FOR 67 ARNIE," a reference to the score Palmer needed to break Hogan's Masters mark of 274. But, for once—maybe for the only time—Arnold didn't take the Hogan bait. Without giving Ben a thought, he shot an intelligent 70.

Palmer's playing partner the last day was Marr, who would win his major championship, the PGA, the following year. A Texan with a dry way of looking at and celebrating life, Marr was wonderful company on and off the course (for the players and the writers alike). "My first Masters," he said, "I played a practice round with Hogan, who didn't say a word to me, not even 'You're away,' until the [par 5] eighth hole. I was in the fairway bunker a couple of miles from the green, taking too much time, I'm sure. Hogan finally said impatiently, 'So, do you think you can reach the green from there?' Then he didn't speak to me again until the back nine, when he turned and said, 'Hold on a minute, this is your first Masters.' He went over to a concession stand, came back with an egg salad sandwich, and handed it to me. After I peeled off the green wrapper and took a bite, he asked, 'Is that any good?' and shut up for the rest of the day."

At the 15th hole, Palmer didn't have to go for the green with a three-wood, but did, of course, and started to panic a little as the ball disappeared into the glaring sun. "Did it get over the water?" he asked Marr. "Hell, Arnold," Dave said, "your *divot* got over."

As Palmer and Marr arrived at the last tee, Arnie had a five-stroke lead over Nicklaus (who closed with a 67 to climb all the way to second place) and a six-stroke lead over Marr. "I have to make a birdie here," Dave told him, "to catch Nicklaus." Nodding, Palmer said, "Is there anything I can do to help you?" "Yeah," Marr said, "you can make a nine." In most retellings, the number is 12, but Marr told me nine.

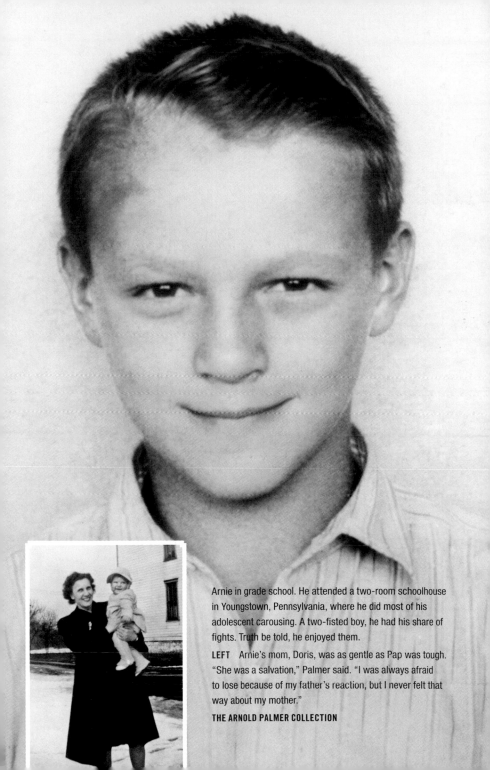

Arnie in grade school. He attended a two-room schoolhouse in Youngstown, Pennsylvania, where he did most of his adolescent carousing. A two-fisted boy, he had his share of fights. Truth be told, he enjoyed them.

LEFT   Arnie's mom, Doris, was as gentle as Pap was tough. "She was a salvation," Palmer said. "I was always afraid to lose because of my father's reaction, but I never felt that way about my mother."

THE ARNOLD PALMER COLLECTION

Arnold met Winnie on a Tuesday and asked her to marry him that Saturday. They eloped. ("I took her out the window, as a matter of fact.") "A golf wife," she said, "can pick her husband up when he's down."

ABOVE First daughter Peggy getting a lesson from Arnie as Winnie looks on. "[Peggy and Amy] don't agree with their father about a single thing," Winnie said, "except the things that truly matter."

BELOW Deacon (far left) and Doris (two places to the right) on the Augusta lawn between the clubhouse and the course around 1959. "Why do I want to win the Masters?" Palmer said. "Why do I want to breathe?"

Arnie was always the most colorful golfer, even when it came to clothing. At a Masters, Phil Mickelson elected a salmon shirt, saying, "It doesn't look good on me, but Arnold Palmer likes to wear this color."

GOLF DIGEST

Most of the good pros before Palmer were purposely stoic. They wanted to hide their feelings. Arnie threw his out there for everybody to see. "He showed up different," Tommy Bolt said.

RIGHT The left seat for 25,000 hours. "I used to think of myself as a realist as a golfer and a romantic as a pilot," Palmer said. "I don't know when I became a romantic as a golfer and a realist as a pilot."

THE ARNOLD PALMER COLLECTION

Walking through a funnel of flowers from the sixth tee to the par 3 green below: 50 Masters exactly, four victories. "Everything about Augusta turned me on," Palmer said. He always knew it would be his home.

DOM FURORE, GOLF DIGEST

Palmer and his assistant, Doc Giffin, in Arnold's office workshop at Latrobe, stocked with some 2,000 old putters. "Maybe Doc's real title should be 'friend,'" Arnold said, "or 'everlasting friend.'"

BELOW Golf's Big Three—Gary Player, Jack Nicklaus, and Arnold Palmer. "At the end of the day," Player said, "the three of us played not for money, not for trophies, not for history, but for each other."

GOLF DIGEST

Palmer and his dog, Mulligan. In the end, Arnie didn't walk Mulligan so much as they walked each other, both allowing for his friend's diminishing capacity. "We'll be old one of these days," Arnie said.

THE ARNOLD PALMER COLLECTION

INSET On a September day in 2016, at Latrobe Country Club and, 10 miles away, over the Palmer statue at Laurel Valley Golf Course in Ligonier, a rainbow appeared. The Arnold Palmer rainbow, Pennsylvanians called it.

GOLF DIGEST

Both of them birdied. Marr and Nicklaus shared second, six strokes back. "Over the seventy-two holes of the tournament," Herbert Warren Wind wrote, "Palmer went over par on only six holes. He birdied eighteen holes, and he parred the rest. This is the equivalent of bogeying only every twelfth hole and birdieing every fourth hole, and that is something!"

"To finally walk the eighteenth fairway at Augusta with no pressure at all, no chance of losing," Palmer said with a sigh. "I wonder what that cost me."

The next day Mrs. Love had the baby out in Charlotte, North Carolina, and, at University Hospital in Augusta, Player had his tonsils out. It was Palmer's seventh major championship, and his last. At the callow age of 34, he was done winning majors. But nobody noticed for 10 years, mostly because nobody wanted to notice, but also because he stayed so relentlessly competitive at U.S. Opens: 1966 (2nd), 1967 (2nd), 1969 (6th), 1972 (3rd), 1973 (4th), 1975 (9th). "How many of them could I have won?" he wondered.

"Nicklaus won majors for twenty-five years," Player said. "I won them for twenty. Arnold for just six. But if you asked the average golf fan, he'd say Palmer did it the longest, and I'm never offended by that. It's fantastic. The people loved him so dearly because he was so charismatic. As Snead said, 'He went to bed with charisma and woke up with more.' It came out of him like sunlight. Because of what he did for golf, the people thought he was still winning majors. And you know what? He was."

"Never saying 'No' cost Arnold something, too," Lee Trevino said. "I don't think he'd change it, though."

Leaning back in his chair, with a faraway look, Palmer said, "Tee to green, I played better golf from the late sixties through the middle to late seventies than I played at any other time in my life. Won less, but played better. If my clubs were right, I thought I could do whatever I wanted to do with the golf ball. That's kind of how I felt about playing. The actual shot-making was better from sixty-five to seventy-six, seventy-seven, but I didn't make things happen like I did in the early years."

Had he lost his edge?

Maybe so, his expression said.

12

1966

WINNER:

Los Angeles Open

Tournament of Champions

Australian Open

Houston Champions International

PGA Team Championship (with Jack Nicklaus)

Canada Cup (with Jack Nicklaus)

"Go ahead, Arnold. You're hot."

"Nobody except Arnie and I remember," Billy Casper told Jack Murphy of the *San Diego Union*, Casper's home paper, "but we were paired at Augusta when he birdied the last two holes to win the nineteen sixty Masters, the year everything started for him really. After two men go through something like that together, they're connected forever. Then nineteen sixty-six came along.

The Olympic Club. Yeah, you could say Arnie and I know each other."

Nineteen sixty-five had been an off year for Palmer, and a disconcerting time, though he won the Tournament of Champions in Las Vegas and contributed four points to helping Captain Byron Nelson and the U.S. Ryder Cup team retain the trophy in England. (Palmer's all-time Ryder Cup record was 22–8–2 as a player, 2–0 as the captain.) Alongside Gary Player, he tied for second at the 1965 Masters, but an awfully distant second, nine strokes behind Nicklaus, who played a game with which Bobby Jones was not familiar.

At 36, Palmer didn't feel old exactly; he just didn't feel young anymore. Lingering bursitis in one shoulder contributed to that. More painfully, his natural advantage—what he called "indifference to consequences"—left him for a time. A certain softness came over him, a slowness, a caution. Perhaps as a delayed reaction to losing the two Open playoffs, Palmer became something he had never been before: careful. As he slipped to 10th on the money list, writers and fans were asking themselves, *What's wrong with Arnie?*

"I still don't know what it was, all these years later," he said. "Was it too much fame, too many business distractions, too great a pressure to please too many people? All I know is, I lost who I was there for a while. I suddenly got to worrying about disappointing everybody. The old me never thought about hitting a putt way by. Hell, I'll make it coming back." But the new Palmer didn't want to risk three-putting, didn't want to risk anything. Under maximum pressure, his hands began to shake. "For the first time in my life," he said, "I guess I was afraid."

But he started 1966 much more like his old self with a string of seven birdies and a comfortable win in the Los Angeles Open, followed by a run of good seconds and thirds at the Crosby and the Hope and in the Lucky International (at public Harding Park across Lake Merced from San Francisco's Olympic Club). Not victories surely, but, as golfers and gamblers like to say, "well-meant." He finished fourth at the Masters, again to Nicklaus, but was competitive this time: back in the game. And his hands had stopped quivering.

Palmer looked forward to the U.S. Open at Olympic, and drew up an aggressive game plan. He knew the golf course well. While it was near enough to the coast to hear and smell the sea, Olympic had no water hazards on it and only one fairway bunker. The challenge was in its claustrophobic tightness. "They pruned a limb off a tree one time," he said, "and more than a hundred golf balls fell out." At Olympic in 1955, his inaugural Open as a professional, he posted a top 25 as Iowa municipal pro Jack Fleck beat Hogan in an 18-hole playoff still counted among the biggest upsets in the history of sports.

Looking at the front nine especially, Palmer decided it was worth the extreme measure of changing his "shape" temporarily, trading in his normal draw for a subtle fade. Left to right, more than right to left, was the order of the week. And this adjustment served him well—for a while.

In the first round, he shot a one-over-par 71, same as Nicklaus and Tony Lema (a month away from his fatal plane crash). A second-round 66, which on a sharper putting day might have produced an Open record of 64 or lower, tied Palmer at the top with Casper. Playing together in the third round (and in the fourth and fifth, as it turned out), Arnold shot 70 to Billy's 73 to build a three-stroke lead. In the pressroom, he was asked prematurely if it pleased him to be out of the shadow of another Open playoff. "Let's put it this way," he said. "I'd just as soon not be in another one." Palmer's shimmering 32 on the front nine of the "final" 18 fluffed his cushion to seven shots with just nine *scheduled* holes to play. Everyone, including Casper and Palmer, believed the tournament was over.

"I wasn't thinking of Bill then, to be honest," Palmer said. He was thinking of Ben.

While Arnold was adamantly the un-Hogan, Billy wanted nothing so much as to *be* Hogan. "When I was sixteen," he said, "I followed Ben around at an exhibition in San Diego. That changed everything for me. Course management. Course management. Course management. From then on, I was purely a percentage player. It's not an exaggeration to say, at every crossroad in every round, I'd ask myself, 'Which way would Hogan go?'"

Palmer and Casper were opposite characters by almost every measurement. Billy's shirts and personality were buttoned snug to his Adam's apple. He grew up a plasterer's son in Chula Vista on the edge of Mexico, putting alone in the dark, postponing his return to a broken home. Casper was a Notre Dame Catholic who converted to Mormonism. He and wife, Shirley, eventually had 11 children, six of them adopted; they forgot which six.

"Our David," as Billy called one of his sons, turned first to drugs and then to guns. "I had a dream one night," Casper said. "In it, David was pacing outside our home. 'Come on in, David,' I said, 'it'll be all right.' But he said, 'No, I'm going the other way.' He committed thirty-five felonies, including armed robberies, and got a hundred and five years in a Nevada prison. Forever. The day they took David away, he left through a door with a small window. I remember looking through that little window and waving good-bye."

Casper hid his considerable human side from the spectators. He played neither to the galleries nor for them. He kept the top button buttoned. He didn't romance the press, either. When in an interview room a reporter asked him why he hadn't removed his sweater as the day heated up, Casper replied in a singsong voice, "Start in a sweater, finish in a sweater." Years later he said, "If I was a little hypnotic on the golf course and in the pressroom, it was because I had to be to play my best golf." The only things the public and press knew about him were he ate buffalo meat and hippopotamus ("a little watery," he said, "just like you might expect"), had a slice of bear Sunday morning at Olympic, and was a hell of a putter.

"I never played for history, either," he said. "I played for money, for my family. That gave me a significant advantage over Arnold, Gary, and Jack. The good player who chokes usually does so because he dwells on what it all means to him. I never did that. I had my share of failures, maybe more than my share, but it was never because I choked."

He was good enough to join the Big Three, to be their fourth, and this nearly happened. But the merger fell through because Casper and Mark McCormack couldn't stand each other, so they went their own ways. The Big Three knew exactly how good Casper was. *Efficient* was Nicklaus's word for him and his game. "No, let me change that," Jack said. "*Extremely* efficient."

"Walking down the tenth fairway," Palmer said, "Bill told me, 'Now I'm going to have to really go to get second.' [Nicklaus, Lema, and Dave Marr were gaining on him.] 'Don't worry,' I told him, 'you'll finish second.'" "It wasn't gamesmanship," Casper said. "I was just being honest. Arnie said, 'I'll do anything I can to help you.'"

By then Palmer wasn't playing in the '66 Open at Olympic. He was playing in the '48 Open at Riviera. "That's where Hogan set the Open record," Palmer said, "two-seventy-six. All I had to do was shoot a one-over-par thirty-six on the back nine and I'd have both the British Open and the U.S. Open records. I thought to myself, 'Wouldn't that be something?' Of course, I completely forgot what Pap had told me over and over when I was a boy." *Never quit. Never look up. And, most important of all, never lose focus until you've completely taken care of business.*

It was George Low in the Augusta gallery all over again.

Palmer bogeyed the 10th; Casper parred it. The lead was six with eight holes to play. Both parred 11 and birdied 12. Six shots still, now only six holes remaining. ("The worst break of all could have been that birdie at twelve," Palmer said. "It convinced me I could break Hogan's record.") He missed the 13th green—Olympic's greens were uniformly small—and made another bogey. Five strokes.

As they approached 15, a par 3, the margin seemed permanently frozen at five. "But I thought to myself," Palmer said, "'now I have to par-in to beat Hogan.'" He aimed directly at a tucked pin, cut beside a bunker in a back corner. Though nicking the green, his ball blew a tire and swerved into the sand. Meanwhile, having asked himself which way Hogan would go, Casper went the surest way, to the heart of the green—fully 30 feet from the cup. Arnie didn't get up and down. Billy made the long putt.

"That changed everything," Casper said. "Now he knew he could lose. And, though still three behind, I knew I had a chance." To Billy, the ocean air felt clean and new. "The gulls were calling to me," he said.

Sixteen, a par 5, brought another two-stroke swing. Palmer's new shape broke down. He should have laid up his second shot out of the heaviest rough, but went for it naturally. "With a three-iron!" Casper gasped. "A three-iron! It didn't go a hundred yards!" Three swings into the hole, Arnold was still nearly 300 yards away from the green. The six he ultimately registered was actually more than remarkable, involving a 265-yard 3-wood, a 40-yard bunker shot inside four feet, and a one-putt.

"I almost said, 'Nice six,'" Casper said, "but I caught myself." Billy had already made his 15-foot birdie putt at 16. "I knew I was going to make it, too," he said. The lead was one.

When Palmer missed a 12-footer for par at 17, they were tied, and, on the 18th tee, effectively changed places. It was Casper who elected the driver, Palmer the 1-iron. The irony was plain to Arnold if to no one else. *Who is the bold one now? Who is being meticulous?*

Twenty-five and 17 feet away from the 72nd hole in two, Palmer and Casper both missed. Before Arnold putted, Nicklaus and Marr, who had just finished signing for third and fourth places, took seats on a hillside to witness the drama. Fairly rare, that. Palmer's first putt was fine for weight but three feet wide. Concerned about standing in his playing partner's line, he asked Billy, "Should I finish?" "Go ahead, Arnold," Casper said, "you're hot."

Tough game, this golf.

Though his 3-footer was treacherous, Palmer handled it. "Believe it or not," he said at his desk, "it was the best putt I hit all week." By just that measure he avoided shooting a 40 on the back. Then he held his breath as Casper pushed his own birdie putt that would have been for 31. Casper said, "I thought to myself, 'You've picked up seven shots on one of the greatest players the game has ever known. Maybe you better just lag this up and putt it in.'" A pair of fours. Eighteen-hole playoff the next day.

In the playoff, like in a lot of nightmares, everything reoccurred exactly as it had before. Palmer went out in 33 for a two-stroke lead but began to unravel again at 10. That subtle fade turned into a rampaging slice, the hacker's calling card. Casper took his first lead by holing a birdie putt at 13 that was every bit of 50 feet. Palmer couldn't avoid 40 this time, for 73. The good player who chokes usually does so because he dwells on what it all means to him. At 18, Casper notched his 33rd one-putt of the tournament, for 69.

"I'm sorry, Arnie," he said. Many years went by before he added in a whisper, "Those of us who play, we understand."

Doesn't 280 win U.S. Opens? Not always. But only one other golfer had ever broken 280 and lost an Open. Like Palmer, Jimmy Demaret shot 278 when Hogan set his record at Riviera. In the days before the Olympic tournament, Palmer had predicted to Marr that it would take a score below 280 to win. "No way," Marr said. For $10, Arnold bet him, "*I'll* break two-eighty." "I never paid him," Marr said years later. "I didn't have the heart."

Early that week, Dow Finsterwald invited Arnold and Winnie on their way home from San Francisco to drop by Colorado Springs, where Finsty served as pro-in-residence at the Broadmoor. "We had dinner at the club the next night," he said. "Dishwashers came out of the kitchen to get Arnold's autograph. He was so nice to them. You would have thought he had won the tournament, not lost it so bitterly. How Palmer handled himself around people was the most amazing of all the amazing things about him. I took a lesson. Not that I'm as good with people. I'm not. But I'm better than I would have been. Watching him that night, you know what I was thinking? I was glad he had his airplane, a diversion. When he got his hands on those controls, he had no choice but to stop thinking about golf. It carried him away from Olympic, into the sky."

To Arnie's Army—disappointed, of course—Olympic humanized him all the more. He won big, he lost big. The plaque on the 16th hole at Royal Birkdale wasn't his only golf course monument from 1961. Another, on the ninth hole at Rancho Park, commemorated the four straight 3-woods he rifled out of bounds (and a fifth onto the green) to make a 12 in the Los Angeles Open. That's who he was. Nobody wanted him to be anybody else. "If you don't think golf is a humbling game," Palmer said, "then you haven't had something like Olympic, something you wish you could be allowed to forget, brought back up to you year after year, over and over. It's not just a humbling game; sometimes it's a humiliating game. But the good thing about the bad losses is they bring you back to earth. And, in my experience, they arrive at just the right time, when you need them most. The moment you become a little too full of yourself, an Olympic comes along to turn you back into a real person again."

Going forward, he continued to be the most asked question called into the night desks on weekends: "What did Palmer do today?" People who didn't follow golf followed him. People who hated golf loved him. That wouldn't change.

13

1973

WINNER:

Bob Hope Desert Classic

"Ol' 'enry was a wise, wise man."

Raymond Floyd was sorry to hear that, contrary to his long-standing recollection, the '71 Hope he lost to Palmer in a playoff was *not* Arnold's final victory on the regular tour. Palmer won the Hope again two years later. That was the finish line.

Floyd so cherished his association with Palmer, he prized even the distinction of losing to Arnold last. "Everybody says he was the swashbuckler who came along at just the right time for television," Floyd said, "but, to me, he was a lot more than that. He was the epitome of a superstar even before the word was coined. In his patience and decency, he set the standard for how superstars in every sport ought to be. The way he always signed autographs. The way he always made time for everyone. I sought him out, as I guess everybody did, as a young player, asking his advice on the practice tee—and you know how dangerous that can be. He said a few things and I immediately started hitting it better. Then he took my club in his hands—those amazing hands—and bent the neck just slightly. I started hitting it even better still. I came across a photograph of Palmer's hands once. I've still got it."

Palmer won that fifth and final Hope in 1973 by two strokes over Nicklaus and Johnny Miller. So, as Arnold had finished second to Nicklaus at Jack's first PGA Tour victory (the Oakmont Open of '62), Nicklaus finished second to Palmer at Arnold's last. During a post-tournament jam session in Indian Wells, a charming if temporary truce broke out in their hostilities. One or the other of them accidentally bumped a female in the crowd, dislodging her blond wig, leaving the poor woman in curlers. Picking up the wig, Arnie asked Jack if he'd care to dance. He said he'd be delighted. Taking turns leading and playing the blonde, they tangoed across the floor, proving the old adage.

Four months after the dance, Palmer returned to Oakmont for another Open without either his airplane or spectacles (with which he lately had been experimenting), because the course was less than an hour's drive from Latrobe and its lines were so indelibly drawn in his head, he could have negotiated it blindfolded. Early Sunday morning, this being a different era in both golf and newspapers, Doc Giffin gathered a gaggle of writers on a screen porch so Arnie could pass some of the long waiting time filling their early columns.

Palmer was in the lead, along with three others, to be sure: Jerry Heard, known then as "the Heard Shot Round the World"; two-time Open champion Julius Boros (the amiable accountant); and Oregonian eccentric John Schlee, who would be Palmer's playing partner that afternoon. Six strokes back in 13th place, Miller was trying to shake off Saturday's 76. As a 19-year-old amateur, he had signed up to caddy at Olympic, his home course, but ended up qualifying and finishing eighth in the Casper-Palmer Open. And, with two top-sevens in '71 and '72, he seemed to be gaining on it.

Oakmont's famously firm greens had been all but drowned by an overnight downpour compounded by a sprinkler malfunction set off by a flash of lightning. The putting surfaces weren't just soft now—they were squishy. It might sound like New Journalism, but Jack Murphy of San Diego was prompted to open the conversation on the porch by asking Palmer, "What if somebody goes out early and shoots sixty-three?"

"There'll be hell to pay," he said, telling the story of Mrs. Fritz at Latrobe and the nickels she used to pay him for hitting her drives over the ditch. "People around here," he said, meaning country club people, "think they can buy anything, and they're not paying for sixty-threes."

Palmer was plainly enjoying himself. He looked confident and on the muscle; in short, like the winner. At a mention of his swing, he said, "Ignoring your descriptions of it, everyone's descriptions of it—even people who know what they're talking about [he looked around pointedly and smiled]—has been crucial to my success."

"Arnie, would you mind giving us an example," said Atlanta's Furman Bisher, flashing a similar smile, "of someone who knows what he's talking about?"

"Henry Cotton, for instance," Palmer said, the Englishman, three-time winner of the British Open, Tip Anderson's father's old employer. "Asked about my style," Palmer said, "Cotton replied, 'Palmer's style? He has no style. No follow-through, either. Never finishes a swing the same way twice. Almost goes to his knees half the time. And don't get me started on that crouching, cringing, knock-kneed putting stance of his. . . .'"

Everyone laughed.

"Ol' 'enry is a wise, wise man," Bisher said.

A writer who arrived a couple of minutes late at the first tee for the Palmer-Schlee pairing was baffled to find Schlee standing there alone with no caddie, no Palmer, and no gallery. He was wearing a Hawaiian shirt that wasn't tucked in, a nod to the Hawaiian Open he had won that year, the only PGA tournament he would ever win. "Hi there," Schlee said pleasantly, sticking a peg in the ground, balancing a ball on it, taking a practice swing, driving the ball away, and quick-stepping down the fairway after it. "See you later," he called.

It turned out, this wasn't his first drive of the day. In fact, it was his third. The second was a provisional, in case the first was out of bounds. When Schlee found his original ball in bounds but unplayable, he had to walk all the way back to the tee with his driver. Nobody went with him. They all stayed with Palmer in the fairway. The U.S. Open was on pause.

A comment of Schlee's the day before made a certain sense now. Asked to rate his chances, he had said, "Well, Mars is in conjunction with my natal moon. So."

Many of the writers took him for a Southerner because he played his college golf in Memphis, looked like a curly-haired cowboy, and spoke with a prairie twang. Also, they associated him with Hogan, so, by extension, with Texas. As the story went, Hogan drove up to him in a cart on a range somewhere and asked if he'd like to have a game. That was more than unusual for Hogan. "I can't remember what we played for," Schlee said. "It wasn't much, but it was all I had. I outhit him by miles. I was more than twenty-five years younger, but I couldn't beat him. It was all I could do to tie him." Schlee became a regular practice companion to Hogan and one of Ben's rare cronies.

Actually, Schlee was from a seaside Oregon town *called* Seaside, where his folks ran a small hotel (with a wishing well?) on the ocean. For dating the daughter of the chief of police more than for stealing golf balls (allegedly), he ended up being browbeaten by his father and the law into choosing between jail and the Army. Whether as a soldier, a college golfer, or a pro, Schlee was hopelessly star-crossed, and knew it. Because he knew stars.

"He didn't only do his own horoscope, he did yours, too," Palmer said. "A decent player and, as far as I could tell, a decent if unconventional guy. Not difficult to play with. Good to play with. I had played with him earlier that year in the Hope." Erasing his double-bogey at the first hole with an eagle at the fourth, Schlee, more than Heard or Boros (or Lee Trevino or Tom Weiskopf), seemed to Palmer to be his primary competition.

Meanwhile, Miller stuck a 3-iron five feet at the first hole, a 9-iron one foot at the second, a 5-iron 25 feet at the third, and a driver, 3-wood, and bunker shot six inches at the fourth. Birdie, birdie, birdie, birdie. Following two-putt pars at five, six, and seven, he three-putted for bogey at eight and two-putted for birdie at nine. Out in four-under-par 32—at a United States Open!

Missing no greens, still throwing feathers at a spongy dartboard, Miller made birdie putts of 14, 15, five, and 10 feet at the 11th, 12th, 13th, and 15th holes, where he took his first lead. His 5-iron approach at 18 went straight at the flag and did its best to climb a dip in front of the hole but couldn't quite make it and rolled back. A 20-footer for an Open and major tournament record 62 hit the left edge and spun right. *What if somebody goes out early and shoots 63?*

One-under-par for the day, four-under for the tournament, Palmer thought he was leading by a stroke when he saw a five-under score being backed in on a leaderboard. That's how they do it. They start with the final number and finish with the name.

"Who *is* that?" Palmer asked Schlee, who said, "Miller," Arnie's playing partner the first two rounds, "didn't you know?"

"I blanched," Arnold confessed later in the press tent—an unusual word for a press tent. "You'd think as long as I've been playing golf, that wouldn't have hit me so hard."

Palmer bogeyed 12, 13, and 14, falling away. Schlee birdied 16 to draw within one of Miller. "Playing with Palmer is roughly a two-stroke penalty," Schlee always said. "Not his fault. But 'Arnie, Arnie.' Hard to concentrate with all that Arnie-ing going on."

Schlee had a putt at 18 to tie, admittedly a 40-footer, but it actually had a chance. He finished second alone. If only he hadn't hit three drives at one. If only.

At age 52 and then 63, Palmer would return to Oakmont for two more Opens, 1983 and 1994, his second-to-last and his last, a total of 32 over a period of 40 years. He made the cut in '83 (Miller didn't) and missed it in '94, finally shooting 81 on a steamy Friday, wearing a planter's broad-brimmed straw hat.

With a white towel draped over the shoulders of a sweat-soaked white shirt, calling to mind a prizefighter once again, Louis against Marciano, he took a seat in the media center. "I think you all know pretty much how I feel," he said slowly. "Most of you I have talked to quite a bit over the years [He wasn't kidding: George Sweda of the *Cleveland Plain Dealer* dragged him along to Sweda's high school reunion, just for the fun of it. Everything was fun then] and, I suppose, the sun got me a little bit. I got a little tired, I guess, and a little emotional coming up eighteen . . . I mean, it is forty years of fun, work, enjoyment. God, I haven't won all that much. I've won a few tournaments. I've won some majors. But I suppose the most important thing [dropping his face in the towel, he took five or so seconds to sob] is the fact that it has been as good as it has been to me."

It embarrassed him to be so exhausted. "I think all of this," he said, "is just being a little sun-whipped and tired, ready to take a little rest. Hopefully a few more tournaments along the way. I think that's about all I have to say. Thank you very much."

He left to a standing ovation of cynics.

Twenty-four-year-old Ernie Els, the young South African who *showed* Palmer instead of telling him ("I guess I kind of like that," Arnie had said), won that '94 tournament, Palmer's retirement Open. "I was on the range, actually, when he finished Friday," Els said. "A lot of players were out there to watch him play the eighteenth hole. He's the King, after all. He's the man. I mean, there wasn't a lot of television yet in Europe when he went to the Open Championship and won it twice. That famous shot he hit at Birkdale on sixteen out of the little bush. He took the whole bush and the golf ball together, and hit the ball on the green and won the tournament. He established the legend over there, just as he had over here. He was a guy everybody wanted to look at, to see. Everybody wanted to be like him. He took the game and moved it forward by himself. And he kept playing the game he loved for a very long time. Also, there's another benefit. He gave young guys like myself an opportunity to play in his tournament. I think he's the most unbelievable example of a sportsman throughout all sport. If you want to emulate a guy, look at Arnold Palmer. Follow what he did. I saw the replay of his press conference, where he got so emotional. That was quite something. Yeah, it was quite a week."

Later in 1994, in the Road Hole Bar at St. Andrews's Old Course Hotel during the Dunhill Cup, a gray-haired English lady drinking Scotch called out from a corner, "Master Els! Come over here, Master Els!"

He walked over and said, "How're you doing, ma'am?"

"Do you know who I am?"

"*No* idea, ma'am."

"Have you ever heard of Henry Cotton?" she said.

"Oh, yes, ma'am," Ernie said. Cotton won his Open Championships at Carnoustie, St. George's, and Muirfield where, eight years later, Els would win one of his.

"I'm Henry Cotton's daughter," she said, "and I want to give you some advice. You're going to have a long career. You're going to be great. But let me tell you something: Don't let anybody ever fuck you around. Do it on your own terms and at your own time. Don't let them fuck you around."

"OK, ma'am," Ernie told her, trying not to laugh. "I'll keep that in mind."

Ol' 'enry's daughter was a wise, wise woman.

14

1976

"I'm going to try to be your best friend from now on."

AMERICA, ESPECIALLY AMERICAN TELEVISION, sees only American golf. Network announcers might calculate a Sergio García or Rory McIlroy victory "drought" in terms of years, even if it had been only weeks. By their count, poor Els won just 19 tournaments, never mind the 50-some world victories he rang up away from the PGA Tour. Even Palmer performed notable feats outside the country that barely registered on home radar.

In 1975, after a fallow couple of seasons, Arnold won the Spanish Open in April, a worthy tournament, and the British PGA in May, a big tournament, to almost no notice. Scottish journalist Renton Laidlaw was with him in Spain. "It meant so much to him," Laidlaw said. "Right after the awards ceremony, I went down with him at La Manga to his condominium right on the course. He ran to the telephone to call Winnie in the States. It was almost as if he had won his first golf tournament. 'Winnie! Winnie! I won the tournament!' he shouted. 'I've won again!' He was so delighted, so elated. Like a young boy, like a twenty-one-year-old boy who had just lifted his first trophy. It was lovely to see. So natural. He was a superstar who was so completely normal. I wrote about that the next day in the paper."

A year later, Palmer shot 64 in Palm Springs and seemed to be on his way to winning again in America, what would have been a sixth Bob Hope. But then something happened and he had to withdraw.

Doc Giffin's best friend since childhood was an insurance salesman, a fellow Craftonite named Bill Finegan. One of Pittsburgh's smokiest bedroom communities was Crafton, the suburb that shaped former Steelers coach Bill Cowher, known for making a sideline face (like a half-chewed caramel) that was a common expression in Crafton.

Finegan married into the Flanagan family; the Flanagans' home served as headquarters and clubhouse for all the neighborhood boys. Bill and Doc (so named, by the way, because his father worked in a drugstore) played golf together growing up and as young adults pooled their modest resources to go in on a partners' membership at an affordable course in Aliquippa.

In 1976 the friends planned a vacation together in Orlando to play Bay Hill. But, riding in the private jet of his richest customer, Finegan disappeared in a storm over West Virginia. The plane was missing for 10 days. Then pieces of it were found in the mountains.

"After the memorial service for Bill," Doc said, "Arnold told me, 'Go take your vacation now, Doc. Go to Bay Hill.'" Deacon came to Giffin and asked, "Would you mind if I tagged along?" "I was surprised," Doc said, "but grateful for the company. 'I'd love that,' I told him."

During the flight to Orlando, they played gin rummy. "He wasn't a man of many words," Doc said. "It was mostly nods and grunts."

But then he stopped dealing the cards, set them down on the tray, and looked Doc straight in the eye. "'You've lost your best friend,' he told me. 'I'm going to try to be your best friend from now on.'"

Accustomed to rising early, the old greenkeeper headed out before daybreak to play nine holes on Bay Hill's short track, the Charger; then, along with Doc, he went 18 more on the big course. Twenty-seven holes in all. "Played nicely, too," Doc said. "We finished up, had a bite to eat, and he went back to the hotel for a nap. We had adjoining rooms with a connecting door. Some of Arnold's workers took me out for a boat ride. When I returned, around dinnertime, the connecting door was open. Something felt wrong. I went into Deacon's room and found him on the floor. He was dead. He'd had a heart attack." Doc called Winnie, who called Arnie, who withdrew from the Hope.

Back in Latrobe, Giffin closed a locker and mounted a nameplate on it for the man who never set foot in the locker room without the express permission of a member. "Milfred J. (Deacon) Palmer, Golf Professional–Course Superintendent, Latrobe Country Club, 1921–1976." It's there today.

"I think Arnold wanted nothing so much in life as his father's approval," Gary Player had said, "and, for all that Arnie accomplished, I don't believe he ever completely got it."

To that, Doc said, "If Arnold *didn't* know how much his father loved him, everybody else did. *I* did."

"Pap played nine holes on the Charger," Palmer said, "had a quick snack, came back, and played a full eighteen on the championship course. Came in, had a drink, said to Doc, 'I'm going to go back and take a little nap. I'll see you at seven o'clock for dinner.' Gone. Whether he was lying down—they said he was—he died. Had a heart attack and died. Now *that* is the way to die."

Doris went three years later, unluckier. "My mother had a tragic death," Palmer said, "and that hurts me a lot." She was tortured by rheumatoid arthritis, undergoing operation after operation, receiving artificial joints in her hands and arms, and the medication sometimes seemed more diabolical than the disease. "For a lot of years, she suffered," he said. "It was a difficult way to die."

Late in his own life, Palmer would say, "I'm more afraid of *how* I will die than of dying. I don't want to linger. That scares me a little. The idea of lingering."

15

1980

"Nobody would have bought into it if he didn't."

PALMER NEVER WON THE PGA Championship, and it is the PGA Championship that seems diminished. For all its fine memories of Walter Hagen and the rest, a tournament that never had Arnold Palmer on its shoulders can hardly feel complete. He considered himself the poorer, of course. "It's a disappointment over a career, a significant missing piece," he said, "especially since my father was a PGA pro. I'd love to be able to say 'Hey, I won the PGA' for him."

Three times Palmer finished second (in 1964, '68, and '70), three other times top 10. In 1964 at Columbus, Ohio, Bobby Nichols opened with a 64 to Palmer's 68. A second 68 drew Arnold within one, but then to his 69–69 on the weekend Nichols went 69–67 to win his only major. In 1968, Julius Boros beat Arnie by a shot on the last day (69 to 70), the margin of victory in the tournament at San Antonio. A sublime 3-wood Palmer hit out of trouble at the final hole, the best shot Doc Giffin ever saw him hit, gave Arnie a chance to tie, but he missed a 10-footer. In '70 he made up three final-round strokes against Dave Stockton at Tulsa—two too few. "You don't dwell on your near misses," Palmer said. "No, as a matter of fact, you do."

In Tom Watson's majors cache, he also lacked the PGA; Lee Trevino lacked the Masters, Sam Snead and Phil Mickelson the U.S. Open, and Raymond Floyd the Open Championship. All of them looked back on their narrowest misses with the same dismay.

Coming to his fifties, Palmer's enthusiasm for the budding senior tour was muted. He disapproved of riding carts, an option available to the liver-spotted geezers. He despised driving from the shorter tees. Returning to Nicklaus's tournament at age 53, Arnold elbowed a writer and whispered jubilantly, "Back to the *real* tees, brother!"

Not that he didn't appreciate the mulligan that senior play represented, especially at the outset, for the likes of Tommy Bolt, Roberto De Vicenzo, Boros, and Snead (while Don January and Miller Barber seemed to do most of the winning). But he didn't care for the joyless cast that came over the tour when the money got serious. "The problem with the senior tour," he said, sitting at his desk, "is the guys who were pricks the first time around are still pricks. They need to remember how things came to be what they are." Raymond Floyd would second that. And Barber said, "The complainers now are the same ones who were complaining twenty, twenty-five years ago when I first went on tour. Shoot, it's a convention of old farts."

In 1980, the first formal year of the Senior PGA Tour, only four tournaments were conducted. The first three, all paying $20,000 to the champion, went to Don January in early June (the Atlantic

City Senior International), De Vicenzo in late June (the U.S. Senior Open), and Old Charley Horse, Charlie Sifford, in November (the Suntree Classic). Charlie sure was a master. The fourth was the PGA Senior at Turnberry Isle in Aventura, Florida, in December, also paying twenty grand.

"It had the name 'PGA' on it," Palmer said. "That's all I cared about."

Arnold opened with a par 72, three shots worse than Paul Harney, a pro's pro from Massachusetts, who 10 times finished in the top 10 at the U.S. Open, failing to join Boros, Cupit, and Palmer in their 1963 playoff by just a stroke. Four times Harney was in the top eight at the Masters, including fifth in 1964, when Palmer won his fourth green jacket. As almost no one but the participants could tell you, Harney and Palmer were paired together on the final 36-hole day in the 1960 U.S. Open at Cherry Hills.

Friday at Turnberry Isle, Arnie shot 69, moving himself into the lead. But neither Palmer nor Harney could manage par the next two blowy days, and they finished tied at the top. In their slipstream was a roll call of the old names: January, Wall, Sifford, Boros, Finsterwald, Ford, Kroll, Dickinson, Souchak.

"If I had made a six-footer at eighteen, I could have avoided the sudden-death playoff with Paul," Palmer said. "I have to admit, that six-footer didn't feel quite as automatic as they used to, but I was still pretty sure I'd make it."

When he didn't, the two men went back to the 15th hole, a 388-yard par four, where Arnold hit a squirter to the right not unlike the one on the 16th at Royal Birkdale in 1961. He was back in his old Latrobe element, in the matted rough. ("Watch me, Pap! Look at me hit this one!")

"Trees were in my way—what else is new?" Palmer said, "and I couldn't hit anything more than a nine iron and still clear the top branches. But I hit the hell out of that nine." His ball landed on the green and moonwalked to within seven feet of the cup. After Harney missed a long birdie putt, Palmer settled in over his shorter one. "This time," he said, "I had absolutely no doubt. It felt automatic again. Automatic. I made the three, looked up at the sky and thought, 'Well, we finally won a PGA, Pap.'"

He won 10 senior tournaments, including another PGA, by two strokes over January; a U.S. Senior Open by two over Billy Casper and Bob Stone (making Palmer the first man to win a U.S. Amateur, a U.S. Open, and a U.S. Senior Open); and a pair of Senior Tournament Players Championships, by three over Peter Thomson, and by 11(!!!) over a gang of four. His victory against the Australian Thomson, five-time winner of the Open Championship, was at Canterbury Golf Club in Cleveland, Arnie's old Coast Guard station. "If I could have—and I couldn't—I wouldn't have dared beat him there," Thomson said.

Nicklaus said, "I doubt the senior tour would have happened without Arnold. Nobody would have bought into it if he didn't buy into it. He played it just a little bit at the start. So, once more, one by one, we all followed him and did the same."

16

1982

WINNER:

Marlboro Senior Classic

Denver Post Champions of Golf

"I live that moment still in my mind."

To ward off the senior malaise, Palmer gravitated toward younger players, like Peter Jacobsen and Rocco Mediate ("Arnold Palmer is timeless," Rocco said, "that's all there is to it"), and several generations of Arnold Palmer and Buddy Worsham golfers at Wake Forest, from Lanny Wadkins and Curtis Strange to Webb Simpson and both father Jay and son Bill Haas. They were all recipients of one of the two golf scholarships Wake established for Palmer and Arnold established for his best friend.

"I know I like to think young," he said. "I'm not much for sitting around and thinking about the past or talking about the past. What does that accomplish? If I can give young people something to think about, like the future, that's a better use of my time."

"I first met Arnold my first year on tour, nineteen seventy-seven," Jacobsen said. "Trying to Monday qualify, I missed out three straight weeks; then, on the fourth Monday, played my way into a field at the AT&T, the old Crosby. I was so excited, nervous. I went back out with just my caddie to play ten, eleven, twelve, and thirteen at Monterey Peninsula Country Club. Now it's, like, five thirty in the afternoon. I jumped across to sixteen to play in, and had hit three drives off sixteen tee, when, out of nowhere, around a corner, came this caravan of four hundred or so people led by Arnold Palmer and Mark McCormack."

Jacobsen suddenly realized he had cut in. "He could have big-timed me," Jake said. "He could have called me out. 'Step aside, kid, I'm coming through.' But instead he walks up to me, tucking in his britches, sticking out his hand, saying, 'How are you? I'm Arnold Palmer. May we join you?' He introduces me to McCormack, who later became my manager for twenty-five years. Then he hands me a sleeve of golf balls. 'Here, these are in the developmental stage,' he says, 'let me know what you think of them.' After we play sixteen, seventeen, and eighteen, he says, 'You've got your card, you're on the circuit, good for you. We'll be seeing each other every week from now on.' And, just like that, I felt accepted. A kid out of Oregon who dreamed of playing golf. I don't have to tell you, golf isn't the most inclusive sport. In all games, for that matter, the stars tend to be exclusive. 'Stay away. Get away. I have my inner circle.' But he included me. He made me feel I belonged. I think he made everyone feel that way."

Jacobsen won the AT&T in time and a score of other tournaments. He served two Ryder Cup teams and played presentably in the majors, finishing as high as third place at the PGA Championship twice, along with a personal best of seventh in a U.S. Open, if you don't count the Open he won in "Tin Cup." Jake was a logical character to portray himself in a movie, being a natural entertainer. He made a lounge act out of practice tee impersonations, dumping a bucket of range balls down his shirt before doing Craig Stadler. Palmer always came last.

"First I'd make sure I unbuttoned my collar and spread the flaps. Then go: 'Huh? Huh?' Snort a bunch of times. Tear out a few chest hairs and toss them into the wind. 'Did you see that lady over there by the tee, Arnold?' 'Talked to her already.' Waggle. Two or three club dips, a neck dip. Then you had to go to the pants with your elbows. Finally that whirligig of a swing. Always followed by 'Where'd it go?'"

Palmer and Jacobsen became regular partners in Fred Meyer Challenges and Shark Shootouts, doubles events in the so-called silly season. But Palmer didn't think they were silly. "I can't add up the number of times I played golf with Arnold," Jacobsen said, "but we were partners in seventeen Fred Meyer Challenges, my tournament in Oregon, and probably ten of Greg Norman's Shootouts. We had a good chance to win Greg's event one year at Sherwood. On the sixteenth, a reachable par five, we were two back and I hit a nice drive and had a long iron or a hybrid into the green. He walked up to me and grabbed me by my shirt. He got that look in his eye and said, 'Do you know how much it would mean to me for us to win this tournament? Knock it on there and make an eagle.'"

Jake did both, "more because of him, less because of me," he said. "But we still lost in the end, and he was so deflated. 'That competitive fire,' I thought to myself, 'it never goes out.' Not in him anyway."

Well beyond his prime, Palmer remained a useful teammate, "because Arnold was still just about the best driver of the golf ball anyone ever saw," Jacobsen said. "It's nice when you can depend on your partner to hit it straight down every fairway with no side spin.

A year finally arrived, as I was calling him to another Fred Meyer, when he told me, 'You know, my game's not what it used to be.' And I replied, 'Arnold, is that why you think I'm playing with you?' He said, 'I don't know, why *are* you playing with me?' The true answer is we had become a team. But the answer I gave him was 'The reason I want to play with you is you're the only one I can outdrive anymore.' 'Screw you!' he said. They punched each other in the arm and played on.

"The hell about a golfer growing older," Palmer said, "is it doesn't happen overnight. It's a process over a period of years. You have that moment after a long lull when you hit a two-iron just right and say to yourself, 'OK, it's back again.' I used to consider myself a realist as a golfer and a romantic as a pilot. I don't know when I became a romantic as a golfer and a realist as a pilot. I just know I did, involuntarily."

In all their many collaborations, never once did Jacobsen see Palmer bristle under the responsibility of being Palmer. "Not a single time, in all the places we went," he said, "when people were falling all over themselves to get a picture or autograph or just shake his hand, did I ever hear him say, 'Geez, get me out of here. This is ridiculous. Get me away from this guy.' And whenever tournament organizers offered him security, say, to escort him to his car, he declined. He'd go with the people, no matter how long it took. And he never hurried them. 'What's your name? Great to see you. Oh, is this your wife? How did you get a wife so good-looking? What do you do? You must be rich.' Everyone felt like they were part of his group. Come on in, join the conversation. He let the whole world inside."

Jacobsen had a theory: "When you're in a position like Arnold Palmer and Muhammad Ali—maybe we should stop with them, though I guess there are a few others. But when you're in that position, I think you have an innate ability to read the people standing in front of you. Not only members of the media, the press, but also everyday fans. It could be an asshole media question—sorry—or a well-thought-out question from just about anyone. He would craft every response specifically to the individual, with graciousness. He was just so accepting. He might be the most accepting person who ever lived. Some people walked up to him a little afraid, others not the least bit intimidated. But, whoever was standing there, Arnold knew how to make it easier for them, and did. Whether it was a five-year old boy, or a forty-year-old trembling woman, or somebody in a wheelchair, or a fellow who actually thought he could outdrive Arnold Palmer. To whomever it was, Arnold adjusted."

It's a natural grace.

Jacobsen's best memory was from a game he had with Palmer, Ben Crenshaw, and Bruce Lietzke. "Arnold jumped on a drive," he said, "and popped one past the three of us. 'Ooh, ooh, ooh,' he said. 'Let me see, now. There's one. There's two. There's three. Looks to me like you boys are away.' We had caught ours pretty good, too, but he was three or four steps out in front, and I'll tell you something, we were just as thrilled as he was. I'd give anything to see that again today. I live that moment still in my mind."

In 1982, Arnie got boiling mad at Curtis Strange, whom he loved.

"I misbehaved a little bit," Strange said, "at the Bay Hill tournament." Curtis doused a photographer with a thousand-gallon flume of profanity and then turned the hose on a female scorekeeper, a long-standing volunteer. "Of course my language got back to Arnold," Strange said, "and he made a public example of me—made me apologize to everyone concerned. The reason he was so goddamned mad at me, I think, was because he *did* like me. I loved him. If Arnold just gives you that wink or grin, or 'Do well,' or whatever, it means everything to you. Then, if you disappoint him, oh, man."

Palmer and Worsham scholars Strange, Wadkins, Haas, Billy

Andrade, were all Arnie's boys but, for some reason Curtis was especially. His father, Tom Strange, was a Virginia club professional who could really play: a five-time winner of the state open, a five-time qualifier at the U.S. Open. He died of cancer when his twin sons, Allan and Curtis, were 14.

"My dad competed against Arnie as an amateur," Strange said, "and served on his equipment staff as a pro. I played Arnold Palmer clubs all through my junior career. Pretty early on, I came to know him and tried to be like him. Arnie played golf with a certain edge. I played with a certain edge, too. We had a conversation about it once. He told me you have to be on edge in order to play well."

When Curtis married Sarah in 1976, they spent their first night as husband and wife at Arnie's house in Latrobe. Strange said, "I was playing an exhibition in Pennsylvania the next day, where he of course was the headliner. I was getting fifteen hundred dollars. I needed it. But being with Arnie and Winnie meant so much more than the money. I say it like this: we all have idols, people we respect as kids, and very few of us are lucky enough ever to meet those people. And many, many times when we do, they don't quite live up to what we hoped they'd be. But Arnie did. That and beyond. For a younger guy, he was a good man to hang out with. He was real. He cared about you, cared enough to get mad at you. When Palmer looked you in the eye and said 'How are you?' he really meant it. Almost everybody says that, but almost nobody really means it."

After Strange won his consecutive U.S. Opens in 1988 and '89—making a commendable run at a third one, too—he and Sarah had dinner with Arnie and Winnie the following week at the Canadian Skins Game. "We talked about our Opens," Strange said, "about all the Opens." Tom Strange's dream at his five Opens had been to play well enough to get into a Masters, which he never did. Curtis qualified for 20 Masters, finishing second in 1985, the year he won his first of three PGA Tour money titles and took a turn as the world's best player. In 1989 he won three tournaments besides the Open and became the first man ever to earn an official $1 million in a season.

Palmer had been the first to win $100,000 in a season, and was the first to win $1 million in a career. It took him 13 years to do it. "When I started out," Arnold said, "we were getting twelve hundred for first place and only fifteen places paid out. I'm pleased to see what has happened to the game and to think that I might have had something to do with it."

Jay Haas and Strange, Wake teammates as devoted to each other as Arnie and Buddy, regularly sought Palmer out at U.S. and British Opens for practice rounds. They knew enough not to give him the dean treatment; instead, to give him their best games, and the business. "We all had the needle out," Strange said, "because that's the way he wanted it and, I think, needed it, to still be one of the guys." Haas, almost the last person you'd associate with off-color humor, collected dirty jokes all year to regale Palmer. "We'd play for five dollars, ten dollars," Strange said, "and never pay. If Jay or I laid up somewhere, he'd say, 'You pussy!' And, let me tell you, he'd rip your heart out to win. Talk about competitive. He just couldn't wait to beat Haas and Strange. He didn't go in for the modern fist-bumping, either, if his opponent holed a putt. Not while the match was still undecided. Uh-uh. Afterward, maybe."

In 2016, when Palmer was 86, Strange dropped by his office at Bay Hill and they talked away an afternoon. "He was giving me a lot of grief," Curtis said, "telling me, 'You might not have been the worst actor on tour, but you were the second-worst.' 'Yeah,' I said, 'and you were a piece of cake, too, a rosebud, weren't you?' He loved it. 'How many times,' I asked him, 'have you gotten so goddamned mad on the golf course that you couldn't spit?' He laughed. I loved to hear him laugh."

Strange said, "Think how normal he seems to you and me. Yet presidents and kings wanted to be Arnold Palmer."

On the second day of 2007, Palmer, Strange, Haas, Wadkins, Andrade, and others—a stunning assembly of gold-shirted Demon Deacons—congregated at the Orange Bowl for about the least likely occurrence any of them had ever imagined happening: Wake Forest's appearance in a Bowl Championship Series football game. The opponent was the University of Louisville. Wearing jersey number 66 (for six-under-par presumably, certainly not for the '66 U.S. Open), Palmer was Wake's honorary captain.

Muhammad Ali, a Louisville native, wore 19 for the Cardinals, presumably a nod to Johnny Unitas, though Unitas's Louisville number was 16. When the Baltimore Colts signed him off a Bloomfield, Pennsylvania, sandlot, 16 was available. But John being John, he took the number the equipment man handed him and said nothing. "That was Unitas all right," Palmer said of his fellow Pittsburgher, whom of course Arnold knew well.

The kickoff was delayed a few minutes because Ali, sitting in a cart, was talking to Palmer about golf. He spoke softly, slowly, and with that horrible palsy, but enough of him was still there. The only two golf swings Muhammad ever tried, splay-legged with an 8-iron at the Stardust course in San Diego's Hotel Circle, came while Ali was training for the first Ken Norton fight, which he lost. Muhammad was trying to tell Palmer something about that, and about lovely little trainer Eddie Futch's belief that it was a fascination with golf that doomed Joe Louis in the first Max Schmeling fight.

"I didn't completely get what Muhammad was telling me," Palmer said, "but I knew that, whatever it was, it was important to him, and I wouldn't let anybody stop him. I was in Ali's company a number of times through the years. He was my friend."

Wake alum Ernie Accorsi, the former Colts, Browns, and Giants general manager, was also at the game, sitting with the golfers. "I'll never forget two things," Accorsi said. "Curtis turning to Andrade, saying, like a twelve-year-old kid, 'Billy, did you ever dream we'd be here in the Orange Bowl?' A guy with two U.S. Open championships. Then the way Arnie's boys followed him with their eyes as he made his way up through the stands . . ."

Louisville won.

17

1986

WINNER:

Union Mutual Classic

"I don't think you can know me if you don't know Doc."

"For as long as I've been with Arnold," Doc Giffin said, "I've never stopped thinking of myself as a newspaper guy."

Doc's first paper was the *Pitt News* at the University of Pittsburgh, where, his junior year, he served as sports editor and, his senior year, as editor in chief. That earned him a scholarship at Pitt and later a starting position in the profession with United Press International in Pittsburgh ($47.50 a week). Ordinarily the *Pitt News* sports editor penned the column, but Giffin deferred to a pint-sized dynamo a semester behind him, Myron Sidney Kopelman, who wrote under the byline Myron Cope.

"'Cope, you're gonna write the column,' I told him, because

I knew he could write rings around me as a columnist." In later years, when Cope was dropping indefinable terms like *yoi* and *double yoi* into Steeler broadcasts while devising something called the Terrible Towel to the enormous enrichment of children's charities, Pittsburgh forgot what a splendid writer Cope was. But the evidence can still be found in the archives of *Sports Illustrated* and the *Saturday Evening Post*.

"Doc's a good writer, too," Palmer said. "I correct his stuff, but that's all right. No, to hear him tell it, everyone else is better. But that's Doc."

It was Bob Drum who put Arnold together with Doc, a fellow scribbler at the *Pittsburgh Press*. Giffin was the man in the composing room who with a radio and a typewriter got out the "extra" when Bill Mazeroski's homer in the bottom of the ninth inning beat the New York Yankees in the 1960 World Series. "We were on the street in ten minutes," Doc said, the excitement still bubbling in his voice. And it was Drum who closed the deal when the tour offered Doc the position of press secretary in the '60s. "Doctor, if you don't take this job," Bob told him, "I'll never speak to you again."

Giffin gave the tour a shot of humanity. Any time Lionel Hebert was in the hunt, for instance, Doc made sure a trumpet was handy. "One year at Memphis," he said, "Hebert, Gene Littler and Gary Player played off. Lionel birdied the first playoff hole to win, and at the awards ceremony, just before he put the horn to his lips, he turned to Gene and said, 'Hey, Lit, do you want me to play you some blues?' Gene laughed. They could get away with things like that in those days because they loved each other."

Doc said, "I've been called Arnold's 'handler,' but while he's trusted my input into places he should go or people he should talk to, I've never been his handler. He doesn't need a handler. I've been asked, 'Why is Arnold Palmer so popular?' The answer is simple. He likes people, and they know it. His public face and his private face are exactly the same. He's not one of those guys who turns it on in public and turns it off in private. He'll tolerate fools that most of us won't, myself included. He just likes people. There are vice presidents and everything else in the company now, but I'm still 'assistant to Arnold Palmer.'"

"Maybe Doc's real title," Palmer said, "should be 'friend,' or 'everlasting friend.'" Ten months Arnold's senior, Doc had similar perspectives and the same memories. At the end of every workday, they convened, just the two of them, for a cocktail and what they called "debriefing."

"We've done that every day, every year," Palmer said, "since the sixties. We enjoy it. They're just bull sessions, really. We start off discussing the tasks at hand but end up talking about everything. Old victories. Old losses. Life. Before he married, I used to call him 'the highwayman.'" In those days, Doc patrolled Route 30 sweet-talking Latrobe's eligible women and teaching its bartenders how to mix a proper Manhattan.

"Doc is someone you can trust with your life," Palmer said, "a good guy who always steers you in the right direction. I can think of a player or two—so can you—who could have used a Doc Giffin. Along with everything else he does around here—and he does a lot—he's been a guardrail for me, and I don't think you can know me if you don't know Doc."

In 1986, Gary Player was lingering beside a par-3 green where he had just putted out, at a senior tournament in a Maryland suburb of Washington. Looking back at the tee, he watched Palmer, playing in the group behind, make a hole in one. "As I was getting ready to swing," Arnold said, "I saw Gary standing there. I got to thinking about him, and us, and everything. You know, I wanted to hit a good one."

"That's it! That's it!" Player said later in the locker room. "He always knew how to share a moment of triumph, yours or his.

Sometimes in life, it can be very hard to find someone to share your moments of triumph."

The next day, at the same hole, with the same 5-iron, Palmer made another ace. Not surprisingly, then, on the third day, he drew a media crowd at that tee. It was a little like going to a random airport just on the chance Amelia Earhart might land. The third shot did not go in the cup. Stop the presses.

In fact, it airmailed the green. A 5-iron was too much club for the new day's conditions, but he was too sentimental to change. Alan Shepard, the first American in space, the fifth human being to walk on the moon, and the only person ever to play golf outside of the atmosphere, brought his collapsible 6-iron and the sock he used to smuggle it aboard *Apollo 14* into a tournament pressroom at Winged Foot. "If you had it to do over, Alan," a comedian wondered, "would you still go with the soft six or change to a hard seven?" "I was committed to the six," he said with a grin, as Palmer was to the five.

When the shot went long, Arnold looked over at the witnesses and said sheepishly, "I didn't want to leave it short."

"Doc," I whispered to Giffin, "*Time* is holding a page for me. I can't wait for the end of the round."

"OK," he said, running to Palmer and back again.

"Can you do it in two walks down the fairway?"

"I've hit my share of unusual golf shots," Palmer said as we walked, itemizing a number of them, like a backhanded wedge out of a gum tree in Melbourne. He slammed drivers off of department store roofs in Japan (where the Japanese regarded him as John Wayne), anthills in Africa ("man-eating ants, now") and volcanoes in the South Seas. Wearing a three-piece pin-striped business suit, he punched a ball down a narrow corridor of Wall Street, and, from home plate at Fenway Park, lifted a short iron over the Green Monster.

"In Paris," he said, "I drove a ball off the top of the Eiffel Tower. It must have carried four hundred yards, straight down mostly, putting a hell of a ding in a passing bus." His eyes were dancing.

"But when that second ball went in the cup yesterday, I don't know how to describe the feeling. I've never felt anything like it. Idiot that I am, I just kept muttering, 'Oh, my goodness, oh, my goodness. Holy mack'rel, Andy.'"

Sometime later I told Palmer, "You know, every one of the writers has the equivalent story of Doc and a deadline."

"I hope so," he said.

18

1995

"A perfectly imperfect man."

PALMER WASN'T A PLASTIC saint. He didn't glow in the dark. For 45 wedded years he worshipped Winnie, but he loved all women, and more than a few loved him back. PGA champion Bob Rosburg, Palmer's occasional roommate in the hungry days on tour, spoke of fielding a phone call once from an especially agitated husband. Rossie said he tried to placate the man but, never wanting to come between Arnie and buckshot, signed off by saying, "My bed is the one by the window."

This is the hilarious way golfers of Palmer's generation, and not just golfers (and not just his generation), dealt with the subjects of sex and infidelity. Remember, Palmer and John F. Kennedy both came to power in 1960, and both knew Frank Sinatra. When I told Rosburg's joke to Gary Player, Dow Finsterwald, and Curtis Strange, all three laughed. None of them said it wasn't a laughing matter. "I heard Rossie tell that story a dozen times," Strange said. "He'd say to Arnie, 'I won't be answering the door tonight.'"

At least once, during the 1980s, Winnie laughed along. Asked about the task forces of women flying reconnaissance missions over her husband, she said, "I don't have a jealous bone. And he *is* handsome and sexy. Sometimes I have to walk away and laugh. In Oklahoma City, two women in the gallery were giggling, each saying to the other that *she* was the one he was winking at. I turned around finally and told them, 'He's winking at me, his wife.' That's the only time I ever identified myself in a gallery."

In 2013, Tom Watson complained to me about a *Golf Digest* cover photo posing 84-year-old Palmer with supermodel Kate Upton in a parody of Grant Wood's *American Gothic*. Mimicking the sober farmer, Arnold is holding a bunker rake instead of a pitchfork. "He looks doddering," Watson said. "If they had only shot him sneaking a peek at Kate—eyes twinkling—that would have been all right. That would have been Arnie."

Winnie was sitting by herself in the grillroom at Royal Portrush in Northern Ireland while Arn (as she called him) was out on the back nine in the 1995 Senior British Open finishing up a 71 on his way eventually to 32nd place. He was playing in a threesome with Englishman Neil Coles, the best and most accomplished golfer America has never heard of, and Irish folk legend Christy O'Connor (*Himself*, as the great man was known throughout the British Isles, especially in the public houses, where he liked to say, "God created Guinness so the Irish wouldn't rule the world.") Christy's grandson/caddie pulled a trolley behind them.

"Is there a big gallery along?" Winnie asked me.

"No, quite small," I told her. "It's a wonderful golf course, but not a layout conducive to big galleries."

"I'm sorry to hear that," she said. "Arn always plays better in front of a crowd of people. He's a ham. He got that from his mom."

The obvious question every writer had for Winnie was: How did she tolerate, or how did she come to terms with, Arnie's well-known womanizing? But no one knew how to put that to her in words that were as gentle as she was. So, instead, she was asked things like "What can a wife do to help a husband who's a golfer?"

"A great deal," she said, glancing out the window at the static clouds and racing years. "She can pick him up when he's down. That's the biggest thing. She can believe in him enough for the two of them when he's momentarily lost faith in himself. She can even give him a golf lesson—'You're moving your head,' 'Crack your knees a little more,' 'Stand closer to the ball,' 'You're *way* too close to the ball'—even if, like me, she doesn't know one thing about it. He'll try whatever she says because he knows she loves him, and that's how desperate he is."

For the advice or for the love?

"For both," she said.

In 1960, when Arnold became the definitive golfer, Winnie was the picture of the golfer's wife. That year, the Associated Press distributed a photograph of "the Palmers at home" with Winnie in a housedress and apron looking like Jane Wyatt, and Arnold in an easy chair and a sweater à la Robert Young. He's glancing up from a magazine and lifting his feet as she pushes a vacuum cleaner under the hoisted slippers. An accompanying article begins: "Mrs. Arnold Palmer, cute as a button in tan shorts and polka-dot blouse, sorted a huge pile of mail in the redwood paneled den of the trim ranch-style house tucked away in the rugged foothills of the Alleghenies hard by Route 30, or the old Lincoln Highway, at Latrobe, Pa. She came upon a familiar envelope and shuddered slightly. It was a telephone bill. 'Here's the war debt again,' she said . . ."

It wasn't exactly like that.

Desperation, advice, love, she had said. Losses:

"Being overtaken at Olympic by Billy Casper wounded Arn terribly, of course. I still think losing the Masters to Gary Player with that bunker shot at eighteen may have hurt him worse. It did me. Gary calls golf 'a game of sorrows.' A wife has to be the first to get over them, so she can help her husband go on. There's always tomorrow."

Winnie wasn't much for expressing her own regrets—although, truth be told, she'd always had a kind of yen to live in New York City, and sometimes wished she'd seen her French studies through to completion at Pembroke. Oh, well. Ray Cave's Sportsman of the Year story in *Sports Illustrated* had a couple of disquieting sentences: "Winnie is not permitted to wear fingernail polish" and "Dyed hair is a Palmer anathema." But maybe that was just 1960.

Arnold and Winnie had daughters instead of sons: Peggy and Amy. ("Amy was supposed to be Arnold II," Winnie said, "so we gave her a name as close to that as we could.") When Amy was five or six and beginning to notice the multitude of writers camped out in Latrobe, she asked her mother, "Why does Daddy have to answer so many questions from all those detectives?"

It's the perfect word. *Detectives.*

("Isn't it?" he said, sitting at his desk.)

If only on their mother's behalf, Amy and Peg must have been awfully mad at him at times. "I felt bad for my mother," Peg once said, referring only to the fact that, like many husbands and fathers, Arnie was gone so much. "But I always understood. It made total sense to me that he didn't want to be sitting around Thanksgiving dinner, learning about everybody's backaches. He always wanted to be doing something. The guilt involved in being a family man and balancing your life—yeah, that's all true, but you have to want to do it. If you don't want to do it, it just isn't that meaningful. He didn't want to be there; he wanted to be out on the golf course, and we were welcome anytime. It was hard for my mother, but there was a thrilling side that she loved in spite of her issues. Everything is a tradeoff."

"They don't agree with their father about a single thing," Winnie said of her daughters, "except the things that truly matter." Then she pointed out a misspelling on the Portrush wall—*Varden* for *Vardon* (six-time Open Champion Harry Vardon)—as an excuse to move the conversation away from the girls.

Winnie Palmer and Barbara Nicklaus were unshakable allies throughout their spouses' cold war. "The ten years difference in their ages might have had something to do with it at the beginning," Winnie said, "but I remember many kindnesses, too, on both sides." "It was certainly never a problem between Winnie and I," Barbara said.

The industry considered Mrs. Nicklaus to be the model golf wife. A girl whose maiden name was Bash could hardly have married anyone else. The extent of Barbara's devotion to her husband *and* his game was as legendary as he was. What other woman on her honeymoon would stay outside Pine Valley's perimeter while her man played the course? Even *she* might not do it today. In the fourth year of their marriage, lying beside Jack on a Saturday night in a Las Vegas hotel, she lost a pregnancy. But, wanting him to get his rest at all cost—he was leading the tournament—she waited until 8:00 a.m. Sunday morning to shake him gently and say, "Jack, I have to go to the hospital." After he took her there, he went out and *won* the tournament. Of course, Barbara knew the other Jack, too, the one who fainted at the birth of every child.

Peg might have exaggerated slightly when she said, "Everything is a tradeoff." But in matrimonial markets, at least, tour golfers do transact a lot of trades. Lee Trevino had two wives named Claudia. How many Claudias have you known in your lifetime? Lee married two of them. And in his heyday as a player, part of Trevino's standard uniform was a Band-Aid on a forearm covering up a homemade tattoo that read "Ann." (His first wife's name was Linda.) Like Johnny Carson and Trevino, John Daly was prone to wed women with the same first name—in Daly's case, Plaintiff. Stepping onto a tee in California, Daly encountered four blondes wearing T-shirts that said, "Bob," "Hope," "Desert," and "Classic." Abandoning Hope, he married Classic. She was his third wife, but not his last.

It's true that there have been great athletes who never let anyone down. Arthur Ashe, Roger Staubach, Wes Unseld, Tony Pérez, Raymond Berry, Stan Musial, Doak Walker, Gordie Howe, Ernie Banks, Brooks Robinson. But the absolute greatest ones, like Babe Ruth, Muhammad Ali, Michael Jordan, and Tiger Woods, seem almost required to have at least one imperfection that should disqualify them as heroes but doesn't.

Ali could be as cruel as boxing. Contemptibly, he socked wife number two, Belinda, while he was breaking in number three, Veronica. Fighters think with their hands. He had many wives and demi-wives, and children with most of them (all of whom he adored). But something else about Ali, not just his love for his own and everyone else's children, was redeeming.

Muhammad was what Waite Hoyt would have called a perfectly imperfect man. "Schoolboy" Hoyt, Hall-of-Fame pitcher for the incomparable 1927 New York Yankees—the kid who said, "It's great to be young and a Yankee"—was one of Ruth's pallbearers in 1948. "Babe was a perfectly imperfect man," Hoyt told me in 1972, riding in a Pittsburgh cab on his way to broadcast a Cincinnati Reds playoff game with the Pirates, "so crude it took your breath away but so generous it made you cry. Not because he was so good at his game, but for some other reason, he was easy to forgive."

"Here," croaked the Babe, wracked with cancer, handing Waite's wife an orchid near the end, "I never gave you anything."

Winnie died of cancer in 1999. Arnold built a second hospital in her name and memory. "She knew me," he said, his voice cracking, "and she knew how to handle me." Strange said, "She had a way of keeping him in line. When he'd get high on his horse, she would kind of rein him in. Sarah and I were staying with them in Latrobe when Winnie called him out on something or other, some story he was embellishing a little. 'Now, Arnie!' she said. '*ARNIE!*'" Palmer lifted his wife up into his arms and danced her around the room, laughing.

A few years after Winnie died, Arnold and Kathleen ("Kit"), a five-time grandmother from California he'd known for years, fell in love. They were married in 2005, when Palmer was 75. "Arnold and I managed a very quiet private wedding in Hawaii," she said. "Those present were Pastor Ron, Arnold, me, and a stray cat on a beach."

Families don't always embrace second wives, but he had someone with whom to unveil the morning again, and his daughters and their children cheered. Quickly, Kit came to know him well.

"He loves to watch Westerns on TV," she said, "he occasionally wins when playing dominoes with me, he can pack away four dozen oysters at a sitting, he would much rather be too hot than too cold, after buying sweatpants he cuts the elastic off the leg bottoms, he often takes a power nap at his desk, he often cries during the National Anthem, his pet peeve is men wearing hats indoors, he considers a drive more than five miles to be a major journey, he loves country-western music, he frets a lot before public speaking, bologna alone could sustain him, he will not have a cat as a pet, he prefers men to be clean-shaven, he often wears loafers without socks, when writing longhand only his signature is legible, he does not care for designer food, and dark chocolate is his all-time fave."

Touchingly, almost unbearably so, Kit was a dead ringer for

Winnie. "I looked at her"—Player shook his head—"and thought, 'This is a twin.' I think it's very sweet." And maybe just a little sad, if tinged with that vague feeling of regretful longing that only old men ever know.

Palmer was a perfectly imperfect man. Not because he was so good at his game, but for some other reason, he was easy to forgive.

19

2000

"I'd be doing everything you're doing."

IT CUSTOMARILY FALLS TO the first grandchild to name the grandparents. "That's right," said Sam Saunders, Palmer's grandson via
Amy. "Emily, my sister, was the one who named him 'Dumpy.' She
tried for 'Grumpy,' but it came out 'Dumpy.'"

Precisely as Pap had placed Arnie's hands on a golf club, Dumpy
carefully braided Sam's small fingers, cautioning him, "Don't you
ever change this grip, boy." "And I never have," said Sam, the father
of two sons now. "Just about as sternly, I told my seven-year-old,
'Here's where your hands go. Don't ever move them.'"

When Arnold Palmer is your grandfather, it takes courage to
choose tournament golf for a life's work. And then, when a trans-
forming success doesn't materialize overnight, it takes something

more than courage to keep going. Not that Saunders didn't have obvious talent: he was a decorated junior golfer and a club champion at Bay Hill multiple times, starting at the age of 15.

When did he first realize Dumpy was Arnold Palmer?

"The way you mean it," he said, "not for a long time, until I was like sixteen or seventeen, and getting serious at amateur tournaments. I always knew he was a very good golfer, of course. I just didn't realize exactly how good, and how important."

At Arnold's final Bay Hill tournament and Masters in 2004, 17-year-old Samuel Palmer Saunders caddied for him. "I had no clue what I was doing," he said. "I wish I could remember more of the little details of those rounds." Facing a second shot on his valedictory hole at Bay Hill, a par four, Palmer was determined to hit a driver off the deck. "I tried to talk him out of it," Sam said, "and into a three-wood. I hated the idea of him possibly going out on a water ball in front of everyone. But he wasn't the slightest bit afraid. Somehow he just hooked that driver right up there and ran it down the left side of the fairway onto the green to within about fifteen or twenty feet of the cup. I can still hear the roar. He two-putted it for par."

Saunders has kept his caddie suit from the Masters, what 1948 champion Claude Harmon called "that white tuxedo" by way of ridiculing one of his sons. ("You just keep wearing that white tuxedo, and I'll take care of the green jacket.") "It's one of my most precious possessions," Saunders said.

While instructing Sam on the practice tee, Arnold was a minimalist, like Pap. Snappy lessons, then go work it out for yourself. "We don't spend hours," Palmer said. "We spend ten, fifteen minutes, and I give him what I think is necessary and he goes with it." "Often," Sam said, "I wished he'd say more, because every simple seed he planted kicked in eventually on the range. Something small about the right hand, or the elbow, would suddenly hit me as I practiced, and I'd get it."

"He is a very polite young man," Palmer said. "That's one thing I'm very proud of. As long as his manners and his characteristics are as good as they are, I'll be happy. But don't forget, I'm not his father." Which was a way of saying he didn't want to poach on Saunders's dad, Roy.

"No, certainly not," Sam said. "Dad and I have a very good relationship. He's the one who took me to all the junior tournaments. I'm grateful that Arnold Palmer is my grandfather. I think very highly of him. I think very highly of my other grandfather, and of both of my parents. I'm proud of my heritage and feel very fortunate to have all of these wonderful people in my life. But only one of them am I able to talk to man-to-man about the ups and downs of a pro's career, about the toughest sides of it, the terrible disappointments."

For a Monday qualifier, Saunders once had to borrow his caddie's irons and shoes, shot 67, and still didn't get in. "Hey, I know what that's like," Arnie told him, "and I know what it's like when you're out on the golf course and everything is out of control and you just want to go hide." Sam said, "It's neat for me to have him, you know, to be able to relate to the bad times, because he had so many good ones. I'm probably able to talk to him probably like nobody else in the family can, and we get along pretty well."

In his support of Sam, Arnie was his mother's son: *"Her mellowness, willingness to feel things and to show her feelings, was a salvation for me. She was a gentle, generous person, but I never felt as if I was being soft by going to her. I sought her out because she was the counterbalance I needed to Pap, who was tough and hard-core and refused to give me a compliment. I was always afraid to lose because of my father's reaction, but I never felt that way about my mother. No matter what, she was the one who understood.*

*She always took up for me. All that was so important—much more important
than I realized at the time."*

Saunders said, "As desperately as I wanted to be my own man, have
my own identity—and nobody ever wanted those things more—I
still needed him to believe in me, to pull for me, and he did. When I
married, when I moved to Colorado, he told me all the things I had
to hear. I went to see him in Latrobe [in 2013] and he said, 'If I were
you, I'd be doing exactly what you're doing, as far as moving somewhere else, starting your own life, getting away from me. I know how
hard it is to be my grandchild and to want to be a tour golfer. And
I know how much more difficult the profession is today, how much
longer the courses are, and how many more competitive players are
out there now. But just keep at it. You're on the right track. I couldn't
be prouder of you.'"

Sam had grown tired of playing the Web.com tour. "I was at the
point of wondering if I was ever going to make it onto the PGA
Tour," he said. "I had one child already, another on the way. Was it
time to do something else? But when he said he was proud of me,
it gave me just that little extra bit of confidence to keep chasing my
dream. He didn't look down on me, saying, 'You should be better by
now.' He said, 'Go get 'em.' The next year I had a great season and
finally got my PGA Tour card."

"I think Sam has taken the right approach," Arnold said. "He's
come a long way in the last couple of years, and I really feel that he
has a shot at it now. But he has to work. He has all the ingredients
that are necessary. It's just going to take time. Stick to the basic
fundamentals of the game of golf. Sure, there's going to be a little
change here, a little change there. But don't listen to all the instruc-
tors out there with a new way. Trust what you have, if it's sound.
Trust yourself."

Though still a journeyman, Sam was on his way. "Of course,"

he said, "I don't expect to have a career even in the same universe as his. But I'm proud of what I've accomplished. The players on tour know who I am, but they also know I don't consider being Arnold Palmer's grandson any kind of accomplishment. That's just being born. They might ask me how he's doing, but they treat me as one of them."

20

2004

"I know everybody by their first names."

On an April Sunday in 2004, his 13th year as a pro, Phil Mickelson surrendered the title of "best player never to win a major." Two days earlier, he heard Sunday roars at Augusta on Friday, "echoing through the valleys and hollows," as he said, "starting at the first hole and building all the way to the eighteenth." That was Arnold Palmer's last round at the Masters.

Palmer played in 50 Masters exactly, missing his 21st straight cut in 2004 at the age of 74. Even "lifetime" exemptions run out, as Billy Casper, Doug Ford, and Gay Brewer learned the hard way, by mail. "I don't want to get a letter," Arnold said, explaining the nice, round number on which he volunteered to take his leave.

Departing the press center for the last time, he felt a muscular arm loop about his waist and looked up to see Tiger Woods on his way in. "How did you do?" Palmer whispered, but Woods didn't mention his 69 or say anything at all, just held on. When Tiger reached the microphone, someone asked if he could see himself still playing at Palmer's age. "I just hope I'm on this side of the grass," Woods said.

Earlier, finding himself deep in the grass on the 15th hole, Palmer jokingly asked the spectators flanking his ball, "With all of my friends here, how can I have such a rotten lie?" A regretful voice in the ranks, speaking for the entire division, murmured, "You should have seen it before, Arnie."

That night Palmer said, "Hell, I know everybody in these galleries by their first names. I'm kidding a little, but not too much. I could probably tell you the first names of thousands of them."

The first name of the guy who called him once on Christmas morning—1:06 a.m. Christmas morning in 1967—was Peter. Peter Deeks. He was a Canadian phoning from Toronto, where Palmer won his first pro tournament. Deeks had just graduated from college and with four of his mates got to wondering whom they hadn't yet wished a Merry Christmas. (Beer was involved.)

"I called information in Latrobe," Deeks said, "and asked if there was a listing for A. D. Palmer. 'No,' the operator said, 'but there's one for Arnold Palmer.' I dialed the number and heard, 'Hello.'

"'Is Arnold there?'

"'This is Arnold speaking.'

"'I hope I'm not bothering you,' I said.

"'No, I'm just putting presents under the tree for Winnie, Amy, and Peggy.'"

They spoke for 12 minutes exactly. Deeks knew this because he kept the Bell Canada bill.

Twenty-two Christmases later, Peter's brother Jim handed him two wrapped gifts, the smaller one marked, "Open me first." It was a video. "On came Arnie," Peter said, "saying, 'Hi, I'd like to wish Peter, Wendy and Sarah and Jocelyn Deeks a very Merry Christmas.

Peter, do me a favor and call me again, but don't make it on Christ-mas Eve, OK?' I was stunned." He opened the next present, and it was that same message written out in capital letters, signed "Arnold Palmer."

In England, one of the heartiest regulars in Arnie's Army was a blue-haired woman named Myra, Myra Leatherdale, whom he called Mrs. Weatherbottom, because she mustered and marched even in sideways rain. When she died in the '80s *at* 80, he mourned.

Palmer also knew the first names of Nate Marcoulier and his brother Adam, just two of the thousands of correspondents who made it necessary, Doc Giffin said, for six figures to be budgeted annually just to answer Arnold's mail.

Dear Mr. Palmer,

One of the greatest gifts that we are given in life is the gift of family. As a son and older brother, I have thoroughly enjoyed the many great times spent with my parents and younger brother throughout my life. I have loved every minute with my brother Nate over our young lives. We are both avid scratch golfers from a small town in Central Massachusetts and have truly looked up to you throughout our entire lives. Your overall attitude and conduct has inspired us to wear our emotions on our sleeve in celebrating our achievements but also being gracious in defeat. You are a true role model for everyone from all walks of life, and we all ought to thank you for that.

Through hard work and a tremendous support network from our parents, both Nate and I have been very successful in both our high school and collegiate careers. While I am a junior at Stonehill College in Easton, MA, Nate is getting ready to graduate from St. Bernard's High School in Fitchburg,

MA this May. Upon graduation, Nate will be joining me once again at Stonehill College where we will continue to have many great times. While I would like to think I am the better golfer, Nate's results speak for themselves. He has won several junior tournaments, including the Massachusetts Division II District Tournament, his biggest win to date. He is a dedicated, hard-working individual who succeeds in most everything he applies himself to. I could not be luckier to have him as a brother and best friend.

As a sibling yourself, I can imagine you can relate to my story and feelings towards Nate. I'm sure you and your siblings looked up to someone and called them your hero. Mr. Palmer, you are our hero. This gets to the root of why I am writing you this letter.

As our hero, I was wondering if you could possibly write Nate a letter wishing him good luck in college and providing him some advice along the way. I don't think there is anyone more qualified to give Nate advice as you have truly been through it all in your life. I would be forever grateful if you would do this for me. It would truly mean the world to Nate—and maybe even provide me with the "Best Brother of the Year" award!

I wish you all the best, Mr. Palmer. Thank you so much for reading this letter, and I hope that Nate will hear from you soon!

Sincerely,

Adam Marcoulier

Dear Nate,

I understand from your brother, Adam, that you are quite a golfer and a great younger brother. I hear you've won several junior tournaments, including the Massachusetts Division II District Tournament. Congratulations!

As you graduate from high school and continue on to Stonehill College, I think you will find life to be enjoyable and fulfilling if you follow this advice:

Courtesy and respect are timeless principles, as well as good manners.

Knowing when to speak is just as important as knowing what you say.

Know how to win by following the rules.

Know the importance of when and how to say thank you.

Never underestimate the importance of a good education.

Good luck in college and study hard.

Sincerely,

Arnold Palmer

Chicagoans Jeff Roberts and Wally Schneider, son of a former minor-league catcher in the Cubs' system, were serving together in the sand hills of Chu Lai, South Vietnam, at the height of the war. Splitting their time between shooting from bunkers and practicing bunker shots, they decided to write Palmer for help with one kind of explosion, addressing the letter simply:

Arnold Palmer

Latrobe, Pa.

Dear Wally and Jeff,

Was great hearing from you both, and I'm extremely gratified by your letter. It's good to see such admirable spirit displayed by our men in Vietnam, and I send my sincere wishes for your return to Chicago safely and soon.

I'm also sending you, under separate cover, two new sand wedges and a supply of golf balls which should be arriving in the very near future from the Arnold Palmer Company in Chattanooga, Tennessee. Hope you enjoy the clubs. However, I hope you won't be hitting too many shots out of bounds. Take care of yourselves and I'll look forward to seeing you in Chicago sometime.

Sincerely,

Arnold

Both men made it home safely. After settling back in Illinois, Roberts went to Olympia Fields, site of the Western Open, and waited outside the clubhouse for Palmer. "I walked up to him and told him, 'I'm one of the guys you sent sand wedges in Vietnam.' He said, 'Are you Jeff or Wally?' Can you believe it? He remembered our names."

Some people wrote Palmer to pass along cure-alls and home remedies for life's and golf's galling maladies, touting the benefits of Sal Hepatica, Squirt, cod liver oil, Heinz Dark Apple Cider Vinegar, and Certo ("You can get it in any supermarket"), not to mention the healing properties of radioactive plutonium (less available in supermarkets) and the benefit of just keeping a potato in your pocket, "making sure to change the potato when it calcifies, every two or three months."

But most of the letter writers wanted only to make a connection.

Dear Arnie:

"You won't remember me, but . . .

Dear Mr. Palmer,

If you don't mind, I'd like to tell you a little bit about something that happened last Saturday . . .

Dear Mr. Palmer:

My sister and my brother and I go to camp every summer in Ligonier, which, I understand, is not far from Latrobe. Last summer, my brother came home with his bag full of clean underwear because he wore only one pair for the whole week. (Ha! Ha!) But that is neither here nor there. The reason I'm writing you is . . .

Picking at the day's stack of letters on his desk (one written in crayon), Palmer said, "I'm kind of like Dear Abby, aren't I? I don't deserve it, but I feel so complimented by it. People confiding their problems and sharing their lives, many of them repeaters, a few of them lost friends who haven't written me in years. Questions and comments of every kind, all of them appreciated. If my secretary, Janet, and I don't stay right on top of it, the pile can grow taller than I am." His original secretary, Winnie, put aside the envelopes with the funniest addresses ("Arnold Palmer, world's greatest golfer") that, like the letters to Kris Kringle in *Miracle on 34th Street*, somehow made it to Latrobe. "I'd read them to him at night," Winnie said, "sitting in front of the television, and he'd tell me what to write back."

One day in Latrobe, in the first decade of the new century, Palmer headed out with a few others—a dentist, an agent, and a magazine editor—to play a lazy round. As they reached the third tee, adjacent to a road, a convertible screeched to a stop and the driver vaulted out. Running to the tee with his hand extended, he shouted, "Mr. Palmer! Mr. Palmer! I've got to shake your hand! I grew up in Pittsburgh! You've been my idol my whole life, since I was a kid! I talk to my own kids about you now! To be able to meet you in person, this is the greatest experience of my life! If I could just shake the hand of Arnold Palmer, it would mean the world to me!"

Arnie beamed, shook the man's hand, and asked him, "Where do you live?" They talked for a few animated minutes, like old barracks buddies. Then Palmer turned to the others and said, "Do you guys know my friend, Bob? He's a Pittsburgher." After about 25 minutes of introductions and small talk, Bob started back to his car. "Hey, Bobby," Palmer called after him. "Do you happen to have a camera with you?" "On my phone in the car," he said. "Go get it!" Arnold said. "Wouldn't it be nice to capture this moment? We'll wait."

The picture was taken, the man drove away, and the game resumed.

This was Arnie and his fans, all of whom he knew by their first names. He was kidding a little, but not too much.

21

2012

"That's an Arnold Palmer I'll never forget."

"THE GAME OF GOLF was sort of in the dark ages," Nicklaus said, "and along came Arnold Palmer." In 2012, when Palmer joined Jackie Robinson, Joe Louis, Jesse Owens, Byron Nelson, and Roberto Clemente as the sixth athlete awarded the Congressional Gold Medal in Washington, Jack was the invited speaker. He stood at a lectern behind a United States Congress emblem, in front of five American flags, House Speaker John Boehner, and Palmer.

Arnold will tell you that when you get to our age, you meet a lot of people who begin conversations with "I remember when." It's not uncommon for a new friend to walk up and say, "I remember I saw you at the nineteen sixty U.S. Open—I was standing behind the eleventh green wearing a green shirt, and you waved at me."

The only proper answer is, "How could I forget?"

In the parts of seven decades that I've known Arnold Palmer, there have been countless "I remember whens" and, most important, even more moments I'll never forget. Moments that I hope provide you a glimpse into the charismatic golfer, the man of unshakable character—father, grandfather and great-grandfather—you're honoring today. He's a golf icon to the world but simply a good friend to me.

When I first saw Arnold Palmer hit a golf ball, I was just fourteen years old. I had just come off the golf course in Sylvania, Ohio, playing a practice round before the Ohio State Amateur. It was pouring down rain.

I was the only person on the golf course. As I walked by the practice tee, there was one person there. I stood and watched him. I didn't know who he was—I just looked at this strong guy with big hands and broad shoulders, hitting these short irons, driving them into the rain. I watched for a while and I said, "Man, is that guy strong. I wonder who he is." I walked into the clubhouse and I said, "Who's the guy out there on the practice range?" and they said, "Oh, that's our defending champion, Arnold Palmer."

That's the Arnold Palmer I'll never forget.

I remember, four years later, I was eighteen when I played with Arnold for the first time: Dow Finsterwald Day. They were honoring Dow for winning the PGA Championship. We had a four-man exhibition in Athens, Ohio, that day. Arnold had just a fair day. He made eight birdies and an eagle and shot a course-record sixty-two. It was my first glimpse of what I felt my future would be. That was an Arnold Palmer I'll never forget.

I remember when we played in a PGA Tour event together for the first time. I was a twenty-two-year-old rookie. It was the nineteen sixty-two Phoenix Open. Arnold won the tournament;

he just nipped me by twelve shots there. But we got to the eighteenth, and he knew I had a chance to finish second. He came over and put his arm around my shoulder, and he said, "Hey, relax. This is not a hard par five. You can birdie it. Just take your time." I birdied the hole, finished second, but here was Arnold, trying to help a young guy while winning the tournament himself.

That's an Arnold Palmer I'll never forget.

I remember when I won my first professional tournament and my first major, fifty years ago this summer, the nineteen sixty-two U.S. Open. Again, I was a twenty-two-year-old with blinders on, in the backyard of the great Arnold Palmer at Oakmont. We tied for the tournament. We got to the practice tee before the playoff—it was customary in those days that the winner of the playoff received the gate—and Arnold came over and put his arm around me again and said, "Would you like to split the gate today?" Here I was, a rookie, and Arnold was thinking of a young guy starting out. And I really appreciated that.

That's an Arnold Palmer I'll never forget.

I'm going to fast-forward here about fifty years. Arnold, Gary Player, and I played as partners in an event down in Texas last May. It was just a scramble, but maybe the last time that we would ever play competitively together. We got to the last green, chose a ball about twenty-five feet from the hole, and Arnold putted first. We needed to make this putt to ensure a win. Arnold just rammed it in. You'd have thought he'd won the U.S. Open or the Masters for the fifth time—to the delight of Arnold, to the delight of us, and of course all of Arnie's Army, which went wild.

That's also an Arnold Palmer I'll never forget.

Mark McCormack, the late founder of IMG [International Management Group], managed both Arnold and me, and because of that he put us together in matches and exhibitions all over the world. We played together, we traveled together, we laughed together, and our wives became close friends, as did we.

Whether it was Oakmont or Baltusrol or many of the other times we competed, I may have had to battle Arnie's Army, but I never had to battle Arnold Palmer. Arnold always treated me as a competitor but, more important, as a friend. I am proud and honored to still call him a dear friend fifty years later.

Arnold and I have played together in numerous team events—Ryder Cups, World Cups—all over the world. We've competed in everything from majors on the golf course, to endorsements, to golf course design. You name it, we've competed. But I'll promise you, if there was ever a problem, I knew Arnold had my back, and he knew I had his.

That's an Arnold Palmer I'll never forget.

Just like the young man I watched that day in nineteen fifty-four—muscles taut, piercing raindrops with every shot—Arnold Palmer was the everyday man's hero. From a modest upbringing, Arnold embodied the hard-working strength of America. He won four green jackets, but he never lost his blue collar.

Arnold was one of the game's all-time greatest competitors, and he came along when golf needed him most. With his shirt hanging out and a hitch of his pants, Arnold played a game we could all appreciate. People loved when he played from the rough like he did, but they could only dream they could recover like he did. When TV first embraced the game of golf, it had a swash-buckling hero in Arnold as the game's face.

Together, Arnold and I won just over ten million dollars in our careers. Today, players make that in a year, and we couldn't be happier for them. But they all should thank Arnold Palmer. They need to understand and appreciate what Arnold did to grow the game, popularize it, and the foundation he created.

The game has given so much to Arnold Palmer, but he has given back so much more. For many years, everyone in this room can say, "I remember when Arnold Palmer deservedly received the Congressional Gold Medal." I just hope they'll never forget why.

22

2015

"He was the boy, wasn't he? For all of us."

On the eve of Open Championships at St. Andrews, the Royal and Ancient Golf Club rounds up as many former winners as possible and sends them off at the Old Course in three-or four-man teams for a four-hole tournament. "Willie," Lee Trevino telephoned his old caddie, Willie Aitchison, Lee's partner for 27 Opens, including two victories, "I'm coming to my last dance. Can you make it, too?" "Try and stop me," Aitchison said.

At 88 years of age, Sam Snead did an old soft shoe on the Swilcan Bridge to the 18th fairway. "And that's what I call," Sam sang, "ballin' the jack."

When Palmer's turn came for a final bow at the home of golf, he was 85. The Wednesday before the 144th British in 2015 was stormy, though not especially for Scotland, until, as 1981 champion

Bill Rogers said, "the Lord saw Arnold Palmer had decided to hit at least one shot, and all of a sudden the sun shined through."

Arnold's team included the Texan Rogers, Ulsterman Darren Clarke, and Paul Lawrie, a Scot. They were up against Team Tony Jacklin (Nick Faldo, Tom Lehman, and John Daly), Team Tom Watson (Louis Oosthuizen, Todd Hamilton, and Ian Baker-Finch), Team Peter Thomson (Phil Mickelson, Ernie Els, and Ben Curtis), Team Bob Charles (Sandy Lyle, Justin Leonard, and David Duval), Team Gary Player (Pádraig Harrington, Mark Calcavecchia, and Stewart Cink), and Team Tom Weiskopf (just Mark O'Meara and Tiger Woods).

"I had never played with Mr. Palmer before," said Lawrie, the 1999 champion, whose Sunday 67 and pristine playoff got lost in Jean van de Velde's baroque collapse at Carnoustie. "As soon as the draw was announced," Lawrie said, "I texted Darren. He was just as excited as I was."

Palmer hit only a shot or two, and didn't have to take a second one at the second hole, where the Scot struck a full-blooded 8-iron into the cup for an eagle. "Playing with him was inspiring," Lawrie said, "and the reception we got at every green was supercool. He was the boy, wasn't he? For all of us."

Sir Michael Bonallack, past secretary of the R&A, twice the low amateur in the Open Championship, was in their gallery. Asked how important Palmer had been to the world's oldest tournament, he answered, "Enormously. Let's face it, he revived the championship. He's the one who got the other Americans to come over. Everywhere he went in golf, they followed."

Team Player was finished and leading by one when Palmer's group reached the last hole. "By then he was riding in a wee buggy," Lawrie said. "I had about a twenty-footer at eighteen, Darren a fifteen-footer, both for birdie. 'One of you *has* to make this putt,' Mr. Palmer said. 'We *have* to beat that [adjectival] Player.' The age of him, and still so competitive. When my putt went in, he came and threw his arms around me. 'But it's only for a tie,' I said. 'No, you don't understand!' he said. 'Combined ages! That's the tiebreaker!' And he knew it going in. [Largely thanks to Arnold, their combined ages were 239.] We won. It was fantastic."

Photographs were snapped on the Swilcan Bridge. The caddies just wanted to touch him. "Everyone was asking him to sign stuff," Lawrie said. Player said, "My God, look at this, isn't it great? He loves it, he really loves it."

To every winner of the Claret Jug, a quiet moment eventually arrives when he is alone with the chalice, to study the engravings in wonder, smearing his fingerprints up and down the silver list of names that now includes his own: Willie Park, Tom Morris Sr., Tom Morris Jr., John H. Taylor, Harry Vardon, James Braid, Ted Ray, Jock Hutchison, Walter Hagen, Jim Barnes, Robert Tyre Jones Jr., Tommy Armour, Gene Sarazen, Henry Cotton, Sam Snead, Bobby Locke, Ben Hogan, Peter Thomson, Gary Player, Arnold Palmer, Jack Nicklaus, Roberto De Vicenzo, Lee Trevino, Tom Watson, Severiano Ballesteros, Greg Norman, Nick Faldo, Nick Price, Tiger Woods, Ernie Els, Phil Mickelson.

Lawrie remembered pausing just an instant at Palmer's name, carved in 1961 and '62, but being a Scot and a European, he took a longer moment at Sandy Lyle's, then stopped entirely, and for some time, at Ballesteros's.

Seve was their Palmer.

"My idol," Lawrie said, "my hero growing up."

The American media never "got" Ballesteros, so the American public never got to know him. A lot of lazy matador-and-cape and hitting-it-into-the-car-park stories were written. Europeans loved Seve not for how much he won (though he won quite a bit, including three Open Championships and a couple of Masters) but for how much he cared, how hard he tried. All champions hug their trophies, but Ballesteros caressed the Claret Jug like an awed parent safeguarding a newborn's head. No other golfer, no other anything, ever bounced in place with the ineffable joy of Severiano. Like Palmer, he played golf the way everyone wanted to.

Seve's birthday always fell during Masters week. In 1997, when Woods won his historic first Masters by 12 strokes, the Spaniard turned 40 the day before the tournament began. Seve, countryman José María Olazábal, and Tiger played a practice round together that morning. Or half of one. Following nine holes, Woods broke off to go another nine alone, with just caddie Mike "Fluff" Cowan at his side.

"And if I could have gone out without Mike, I would have," Tiger told me that night. "I just wanted to try some things Seve showed me with nobody watching."

For the rest of Seve and José María's round, they capped each hole with a putting contest, a 100-footer to a wooden tee they stuck in the green. Coaxing the slow-rolling balls up, down, and around Augusta's penny arcade, they cheered like schoolboys.

When Seve walked off the 18th, passing under a spreading oak by the clubhouse, a writer standing there asked him, "Does forty feel any different?"

"How you know I shoot forty?" he said.

"Happy birthday."

Ballesteros walked over with enfolding arms, and said, "*Mi amigo.*"

How do you explain this man to the public?

"He was a man," Player said, "you wanted never to be unhappy. We were paired together when I won my third Masters. [Seve was 21.] He ran across the eighteenth green and just put his arms around me, saying, 'I'm so happy for you, Gary.' I said, 'I'm sorry for you.' 'No, no,' he said, 'don't you see? You teach me to win Masters today.' Which he did two years later, and again not long after that.

"The last time I saw him was very sad [at the 2007 tournament]. I had just come out of the bottom locker room and was standing in front of the clubhouse as his car was going by. I called out, '*Adios, compadre!*' He stopped, turned the window down, and said, 'Gary, why are you always so happy?' 'Well, because I've got a great wife, because I've won a lot of golf tournaments, because I have my health . . .' He said, 'I wish I knew how to be happy,' and a tear rolled down his cheek. '*Adios, amigo,*' he said."

Ballesteros's brain tumor had been stalled (but not stopped) by the spring of 2009 when a photograph postmarked Pennsylvania arrived in northern Spain. With a needed laugh, Seve told a friend, "Arnold Palmer just sent me a dog [a big yellow dog]. In a picture. His dog, called 'Mulligan.'" The Spaniard got the message and understood it for what it was: a prayer. ("Palmer always did the right thing," Player had said. "More than anything else, always doing the right thing was what made him Palmer.")

"The doctor saved my life," Seve said, "and now I use my mulligan." Adopting his own yellow Labrador puppy (that could have been Mulligan's offspring), he named it for the Palmer who followed him.

Phil.

Alicia Nagle represented her grandfather, Kel, in the champions' gathering at St. Andrews. "Mr. Palmer was sitting behind me at breakfast," she said. "I wasn't going to bother him at first, I didn't want to intrude. But when I stood up to get a coffee, he smiled at me such a welcoming smile that I told him who I was, and he jumped up and shook my hand, and kissed me on the cheek, and said, 'Your grandfather beat me here in nineteen sixty.' 'Yes,' I said, 'but you beat him at Troon two years later.' 'Aw,' he said, 'I was lucky. Kel was a great golfer and a great guy.'"

Six months earlier, she had received a call at her London home to come to Sydney, and hurry. "He was ninety-four," she said. "We only had ten days left, but we had some lovely chats during that time. In our final conversation, I promised him I'd go to St. Andrews in his place."

Palmer told her, "It's so wonderful that you're here. What a gentleman Kel was. Gary! Gary! Here's somebody you have to meet!" Player won an 18-hole U.S. Open playoff against Nagle in 1965 at Bellerive in St. Louis. "Gary had lots to say," Alicia said. "He's so full of life. He told me he had made thirty-one trips to Australia. [*See these hands? They're going to hit more golf balls, and I'm going to travel more miles to do it, than any man who ever lived.*] And he said, of all the men he has known in golf, my grandfather was the finest. I've heard that so many times, it must be true."

Palmer and Player took Alicia, each by an arm, and walked her over to the 18th grandstand to show her Kel's name on the list of champions, the registry of saints. "'See,' Mr. Palmer said, 'he's looking down on St. Andrews, and he's looking down on golf, and he's looking down on you.' I cried."

23

2016

"I couldn't have enjoyed it more."

A THURSDAY CAME AGAIN. ANOTHER U.S. Open was under way at Oakmont, 42 miles to the northwest. In Latrobe, Doc Giffin had said on the phone—"How about eleven?"—and it was almost that time now. Traffic was light on State Route 30 driving past Arnold Palmer Buick, Arnold Palmer Cadillac, and Arnold Palmer Motors, rolling under an overpass carved in concrete "Legend Arnold Palmer" on one side and "It's a Beautiful Day in the Neighborhood" on the other, turning left at the sign for Arnold Palmer Regional Airport, veering right onto Arnold Palmer Drive, and then left at Legends Lane, parking in front of the familiar building that held his office.

Years earlier, sitting in that office, Palmer was on the telephone giving somebody the bum's rush, saying, "Listen, I have to go. There's a guy here in my office. Talk to you later."

"Who was that?"

"The king of Spain."

Of course it was.

"Pardon me for not getting up," Palmer said now, already seated behind his desk. Moving at all, especially walking, had become an ordeal. (Though he had been trying to chip golf balls just an hour before, slapping rubber. "Golf never ceases to be a challenge, even when it really is just you and the ball out there and nobody else.")

"How many times have you sat in that chair?" he asked. "Four or five," Doc estimated from across the room. "I thought so," Palmer said. "Do you remember when I asked you, 'Doesn't your ass hurt from all this sitting?' and we went and played a few holes?"

Arnold was vain about his unfailing memory. During the last press conference he was able to tolerate, the day before round one of his Bay Hill tournament in 2015, a local reporter inquired, "Mr. Palmer, on your love for the Central Florida region, the very first time you visited Orlando, I read Wake Forest had a match against Rollins College. I'm wondering if you recall the very first time you played a match here at Bay Hill with Don Cherry, Jack Nicklaus, and—"

"Dave Ragan," Arnold said. "No, I don't remember."

Along with everyone else, he laughed. "Well, there are some fun things about what you just went over. I came here in nineteen forty-eight. I was a sophomore at Wake and we played the men's golf team at Rollins. Our coach was a guy named Johnny Johnston and he asked us what we wanted to do. 'We can stay here and practice or we can go on to the next stop.' We all voted to stay at Rollins because we could play the *girls'* golf team for the next two days. That was a hell of a lot more fun than playing the men's golf team. Betty Rowland played for them. She became a national amateur champion and she's still a good friend of mine from Chattanooga, Tennessee. Bud Worsham was my roommate at the time and we were both approached by Rollins with an offer to transfer, but we stayed at Wake. Have I answered the question?"

Sitting at that press conference, alongside comedian Kevin Nealon and NASCAR's Brian Vickers, his fellow Xarelto pitchmen, Palmer for the first time looked fragile at 85. He had tripped on a rug at home ("Did a three-sixty," he said), unhinging his right shoulder. That expressive putty face wasn't just pale, it was gray. The hearing aids he'd worn for decades didn't seem to work anymore. "Don't use the microphone, just talk to me," he kept telling the questioners. ("It's genetic. My grandfather lived to a hundred and wore hearing aids for fifty-five years.") But his mind was terrific, his memory astonishing, and his sense of humor intact.

"As I told someone who asked me about my prostate problem [cancer, in 1996], 'I don't have a prostate problem. I don't have a prostate.' I got rid of that thing twenty years ago and moved on. Oh, and I have a pacemaker in my heart [as of 2014]. Big deal."

When he saw me in Orlando, he asked, "What are you doing here?"

I had come just to look at him, to see if he was OK.

"What do you mean? This is a big tournament."

"Don't give me that shit," he said.

Now, at 86, he looked much worse, but, having to do with the nature of expectations or something—wishes, hopes, I don't know, something—he seemed a little better. He was wearing a bright plaid sport shirt, not a golf shirt, with a couple of top buttons unbuttoned. A V-neck white undershirt showed underneath. He was so gaunt that he swam in both shirts. His smile looked different, too, sawed-off somehow. His thinning white hair gleamed like wadded cotton.

We talked about nothing and everything—for instance, Mark McCormack. I mentioned the "Pope and a Smile" headline. After he and Doc had a laugh, Palmer said, "Ours was a successful partnership, but I didn't agree with him, either." We spoke of Johnny Unitas (who in retirement needed a strip of Velcro to hold on to a golf club, even a putter, his hands were so badly damaged from football) and of Muhammad Ali, who had died 13 days earlier. I said, "Ali always greeted me the same way. 'How's Angie? I like her better than you.' And he never met her." One time, unable to get off the phone with Ali as the deadline was bearing down, I handed it to her and went into the next room to write a column. An hour and a half later I came out and they were still talking. "I can believe it," Palmer said. "I spoke with him on the phone a number of times. Sometimes you could hardly hear him. Other times he hurt your ears."

Doc said, "Arnold, Ali, Kareem Abdul-Jabbar, Ted Williams, Wilma Rudolph, and Arthur Ashe were honored once at the White House with what was supposed to be an annual sports award, called the National Sports Award, but it turned out to be a onetime thing."

Palmer picked up the thread: "I was seated next to Ali, and when President Clinton called him 'a man who has unfailingly stood by his principles and his beliefs,' I reached over and squeezed his arm. He gave me the most beautiful smile."

Of Palmer, Clinton declared, "He revolutionized his sport. It's been said that when television discovered golf, the world discovered Arnold Palmer. Fans all over the world grew to love his unique style, his boldness, and his daring. To many he is the American ideal: the perpetual underdog falling behind and then charging down the stretch and tearing up the golf course.

"Who could forget the nineteen sixty U.S. Open? Before the final round he trailed in fifteenth place, and a reporter [Bob Drum] said he was no more in contention than the man operating the hot dog concession. In one of the most memorable examples of grace under pressure, he birdied six of the first seven holes and went on to win the tournament. Of all the perks that have come along with being president of the United States, the best one was being able to play eighteen holes with Arnold Palmer this morning. I saw that, even today, when he tees it up, Arnie's Army is as faithful and enthusiastic as when he marched through Augusta to win his first Masters. We thank him tonight for all he has given us, for all the thrills. And I can tell you that, on the basis of a wonderful few hours, he's just as much of a gentleman and a competitor as he always seemed to the public. Congratulations, Mr. Palmer."

I'd been wondering something: "Are all Western Pennsylvanians the same guy?" Along with incredible memory banks, both Palmer and Unitas had that unusual blend of humility and self-confidence. Doc, Drum, Art Rooney, too.

"I think probably so," Palmer said, his face alit with mischief.

Mr. Rooney enjoyed the company of sportswriters more than of his NFL partners. Avoiding owners' boxes and suites, he sat with Drum in the back row of the press box watching his Steelers play. The Drummer died a few weeks after the 1996 Masters, of heart failure officially, of everything, really. "When I think of Drum," Dan Jenkins said, "I think of laughter." During the '97 Masters, early in the morning, sons Bob Jr. and Kevin carried their father's ashes out to Amen Corner, sprinkling them in the azaleas at the 13th hole. "We said some prayers and we cried a little," Bob Jr. said. "Then we thought it would be great to have a beer. Dad would want us to have a beer. So we went to a concession stand and had a beer."

The photographs surrounding Palmer in his office had been shifted around. Babe Didrickson Zaharias was reassigned to an adjoining room. Norman Rockwell's painting of Arnie was brought from the main house to an alcove of the office building not far from *Sports Illustrated*'s Sportsman of the Year amphora and the Associated Press's Sportsman of the Decade (the sixties) proclamation. But the low table inlaid with gold and silver medals hadn't moved, continuing to show three openings.

"They still would be nice to fill, wouldn't they?" Doc said.

"Oh, boy," said Palmer, "I would do it."

Two of the choicest slots belonged to Royal Birkdale (1961) and Troon (1962). In 1989, when he and Tip Anderson returned to Troon for another Open Championship, Arnold confused the two courses. "I can't find our monument," he told Tip, rooting around the 16th hole. "Where is it?"

"About two hundred miles that way," Tip said, "you senile git."

(Palmer took that from him. What a grand man he is.)

Tip died in 2004 at age 71. They had been comrades for 22 Open Championships.

Arnold began to talk about flying, his favorite subject.

"I started out loving airplanes," he said, "and haven't ever finished. Still love them. I logged twenty-five thousand hours in the left seat, not giving up my personal flight certification until twenty-eleven [at age eighty-one]. Every year I took all the tests again and passed them all again."

"The examiners had a nickname for him," Doc said. "'Flying Colors.'"

"That's a lot of hours in the air, you know," said Palmer, "in just about everything that flies."

Including jumbo jets?

"Oh, yeah. I went out to Boeing. I knew the chairman of Boeing. [Of course he did.] He asked me, 'Would you like to fly a 747?' I said, 'I'd *love* it.' 'Well, we're about to do some testing on one. You can take her up.'"

That must have been like piloting a skyscraper.

"From the top floor," he said.

Palmer once spoke of flying with the Navy's acrobatic Blue Angels in an F9F Panther two-seater. "We're 50 feet off the ground and the pilot says, 'All yours, Arnie.' The first thing I know, I've got her in a six-g turn. We gain some altitude, and the pilot tells me how to roll

her. I give her a little flip, and there we go corkscrewing across Florida. We get up to twenty thousand feet and the pilot says, 'Point her
straight down and I'll pull her out.' So I stick her nose at the beach
and down we go at six hundred fifty mph. We pulled out at fifty feet."

Just then a beam of light came through the office window,
swooping and soaring, like an F9F Panther over Latrobe, carrying
him back to the beginning. ("When I think of Palmer," Herbert
Warren Wind wrote, "I think of a burst of sunlight.")

"I played some golf with the brother of a close friend of mine at
the club," Arnold said. "This guy was ambitious, dreamed of flying
in the Army Air Corps, and ended up a glider pilot in the war. Just
to be around airplane talk, I hung out with him as much as I possibly
could, pressing him endlessly about anything to do with aviation.
Eventually he took me up for a wild first ride. I enjoyed it. I loved it.
It was exciting, almost like playing golf."

All of Palmer's many planes came spinning back to him then,
from props to jets (even a helicopter, a McDonnell Douglas 500E
jet), starting with the little ones he first rented, leading up to the
Aero Commander 500 he bought (secondhand, for $27,000) in
1961, moving on to an Aero Commander 560F and then a Learjet
before many generations of roomier and roomier, more and more
powerful, faster and faster Cessna Citations, ending with the speed-
iest private jet money could buy ($15 million). "A wonder ship," he
called it. The boy who with Fred Rogers had built models of balsa
wood and glue now had exact metal replicas of the real things lined
up on a shelf like on a tarmac. The most colorful was a plump jet
outfitted with extra fuel tanks on whose side was painted in brilliant
red, white, and blue "Freedom's Way USA."

"That was 'Two Hundred Yankee,'" Palmer said, "the plane I
flew around the world, the bicentennial year [1976], to set the record
for her class." Two other pilots and a wire service journalist, screen-
writer Rod Serling's brother Bob, went with him.

"How much of the actual flying did *you* do?" I asked.

"Did *all* of it," he said, mock-indignantly. "Every bit of the way. Through the darkest night over the Indian Ocean, while everyone else was asleep."

From Denver (the airplane started approximately where the legend did, Cherry Hills Country Club) to Boston to Wales (an unscheduled stop, for fuel) to Paris to Tehran (where the Shah was still in power) to Colombo in Sri Lanka to Jakarta in Indonesia to Manila (where he was saluted by President Ferdinand Marcos, who regularly hit the first tee ball, a slice, at the Philippine Open) to Wake Island to Honolulu and back to Denver in 57 hours, 25 minutes and 42 seconds.

"Every now and then," Palmer said, "I'd get off to ride an elephant."

Was it so long ago when he sat in the Latrobe flight room by a potbelly stove and listened to the grizzled pilots dramatizing their closest calls? Now he had his own close calls to dramatize.

"What do you think, Doc?" he said. "Was Monterey the closest?"

"That was as close as you want to get," Doc said.

"I had been in the Far East," Palmer began to tell it, "and came back through Hawaii, where I picked up my own plane. Now I'm going to fly to California. My golf course architecture team was aboard, five or six guys. Halfway to San Francisco, past the point of no return, headwinds picked up, and picked up, and picked up, until they became unbelievable. I'm doing the fuel calculations as frantically as I can. There was no way we were going to make it to San Francisco. I plotted a new course to the Monterey airport, and hoped. Flying had always allowed me immediately to get my mind off golf. That was the great benefit of having a plane. But now my mind was on everything."

Like John Wayne in *The High and the Mighty*, he was about to order all of the passengers to jettison their luggage, when the airstrip came into view.

"The tower wanted me to go around one more time," he said. "I told them, 'Uh, I don't think so.' After we landed, the maintenance crew said we wouldn't have made it around again. We were bone-dry. There were a few other close shaves, a thing with the rudder once (or, I should say, without the rudder), and I had to shut down an engine in a flight out of Los Angeles, making an emergency landing in Las Vegas. Also, in the early days, I couldn't always find the right airport on the first try. But most of the chills I threw my passengers, like Gary and Jack, were intentional."

"'Can I drop you someplace?' Arnold would ask you," Peter Jacobsen said. "Then he'd add: 'I don't mean literally drop you, of course. Probably. We'll see.' Getting on the plane, he'd say, 'By the way, have you ever flown with me before? No? Oh.' Then he'd jump into that left seat the same way he hitched at his trousers, and proceed to show you exactly how good he was. He'd barrel-roll you a full turn one way, then he'd barrel-roll you a full turn the other way. 'Sorry,' he'd tell you while you were looking around for your stomach, 'but I had to return you back around to where you started. It has to do with vectors.'"

"One time in Houston," Tony Jacklin said, "he took a bunch of us British Ryder Cuppers up for a death-defying spin. George Will, a Scot, was one. Good player. Jimmy Demaret was there, too. ["I remember that," Palmer said. "They all got sick."] Well, when Arnold finally turned the plane right side up, somebody on the ground called on the radio, some authoritative figure, reaming out the co-pilot for the shenanigans. Arnold grabbed the mike away from his assistant and abjectly took full blame. After he signed off, he told his man, 'If you get in trouble, you might lose your livelihood. I'll just lose the ability to fly.' I thought to myself, 'That's Palmer. Even when he does the wrong thing, he does the right thing.'"

In Palmer's final turn at the throttle ever, an 1,800-nautical-mile trip from Palm Desert to Orlando, controllers all across the country chimed in one after another to wish him farewell and Godspeed. For three hours and 17 minutes, his spine never stopped tingling. It was the Scots engulfing him at Troon all over again.

"This is what I fly now," he said, pointing to the largest model, a Citation X with the markings N1AP. "Aren't I lucky?"

He once said, "Some people think of me as just plain lucky. I can't argue with them. I'd like to say, however, that a man might be walking around lucky and not know it unless he tries."

Palmer was never much for cursing his luck, or regretting anything about his career, as he framed it perfectly for Bob Verdi in a *Golf Digest* Q and A:

"If you had spent less time concerning yourself with the other side of the ropes, if you had had more tunnel vision about your game, would you have won more?"

"Perhaps," Palmer said. "I think I know what you mean, but I want to make sure. You mean if I had gone to hit balls after every round instead of mingling with sponsors and fans and you guys in the media?"

"Exactly."

"Well, I couldn't have enjoyed it more than I did if I had devoted more time to my golf itself. If golf itself had been all that mattered, I can't imagine I would have had a better time, even if I had more trophies. Sure, I would love to have won the four U.S. Opens I almost won, or the two or three PGAs I barely lost. But if I had it to do over again, would I take a different approach? I wouldn't. Let's say I could start over. I could have five Opens and two PGAs and six Masters and a couple of more British Opens, but not as many friends? No. No way, José. Keep the trophies. I mean, I remember teeing off in Palm Springs at the Bob Hope and, because I had a couple of bad rounds, I'm starting early. Real early in the morning. Maybe seven o'clock. And here comes Arnie's Army in their pajamas and robes at the first tee."

He never insisted that his way of doing things was the only way to do them. "I wasn't perfect," he said. "Never intended to be."

At Bay Hill one time, when only the two of us were talking, I brought up a subject he didn't want to go into: Tiger Woods, who was just coming undone. After a hesitation, Palmer said, "Let me make sure I say exactly what I want to say." Staring out a window, he waited a moment longer. "Let's not put a name on it," he said finally. "Let's not talk about anyone specifically, do you mind? Let's just say that not everyone in golf or sports wants to share his life with the public, or for that matter with anyone else at all. I think that's the simplest way to put it. I've liked sharing my life. I think being out there among the people, letting them know you and sincerely wanting to know them, too, is the happier way to go. But everyone has to go his own way."

Then he said, "I think when Tiger lost his father, he lost himself. My wish for him is not to come back as a player but to come back as a man."

His wish for the game of golf was equally straightforward: "That every twenty handicapper who goes to the first tee with a knowledge of the game should pass it on to someone who doesn't know or doesn't seem to care. Think of those who came before, think of those who are coming next, like your children. An athlete must have a certain cockiness to succeed and win, but an athlete must also care about the game he or she plays. For every swing lesson a golfer takes, take a lesson in rules and etiquette. Preserve what we have."

Here are some of Palmer's lessons in etiquette:

DON'T BE THE SLOWEST PLAYER
"Evaluate your pace of play honestly and often, and if you're consistently the slowest one in your group, you're a slow player, period.

Play 'ready golf.' Hit when ready, even if you aren't away, until you reach the green, be prepared to play when it's your turn on the tee and green, and never search for a lost ball for more than five minutes."

KEEP YOUR TEMPER UNDER CONTROL

"Throwing clubs, sulking, and barking profanity make everyone uneasy. We all have our moments of frustration, but the trick is to vent in an inoffensive way. For example, I often follow a bad hole by hitting the next tee shot a little harder—for better or worse."

RESPECT OTHER PEOPLE'S TIME

"Because time is our most valuable commodity, there are few good reasons for breaking a golf date. Deciding last-minute to clean the garage on Saturday, or getting a call that the auto-repair shop can move up your appointment by a day, just doesn't cut it."

REPAIR THE GROUND YOU PLAY ON

"I have a penknife that's my pet tool for fixing ball marks, but a tee or one of those two-pronged devices is fine. As for divots, replace them or use the seed mix packed on the side of your cart. Rake bunkers like you mean it. Ever notice that the worse the bunker shot, the poorer the job a guy does raking the sand?"

BE A SILENT PARTNER

"During one of my last tour events as a player, I noticed another pro making practice swings in my field of vision as I was getting ready to hit a shot. I stopped, walked over, and reminded him—maybe too sternly—that it was my turn to play. The point is, stand still from the time a player sets himself until the ball has left the club. Even with the advent of spikeless shoes, the etiquette rule of never walking in someone's line of play on the putting green is an absolute. The area around the hole in particular is sacred ground. The first thing to note when you walk onto a green is the location of every ball in your group, then steer clear of their lines to the hole. When a player is about to hit a shot, think of the fairway as a cathedral, the green a library."

MAKE YOUR GOLF CART "INVISIBLE"

"Your goal when driving a cart should be to leave no trace you were there. Because we tend to look where we're going and not where we've been, it's easy to damage the turf and not realize it. Avoid wet areas and spots that are getting beaten up from traffic. Golfers tend to play 'follow the leader' and drive in single file out to the fairway before branching off. It's usually better to 'scatter'—everyone take a different route—so cart traffic is spread out."

ALWAYS LOOK YOUR BEST

"From Bobby Jones and Walter Hagen to Ben Hogan and Sam Snead to Tiger Woods and Phil Mickelson, the best players have been meticulous about their appearance. Their clothing has been sharp, and not one of them has shown up on the first tee with his cap backward, mud caked on his shoes, or his shirttail hanging out. (My shirt often came untucked, but it was my swing that did it. I started with it tucked in!) Give the impression the golf course and the people there are special."

TURN OFF THE CELL PHONE

"Nobody knows less about technology than I do. But I know enough to recognize a cell phone when it rings in my backswing. If I had my way, cell phones would be turned off at all times on the course, but most clubs have given in to the fact that people are going to use them. I don't know all the gadgets and settings on those phones, but do whatever you have to do to keep it quiet. And if you absolutely have to make a call, move away from the other players. And keep the call so brief that they don't even know you made it."

LEND A HAND WHEN YOU CAN

"It's easy to help out your fellow players if you just pay attention. One obvious way is looking for lost balls—better yet, watching errant shots so they don't turn into lost balls. Pick up that extra club left on the fringe or the head cover dropped next to the tee, and return it to its owner after saying, 'Nice shot!'"

A CONSIDERATE HEART

"There are a hundred bits of etiquette I haven't mentioned, like laying the flagstick down carefully, tamping down spike marks when you're walking off a green, letting faster groups play through, and so on. All of these things are learned by observing, with a sharp eye and a considerate heart. Just know that golf has a way of returning favors, and every piece of etiquette you practice will be repaid tenfold."

And take your goddamned hat off indoors.

I switched off the tape recorder. ("That's all right," he had told the kid who forgot to turn his tape recorder on at the Western Open, "let's start over and do it again.")

A considerate heart.

"You got enough?" he asked me, the perfect thing to ask. "Well, anything you need while you're here, we'll take care of it. Just holler. Nice to see you. Thanks for coming. Come back. And, again, excuse me for not getting up."

Outside, it was a pretty day in Latrobe (a bogey-free day for

Dustin Johnson at Oakmont). Back at the tournament, a few writers and players who knew I was going to see Palmer asked, "How was he?"

He was equal parts humble and proud.

He was equal parts commoner and king.

He was equal parts iced tea and lemonade.

"He was himself," I told them.

24

SEPTEMBER 25, 2016

Fifty-eight years to the day since his first round with Jack.

TIGER WOODS

"I think Arnold and I had a great relationship. I was always able to talk to him about anything, not just golf. He'd take the time to listen, talk to you honestly, and then tell you exactly what he thought. He had a way of making you feel comfortable and at ease. The first time I ever met him was at Bay Hill. I was fifteen, playing in the U.S. Junior, and he was the keynote speaker. I was honored to meet him. Later, when I was at Stanford, we had dinner in Napa and we spent a while just talking. It was really cool having dinner with Arnold Palmer, and he made you relax and enjoy the evening.

"Arnold enjoyed being Arnold Palmer. No one did it better. He truly liked people and wanted to be with them. Arnold, as much as anyone, had been instrumental in the growth of the game. His outgoing personality and style of play were made for TV. But what might be his most enduring legacy is his philanthropic work. He

did so much for so many people. My kids were born at the Winnie
Palmer Hospital and I'll always be grateful for his, and the staff's,
support and kindness. Arnold will be remembered for that along
with what he accomplished on the course.

"I've been fortunate to have won Bay Hill a few times [eight],
and that's meaningful to me. It's like winning Jack's Memorial or
the Bryon Nelson when Mr. Nelson was alive. It's just different.
Knowing Arnold was waiting for you at the end of the tournament,
and that he'd put his arm around you and you'd share a laugh, made
a win there extra special."

PHIL MICKELSON

Before the third round of the 2015 Masters, Mickelson pulled out a
salmon shirt. "It's not my color," he said. "It doesn't look good on
me. But Arnold Palmer likes to wear this color, and after spending a
little time with him, I had a premonition. I just had a feeling that I
needed to make a move." Phil shot 67 in the salmon shirt.

"I remember the last of Arnold's U.S. Opens [1994] and the
hour and a half he spent in the volunteer tent, meeting the people
who do the work, finding out their names, signing autographs for
them. He always took the time. As an amateur I played my first
Masters practice round with Arnold at his invitation. I saw how he
kept looking over at the spectators, smiling at everyone, giving the
two thumbs-up, and really *seeing* them. 'Don't ever walk by them as
though they're not there,' he told me. 'They're there.'

"In nineteen ninety-six, the tour set aside an area for autograph
signing. I don't know why, but it never really took and they dropped
it after that one year. But it worked for me, helped me organize my
practice day. I still do it. Practicing is more demanding than playing, you know. You're concentrating just as hard, but you're hitting
three times as many shots. I found myself avoiding the people during
practice, and I didn't like that feeling. So being able to block out a set

time for autographing helped me. And, at Arnold's urging, I've tried to make my signature a little more legible. 'Sometimes,' he said, 'you only have a few seconds to make the only impression you'll ever make on that individual. Take the full time. These are the people who make it possible for us to play golf for a living.' He was always the one to emulate, wasn't he? And there was never anything phony about it.

"You mention Seve. I had a special relationship with him. I was too young to see Arnie at his best, so Seve was the one I was able to watch. From the moment I met him, Seve was so great to me, so generous. Both of us had Hugo Boss among our sponsors, and so we did some photo shoots together. We were like playful kids. I knew about Arnold sending the picture of Mulligan to Seve, and Seve naming his own dog after me. If anyone wants to put me in a line with them, I'll take it.

"I think of the young guys on tour who never had the privilege of playing golf with Arnold Palmer and Jack Nicklaus, or of going to dinner with Byron Nelson at his home the week of Byron's tournament. I'm so grateful for all of that."

(Palmer made up games in the Latrobe rough, like Phil Mickelson in his backyard in San Diego, concocting unplayable lies and then playing them. "I'd have two or three balls going at a time," Palmer said, "make a tournament of it. One ball would be Byron Nelson's, my favorite golfer, another would be Ben Hogan's, and the third would be mine. You might not be surprised to hear, mine was usually the best.")

"I'd have a few balls going, too," Mickelson said with a soft laugh. "One would be Arnie's, one would be Jack's, one would be Tom Watson's, and one would be mine, and I never lost."

TOM WATSON

"Arnie was nicknamed 'the King' for one reason . . . he was. When I was fifteen, I was asked to play with him in a benefit for multiple sclerosis in Kansas City. I was thrilled. It was sponsored by TWA [Trans World Airlines] and the Clipped Wing Society—stewardesses, as they were called then, who had to quit flying when they married. Times have certainly changed, haven't they? My teacher, Stan Thirsk, was in the group, and I played pretty well for a while. I tied Arnie on the front nine with a thirty-four. But then he shot thirty-four on the back, too, to my forty. He complimented me just enough, built me up in the most generous way, without being condescending. Treated me like a real player. I learned a lot that day.

"I saw how he looked everybody in the eye, drew everybody in, didn't shut anybody out. My father was there. His hero was always Snead, mine was Arnie, and Jack was the villain in those days. After our round, when Arnie was out of the shower and getting dressed, Dad asked him, 'What will help my son become a better player?' He said, 'Competition. As much competition as possible.'

"The first time I played with him on tour was at the Hawaiian Open in the early seventies, and every time after that I learned something new. Even in practice rounds. We played a few Tuesday money games with Lanny Wadkins and that crew. Arnie just loved to compete. He wanted to beat you. He was all in, all the time. That was the way I went at it, too. In my opinion, Arnold, Mark McCormack, and ABC were the real Big Three. Arnold knew how to do it, McCormack knew how to sell it, and television knew how to show it. At that last champions' dinner during Masters week, he looked so frail. He obviously didn't like the situation his body was in. But he was standing up to it, the way you knew he would. Competing."

(Palmer said, "I've laughed about the nickname 'King,' kidded about it. People have used the term as a fun thing and I appreciate it because I think I know where they're coming from. Everybody has a different definition of what it means, and my definition is that there's no king in golf. Certainly not me, and I've taken more from this game than given.")

BEN CRENSHAW

"My dad, like all the other dads around the country, loved Arnold. One shot in particular, at Brackenridge Park in San Antonio, stayed with my father the rest of his life. He never stopped talking about it, the sound it made, 'like a high-powered rifle going off,' he said."

(The first time Ben heard that sound was in the Texas Open of 1962, when he was 10 and Palmer was winning his third Texas Open in a row.)

"I'll never forget being swallowed up by that crowd when it seemed to a little kid like the whole world was trailing Arnold Palmer."

(Then, at a Texas Open Junior tournament in 1970, 18-year-old phenom Crenshaw was selected to play nine holes with Palmer.)

"He was so considerate to me that day, and to everyone. No one loved golf more or got more excited if you loved it too. That was the thing about Arnold. What thrilled him most of all was the fact that *you* were thrilled. It was never about him. It was always about the game. Loved being in the fray, but loved people even more. He was a father figure to a lot of us. Talking to him, anyway, was like talking to your father. In my second Masters [first as a pro, 1973] I drew Arnold on Thursday and Jack on Friday. How's that?

"At Bay Hill once, I was hitting balls on the range next to Dave Marr, not far from Arnold. [In the warm-up Ben had been having trouble adjusting to his driver and was hoping it could be adjusted to him.] 'Dave'—I turned to Marr—'do you think anybody here might have some lead tape?' 'Are you kidding me?' he said. 'That guy over there eats lead tape for breakfast!' Arnold pulled out his entire tool kit, full of saws and scissors, and reweighted my club head just in time."

(Palmer told Ben, "That'll be a dollar fifty.")

RORY McILROY

"It's a little different for a European. Seve was our Arnie. Everyone says that, and it's true. The way Arnie brought golf to the masses, Seve brought it to us. I didn't grow up thinking of Arnie, but once I came over to the U.S., and learned what he did for the game, and all he meant to the tour, I got it. It was nice to come to his tournament, to honor him and all that he did for our game. Would there have been a Seve without him? Sure, but not the same Seve. None of us would have been the same. Golf wouldn't have been the same."

("If you ever need anything," Palmer said to McIlroy, "here's my number. Call me." "All I need, Mr. Palmer," Rory told him, "you've already given me.")

JORDAN SPIETH

"In the weeks before Christmas after I won the Masters, I came back to Augusta National to play the course a couple of days with my dad. You know, you can take the green jacket home with you for a year, but then you have to bring it back. I was already feeling my time with it kind of running out. I didn't wear it around Dallas a lot—it pretty much stayed in my closet, in a garment bag that said '2015 Champion.' But I would put it on at home when friends came over, and I wore it while doing crazy stuff, like grilling. Making memories. So now my father and I are walking upstairs to the Champions Locker Room, and I'm trying to soak in this feeling and make it last a lifetime. How often do you get to go and see your name in the Champions Locker Room at Augusta National for the first time? I had no idea—no one had told me—whom I'd be sharing a locker with. Arnold Palmer."

NICK PRICE

"There are only two people I've met in my life who had that sort of—I want to say 'It.' Arnold was one and Seve the other. Because I knew Arnie and he made it so easy for me to know him, it was good to look at him at times through others' eyes. My father-in-law, Jim, was the senior partner of a big law firm in Rhodesia—Zimbabwe—a very respected man in the community, president of the golf club, served on many, many boards of big companies. A very traditional man brought up in an English background and environment where manners and etiquette were everything. And he was a huge Palmer fan. Anyway, he came to Bay Hill not long after Sue and I were married. Nineteen eight-eight or so. I asked Arnold if I could bring him by. When I introduced him to Arnold Palmer, Jim was as nervous as any person I have ever seen in my life. I'm telling you, in Arnold's presence he was like a kindergartner. That's what Palmer could do to people. It wasn't something he tried to do. In fact, he tried not to do it, to put everybody at ease. But I'll never forget Jim's nervousness as long as I live.

"My other memory: Sue and I were applying for our green cards, and because I didn't know the president of the United States, I went to Arnold to ask if he'd do a character reference for me. Geez, I'll tell you what, he wrote the most glowing letter on my behalf. I pictured the INS [Immigration and Naturalization Service] officer seeing 'Arnold Palmer' at the bottom and stamping that thing straightaway. For years, every time Arnold saw me, he reminded the people in the room, 'I got Nick into the country.'

"All golfers, every single one of us, has learned from him in some form or fashion. My career, Tiger Woods's career, even Jack Nicklaus's career, all owe something to Arnold. Golf won't ever be able to repay him for what he did for the game. Last time I saw him was at Augusta. He was sitting in the cabin there and called me over. He grabbed my hand, just held on to me, and said, 'It's so good to see you, Nick.' He told me he had been surrounded by old people all day—and I'm no spring chicken myself—but I was like the youngest guy who had come to see him. 'Tell the other kids not to forget me,' he said."

GEOFF OGILVY

"There are people in the world—every now and then you bump into them—who have good energy. You just want to be friends with them. Everyone wanted to be friends with Arnold Palmer: women, men, young people, old people. Any interaction you had with him, you walked away thinking, 'You know, I really like that guy.' I think one of those natural laws of the universe, or the world, or whatever you call it, is that we are drawn to people who enjoy what they do. When you see somebody really *loving* what they're doing, whatever that happens to be, it lifts you up for some reason. And so many golfers, because of the nature of the game, look like they're not enjoying it at all. He always seemed like a kid having fun at the golf course. He loved playing golf, and that carried over into everything else he did. Every side success was just a happy by-product to the pleasure he got playing golf. He was a golfer.

"Tiger in the early days, when he seemed to love it, was so great to watch. But even before everything went bad, the fun had already gone out of it. He was still good, still winning, but it wasn't the same. It looked like he was hating it. I shouldn't say 'hating it,' but he wasn't doing it joyfully. He was just doing it to do it. Even after Palmer lost his game, he never lost his joy.

"Generally speaking, he was a little too early for me, but I'm a little different. As a boy in Australia, I read Jones's books, Byron's books, Jack's books, Arnie's books. But Palmer was mostly just a great name out of the past until I came over and met him. He was still playing at Bay Hill, where the people didn't care at all what he shot. They were just so happy to watch him. I think the character he was and how big he got came to outweigh his career a little, which is kind of a shame, really. But if Nicklaus and Tiger and Hogan had slightly better playing careers, none of them had anything like Palmer's impact on the game. If Arnold hadn't been around, there'd be a PGA tour but it wouldn't be quite the same. From a professional's standpoint, anyway, he's the most important *guy* in the last hundred years of golf.

"Especially to this latest generation, Tiger was very important, too, obviously. To Australia, Greg Norman was important. For Palmer, Norman, Tiger—and Seve—there was only ever a gallery on one hole, wherever they were. That magnetism and showmanship was handed down to the others by Palmer. He made golf more attractive to watch and easier to sell.

"I heard from him when I won the Open, but the best time I heard from him was when I won Reno after two or three bad years. He sent me a little note Monday or Tuesday saying, 'Well done. Welcome back. I know it's hard to win again after a bad patch.' So he noticed. He didn't have to be noticing who wins in Reno, but he did. Pretty cool."

NANCY LOPEZ

"I guess I did have a sense of history growing up, but more Arnold than anyone. Of course, you hardly ever saw the women on TV then. But JoAnne Carner was my female idol. Whenever the women were on, my dad would always say, 'Let's watch *them* today,' and JoAnne stood out."

(The legend of JoAnne Gunderson Carner—"the Great Gundy"—included the fact that she outdrove Palmer once. It was at an exhibition. Both hit long drives into the fairway off the first tee. With a swagger, Arnold bypassed the shorter ball, bent down to identify the longer one, then withdrew backward with a look of chagrin. If asked, he would get up from his desk and reenact that embarrassing moment, and love doing it. "I birdied the hole," he said, "a par five. She eagled it.")

Nancy continued: "The first time I played with Arnold was at the Bing Crosby when I was fifteen. Mr. Crosby invited me and another amateur, Marianne Bretton, to play in his tournament. We played a practice round with Arnold and Mark McCormack, which was pretty cool. From there on, Arnie and I came to do a few clinics and outings together and to really get to know each other. I started a women's golf club company in conjunction with his and that led to doing more things with him, like the PGA show. I just adored him and loved being with him, and I think he felt the same way about me. He was such a sweet, sweet man.

"I was at the Masters this year and for him not to be well enough to hit the opening tee shot with Jack and Gary broke my heart. He's so proud, and I could see it was killing him to be sitting there watching. I went to hug him, and that was the first time he didn't stand up to give me a hug. So I kind of knew. He had such a character about him. That's why the fans loved him. They knew how close they were to him, but I don't think they realized how close he was to them. He got choked up talking about his fans. And thinking of that makes me cry. The reason he always gave so much of himself to them was because he loved them.

"Arnold started out better with people than Jack was, but Jack became better just from being around Arnold. I think of Winnie and Barbara, too. A big part of Arnie's and Jack's success had to be what their wives went through, basically having to share their husbands with the world. I know Winnie had to do that."

(Gary Player always insisted, "Vivienne, Winnie, and Barbara were the real Big Three.")

"I like that," Nancy said, hearing what Player said. "I agree with that completely."

BERNHARD LANGER

"We played together first in Australia. He was a worldwide player, of course. Went over to the British early, went everywhere eventually. International golfers probably appreciate him even more than Americans do because of that. They know how much his presence meant to kids in countries like Germany, where golf wasn't the biggest sport. He invited me to play in his tournament at Bay Hill, and that meant a lot, too. When I think of him, I think of those enormous hands, one of his fingers like two of mine, and I think of how he always looked you straight in the eye, never giving you less than his complete attention. He was the superstar who cared about other people more than himself. In the twenty years since I won my first Masters, I've had all of those Champions' Dinners with him. I'm blessed for that. I'm blessed to have known him. I'm sure others have told you, he never failed to send a note congratulating you on your successes. Seeing his name at the bottom of that note did something to you."

PETER ALLISS

"Arnold and I had a few games together, including at Royal Lytham and St. Annes in his first Ryder Cup. Was that nineteen sixty-one? My father [an honored golf instructor], who was a great friend of Bobby Jones and Walter Hagen, almost immediately pegged Palmer as their natural heir. As it turned out, of course, he was right.

"My first impression was just how indomitably confident he was. Damnably confident, I should say. As if there was absolutely no doubt in his mind he was going to beat you. It was infuriating. We tied at Lytham, you know. But he seemed to believe I had been lucky to tie him—even though he holed his ball from off the green four times. *Four times!* We played another singles match in the next Ryder Cup. I'm too modest to say who won, but he lost. On the golf course, Arnold could be strangely aloof to his playing partner but he was never that way to the public. The uniqueness was obvious. The flamboyance. The excitement. The charisma. Majestic at winning, majestic at losing. A bit crash-bang-wallop. Uniformly wonderful long game, not always so wonderful short game, though he was among the best chippers I ever saw. Not pitchers, chippers. He just played in this unbelievably bold style, going for absolutely everything, committing the silliest mistakes along the way, schoolboy mistakes. But making up for them most of the time.

"As a person he was utterly real. Authenticity always takes some time to verify. There was a slightly cruel joke going around golf at the start of the Palmer era, told by inferior players who are deservedly forgotten. 'Where's Palmer?' 'Oh, he's out in the car park waiting for someone to ask him for his autograph.' Once we became friends, he scolded me about my signature. 'Only old prospectors make their X,' he said. 'Stop scribbling and start signing.' What he was really saying was 'Take a bit of time for the ones who make all of this wonderful stuff possible.' They say he liked all people, but I think he just didn't mind them. He was a happy man, and made even grumps like me a little happier. He drank from the cup of happiness."

(Palmer said, "Believe Peter's license plate, '3 PUT,' at your own risk.")

BUBBA WATSON

"I was feeling a little tightness in my back, and with the Olympics and everything coming up, I thought the responsible thing to do was withdraw from Bay Hill. But I had too much respect for Arnold to do that on the telephone. I went to his office in person and brought Caleb [Watson's four-year-old son] with me, figuring it might go a little better for me having Caleb there. But Arnold made it easy, as always. He didn't talk about Bay Hill, the tournament, or golf. He talked about Caleb, about life. He looked worn-out. I tried to give him some energy, to encourage him as much as I could, if he even needed it from me. He was the one who picked Caleb up and put him in his lap. I didn't do it. I didn't stage it or anything. I asked him, 'Do you mind if I take a picture?' And after I left, I called back and asked if it was OK to post it on social media." Caleb and the King.

JAMES GARNER

"We aren't just acquaintances, we're friends. Though I'm sure everyone says that. My brother is a club pro at the Oakmont out here [Los Angeles] and we talk about Arnie constantly. So do Dan Jenkins and I in the Lodge bar [at Pebble Beach], where I gave Dan the title for one of his books, *Baja Oklahoma*, and he gave me absolutely no credit. Jenkins likes to say, 'Bob Drum invented Palmer,' but I say God invented him, and is damn proud of it, too. I think Arnie likes me because I was Maverick on TV. He likes TV cowboys, being a kind of TV cowboy himself. Like Clint Eastwood, *Rawhide*. Though I think Clint would prefer to be Arnold Palmer."

DAN JENKINS

"In the 1970 PGA at Southern Hills, my good friend and fellow typist Bob Drum and I spent the week rooting shamelessly for Arnold Palmer, who was playing superbly tee to green and contending for the only major title that had been escaping him. Palmer would have been the best story, and we root for good stories.

"Unfortunately, the relatively unknown and more or less invisible Dave Stockton was in a 'putting coma,' sinking twenty- and thirty-foot putts for pars and bogeys all the way, and he wound up winning that PGA by two strokes over Palmer and Bob Murphy.

"I couldn't resist writing a story [in *Sports Illustrated*] that was more about Arnold regrettably losing than it was about Stockton winning. The tournament in boiling-hot Tulsa turned out to be the last time Palmer had a serious shot at the PGA.

"Stockton wasn't happy with my story. Two weeks later at a tournament in New Jersey, he ran into Drum and said, 'Is Jenkins here? I need to have some words with him.'

"Drum reported my absence, and said, 'Whom shall I say is asking?'"

ARCHABBOT DOUGLAS NOWICKI

"I had the opportunity to meet Pope John Paul II. The archbishop conducting the visit introduced me as the archabbot of Latrobe, Pennsylvania. Pope John Paul immediately responded, 'Arn-old Palmer.'"

GEORGE W. BUSH

"I gave him the Medal of Freedom for a reason. His impact on American sport, but also his impact on American character."

The first recipient of the Medal of Freedom, in 1776, was George Washington.

("Contrary to what you may hear," Palmer said, "I never knew George Washington, but if I met him, I'd shake his hand and say, 'You were the first, and I won't be the last.'")

25

TRIBUTE

"A good man."

O N A SHIMMERING DAY in an ornate basilica at a small Catholic college two miles from Latrobe Country Club, hands clapped, voices rang, a guitar played, and the eyes of a thousand mourners inside the church—five times that many on an adjoining football field, and a national television audience—glistened in the sweet celebration of "a good man," Arnold Palmer. In the welcome of Pope John Paul II's friend, Archabbot Douglas Nowicki, the familiar words of the "valley of death" psalm, "green pastures," "still water," for the first time brought to mind a golf course.

Bob Goalby, who won the 1968 Masters when Roberto De Vicenzo signed for one more shot than he took, and Dow Finsterwald on a cane, both born in Palmer's year, 1929, were his oldest colleagues there. "A lot of the guys our age can't fly," Goalby said. But 83-year-old Doug Sanders made it. He got the message.

Arnold's youngest fellow pros who were present included Rickie
Fowler, who brought the Ryder Cup, retrieved by the U.S. just a day
and a half earlier. Captain Davis Love III, whose dad was tied with
Palmer for the Masters lead in 1964, was in attendance, too, along
with Phil Mickelson and assistant captain Bubba Watson. Though
the seventh-ranked player in the world, two-time Masters champion
Watson was skipped over in the Ryder Cup selections because the
other players on Love's team didn't like him. His reaction was to ask
to be included anyway, to root them on. He won more than anyone
that week.

"We were looking down at the airstrip," said Ernie Els, who
flew in from Florida, "and the fog just suddenly lifted." Other
major winners in the chamber included Tom Watson, Lee Trevino, Curtis Strange, Nick Faldo, Hale Irwin, Craig Stadler, Mark
O'Meara, Mike Weir, Fuzzy Zoeller, Nancy Lopez, Juli Inkster,
Annika Sörenstam, and, of course, Jack Nicklaus. The greatest (or
second-greatest) player who ever lived. The only other candidate,
Tiger Woods, was missing. But Muhammad Ali was probably sitting
there, maybe next to Pap and Doris.

Golf's rank and file was well represented, too: Peter Jacobsen, Jay
Haas, Scott McCarron, Tim "Lumpy" Herron, Bobby Clampett,
William McGirt, Billy Andrade, Jerry McGee, Chris Perry. Faces
out of the past dotted the congregation, like Bob Drum's son, Kevin,
and old Bob Murphy, who tied Palmer for second in Arnold's last
good shot at a PGA. There might have been a more amazing assem-
blage of golf people sometime, but I doubt it.

Sam Saunders told a story of his grandfather, Dumpy. ("He's
still Dumpy in my phone, and [like hands on a golf grip] I'll never
change it.") "He'd always take my call no matter where he was, and
he'd always begin by saying, 'Where are you?'" At 4:10 on Sunday
afternoon, September 25, 2016, Sam called Palmer at the University
of Pittsburgh Medical Center. "He asked me where was I? 'I'm here

at home,' I said. 'I'm thinking about you today—we all are.' He told me to take care of my babies, take care of the children and my entire family. I told him I loved him, and he told me he loved me back. It was the last thing we said to each other, and I will be grateful for that the rest of my life."

It reminded him of another phone call once, when Saunders dialed Dumpy and, flipping the script, Sam opened the conversation with "Where are you?"

"I'm with the president," Arnold replied.

"The president of what?"

"Of the United States."

"Why did you answer the phone?"

"Well, I wanted to talk to you."

Against everyone's counsel, but being a competitor, Palmer was in the hospital preparing for heart surgery that offered but didn't promise an improved condition. He was awaiting a test when he died exactly as Pap had, just that suddenly. He didn't linger. By the way, it wasn't a rug on which he tripped, which separated the shoulder that never healed and started his decline. It was Mulligan, the dog. He said it was a rug because he didn't want anyone to blame his old friend.

Arnie's ashes were spread on top of Winnie's at a particularly leafy and lovely spot by Latrobe's ninth green. At that moment, a rainbow appeared.

Filing out, his friends paused on the church steps, listening to a piper and watching the jet with N1AP markings shoot straight up into the sky, on its way to heaven.

APPENDIX

Compiled by Cliff Schrock

HIGH SCHOOL VICTORIES

Western Pennsylvania Interscholastic Athletic League Championship:
   1946, 1947

Pennsylvania Interscholastic Athletic Association Championship: 1946,
   1947

COLLEGIATE AND AMATEUR VICTORIES

Southern Conference Championship: 1948, 1949 (runner-up in 1950
   when Wake Forest won team title)

Medalist, National Intercollegiate (NCAA): 1949, 1950

Medalist, Southern Intercollegiate Championship: 1950, 68–72–68–
   72—280, Athens, Ga.

ACC Championship: May 1954, Old Town Club, Winston-Salem, N.C.
   (first time held)

AT U.S. OPEN AS AMATEUR

1953, Oakmont Country Club, 84–78—162, Missed Cut

1954, Baltusrol Golf Club, 81–73—154, Missed Cut

UNITED STATES AMATEUR CHAMPION
1954, Country Club of Detroit, Aug. 23–28

Round 1—defeated Frank Strafaci, Garden City Country, N.Y., 1 up

Round 2—defeated John W. Veghte, Pine Brook, N.Y., 1 up

Round 3—defeated Richard L. Whiting, Red Run, Mich., 2 and 1

Round 4—defeated Walter C. Andzel, South Shore, N.Y., 5 and 3

Round 5—defeated Frank Stranahan, Inverness, Ohio, 3 and 1

Quarterfinals—defeated Don Cherry, Wichita Falls, Tex., 1 up

Semifinals (36 holes)—defeated Edward Meister Jr., Kirtland, Ohio, 39 holes

Final (36 holes)—defeated Robert Sweeny, Sands Point, N.Y., 1 up

PGA TOUR VICTORIES (62, FIFTH BEST ALL-TIME)

(Played 734 tour events, making 574 cuts, playing 2,567 rounds. He had 62 firsts, 38 seconds, 27 thirds, 245 top-10 finishes, 388 top-25 finishes, a 14–10 playoff record and prize money of $1,861,857.)

1955 Canadian Open

1956 Insurance City Open, Eastern Open

1957 Houston Open, Azalea Open, Rubber City Open, San Diego Open

1958 St. Petersburg Open, Masters Tournament, Pepsi Championship

1959 Thunderbird Invitational, Oklahoma City Open, West Palm Beach Open

1960 Palm Springs Desert Golf Classic, Texas Open, Baton Rouge Open, Pensacola Open, Masters Tournament, U.S. Open, Insurance City Open, Mobile Sertoma Open

1961 San Diego Open, Phoenix Open, Baton Rouge Open, Texas Open, Western Open, The Open Championship

1962 Palm Springs Golf Classic, Phoenix Open, Masters Tournament, Texas Open, Tournament of Champions, Colonial National Invitation, The Open Championship, American Golf Classic

1963 Los Angeles Open, Phoenix Open, Pensacola Open, Thunderbird Classic, Cleveland Open, Western Open, Whitemarsh Open

1964 Masters Tournament, Oklahoma City Open

1965 Tournament of Champions

1966 Los Angeles Open, Tournament of Champions, Houston Champions International

1967 Los Angeles Open, Tucson Open, American Golf Classic, Thunderbird Classic

1968 Bob Hope Desert Classic, Kemper Open

1969 Heritage Golf Classic, Danny Thomas–Diplomat Classic

1970 National Four-Ball Championship

1971 Bob Hope Desert Classic, Florida Citrus Invitational, Westchester Classic, National Team Championship

1973 Bob Hope Desert Classic

NON-PGA TOUR AND INTERNATIONAL VICTORIES

1956 Panama Open, Colombia Open

1957 West Penn Open (won by six strokes at Fox Chapel Golf Club with scores of 70–72—142), Mountain View Open, Roanoke, Va.

1960 World Cup (Team, with Sam Snead)

1962 World Cup (Team, with Sam Snead)

1963 Australian Wills Masters, World Cup (Team, with Jack Nicklaus)

1964 Piccadilly World Match Play Championship, World Cup (Team, with Jack Nicklaus)

1966 Australian Open, World Cup (Team, with Jack Nicklaus), PGA Team Championship (with Jack Nicklaus)

1967 Piccadilly World Match Play Championship, World Cup (Individual and Team with Jack Nicklaus)

1971 Lancôme Trophy

1975 Spanish Open, British PGA Championship

1980 Canadian PGA Championship

YEAR-BY-YEAR PROFESSIONAL RESULTS

Lists event, date, round scores, final position, money earned ("No Money" indicates Palmer didn't finish "in the money"). Excludes weekly, one-day PGA Tour pro-ams, and various exhibitions. Some dates and prize money missing. PGA Tour summaries only include official events/money and do not include non-tour and foreign events. The letter *T* denotes tied for position.

1954

Miami Open, Miami Springs, Dec. 9–12: 78–74—152, Missed Cut

1955

Panama Open, Jan. 16 (final day): 65–68–70–71—274, T-2, $900

Imperial Valley Open, Jan. 27–30: 72–68–67–70—277, T-17, No Money

Phoenix Open, Feb. 3–6: 69–68–71–73—281, T-10★

Tucson Open, Feb. 10–13: 68–71–74–73—286, T-43, No Money

Texas Open, Feb. 17–20: 69–70–64–67—270, T-6★

Houston Open, Feb. 24–27: 74–68–68–73—283, T-22★

Baton Rouge Open, March 3–6: 70–73–73–72—288, T-40, No Money

St. Petersburg Open, March 17–20: 71–70–68–75—284, T-17★

Masters Tournament, April 7–10: 76–76–72–69—293, T-10, $695.83

Greater Greensboro Open, April 14–17: 72–75–71–73—291, T-33, No
    Money

Colonial National Invitation, May 5–8: 81–79–80–72—312, 43rd, No
    Money

Kansas City Open, May 19–22: 73–75—148, Missed Cut

Fort Wayne Invitational, May 26–29: 69–72–72–74—287, T-25, $145

U.S. Open, June 16–18: 77–76–74–76—303, T-21, $180

Western Open, June 23–26: 76–66–70–72—284, T-16, $230

British Columbia Open, June 29–July 2: 70–74–68—212, Withdrew

St. Paul Open, July 7–10: 65–67–70–71—273, T-3, $1,300

Miller High Life Open, July 14–17: 75–71—146, Missed Cut

Rubber City Open, July 28–31: 71–69–72–73—285, T-36, No Money

All American Championship, Aug. 4–7: 68–75–73–74—290, T-26, $205.83

World Championship of Golf, Aug. 11–14: 74–74–75–73—296, T-55, $160

Canadian Open, Aug. 17–20: 64–67–64–70—265, 1st, $2,400

Labatt Open, Aug. 25–28: 72–71–65–71—279, T-8, $760

Insurance City Open, Sept. 2–5: 71–73—144, Withdrew

Cavalcade of Golf, Sept. 8–11: 78, Withdrew

Philadelphia Daily News Open, Sept. 15–18: 78–68–69–70—285, T-34, No Money

Carling Golf Classic, Sept. 22–25: 71–74–73–81—299, T-39, $241.66

Long Island Rotary Open, Sept. 29–Oct. 2: 71–70–68–72—279, 6th, $800

Eastern Open, Oct. 6–9: 71–76 73–70—290, 16th, $320

Havana Invitational, Dec. 1–4: 75–75–71–73—294, T-25, $115

Miami Beach Open, Dec. 8–11: 70–65–71—206, T-8, $520

Mayfair Inn Open, Dec. 15–18: 72, Withdrew

*Ineligible for money during six-month probationary period after turning professional.

PGA Tour summary: Official events entered 30, money $7,958, scoring average 70.99

1956

Los Angeles Open, Jan. 6–9. 72 71 67–74—287, T-27, $250

Panama Open, Jan. 15 (final day): 68–72–75–68—283, 1st, $2,000, defeated Sam Snead in six-hole playoff

Colombia Open, Jan. 21 (final day): 69–75–71–65—280, 1st, $1,800

Thunderbird Invitational, Jan. 26–29: 70–70–72–67—279, T-6, $365

Phoenix Open, Feb. 2–5: 70–76—146, Withdrew

Texas Open, Feb. 16–19: 71–73–73–71—288, T-43, No Money

Houston Open, Feb. 23–26: 74–73–71–72—290, T-35, $101.11

Baton Rouge Open, March 1–4: 70 70–75–71—286, T-18, $155

Pensacola Open, March 8–11: 78–66–73—217, Withdrew

Miami Beach Open, March 22–25: 73–69–77—219, Withdrew

Azalea Open, March 29–April 1: 67–70–73–70—280, T-8, $416.67

Masters Tournament, April 5–8: 73–75–74–79—301, 18th, $630

Tournament of Champions, April 26–29: 74–76–71–72—293, 12th, $1,180

Colonial National Invitation, May 3–6: 73–71–76–76—296, T-28, No Money

Carling Open, May 10–13: 71–74–71–73—289, T-28, $155

Kansas City Open, May 17–20: 68–69–71–72—280, T-11, $550

Dallas Centennial Open, May 24–27: 73–66–70–72—281, T-29, $184.28

Texas International Open, June 1–4: 69–70–71–74—284, T-58, $139.85

U.S. Open, June 14–16: 72–70–72–73—287, 7th, $600

Philadelphia Daily News Open, June 21–24: 70–69–64–70—273, 6th, $1,000

Insurance City Open, June 28–June 1: 66–69–68–71—274, 1st, $4,000, defeated Ted Kroll in two-hole, sudden-death playoff

Canadian Open, July 5–8: 72–72–68–68—280, T-8, $550

Labatt Open, July 12–15: 70–70–73–74—287, T-26, $177.50

Eastern Open, July 26–29: 70–66–69–72—277, 1st, $3,800

All American Championship, Aug. 2–5: 72–69–74–76—291, T-33, $117.50

World Championship of Golf, Aug. 9–12: 70–73–68–73—284, T-25, $343.75

Miller High Life Open, Aug. 16–19: 67–73–71–71—282, T-34, $150

St. Paul Open, Aug. 23–26: 73–70–70–66—279, T-17, $296

Motor City Open, Aug. 30–Sept. 2: 77, Withdrew

Rubber City Open, Sept. 6–9: 67–68–68–69—272, 2nd, $2,000

Fort Wayne Open, Sept. 13–16: 76–69—145, Withdrew

Mayfair Inn Open, Dec. 13–16: 66–68–67–71—272, T-7, $528

PGA Tour summary: Official events entered 29, money $16,145, scoring average 71.14

1957

Los Angeles Open, Jan. 4–7: 77–71–77—225, Missed Cut

Thunderbird Invitational, Jan. 24–27: 71–69–80–68—288, T-32, $112.50

Phoenix Open, Jan. 31–Feb. 3: 66–70–70–71—277, T-5, $787.50

Tucson Open, Feb. 7–10: 68–70–69–70—277, T-20, $175

Texas Open, Feb. 14–17: 68–68–70–68—274, T-3, $1,300

Houston Open, Feb. 21–25: 67–72–71–69—279, 1st, $7,500

Baton Rouge Open, Feb. 28–March 3: 68–72–73–78—291, T-34, No
    Money

Pensacola Open, March 7–10: 72–71–75–71—289, T-26, $85.72

St. Petersburg Open, March 14–17: 69–69–71–72—281, 13th, $370

Azalea Open, March 28–31: 70–67–70–75—282, 1st, $1,700

Masters Tournament, April 4–7: 73–73–69–76—291, T-6, $1,137.50

Greater Greensboro Open, April 11–14: 74–72–73—219, Withdrew

Tournament of Champions, April 18–21: 72–73–74–73—292, T-9, $1,270

Kentucky Derby Open, April 24–28: 71–75–75–68—289, T-20, $413.75

Colonial National Invitation, May 2–5: 70–74–75–79—298, T-32, No
    Money

Kansas City Open, May 23–26: 74–72–69–82—297, T-39, No Money

Rubber City Open, June 6–9: 71–66–67–68—272, 1st, $2,800, defeated
    Doug Ford in six-hole, sudden-death playoff

U.S. Open, June 13–15: 76–76—152, Missed Cut

Carling Open, June 20–23: 67–74–66–73—280, T-4, $1,425

Western Open, June 27–30: 75–72—147, Missed Cut

Labatt Open, July 4–7: 72–70–73–68—283, T-8, $950

Canadian Open, July 10–13: 70–70–70–70—280, 11th, $850

Erie Open, July 21: 69–71—140, T-6, $325

Eastern Open, July 25–28: 71–71–72–69—283, T-8, $825

All American Open, Aug. 1–5: 69–73–72–71—285, T-14, $675

World Championship of Golf, Aug. 8–11: 70–70–74–71—285, T-10,
    $1,500

St. Paul Open, Aug. 15–18: 72–67–68–69—276, T-17, $430

Miller High Life Open, Aug. 22–25: 72–75–69–72—288, T-54, No Money

Insurance City Open, Aug. 29–Sept. 2: 67–68–67–77—279, T-10, $670

Dallas Open, Sept. 13–16: 71–73–71–71—286, T-38, $200

Mountain View Open, Sept. 22 (final day): 67–68—135, 1st, $350

Hesperia Open, Oct. 24–27: 68–71–70–70—279, T-3, $1,033.33

San Diego Open, Oct. 30–Nov. 3: 65–68–68–70—271, 1st, $2,800

Mayfair Inn Open, Dec. 12–15: 73–69–69–69—280, T-22, $175

PGA Tour summary: Official events entered 31, money $27,803, scoring average 71.09

1958

Los Angeles Open, Jan. 3–6: 73–74–70–72—289, T-32, $208.33

Bing Crosby National Pro-Am, Jan. 9–12: 75–70–72–74—291, T-16, $650

Tijuana Open, Jan. 17–20: 70–70–71–70—281, T-2, $1,150

Panama Invitational, Jan. 23–26: 66–73–71–69—279, T-7, $612.50

Phoenix Open, Jan. 30–Feb. 2: 73–74—147, Missed Cut

Houston Invitational, Feb. 20–24: 73–79—152, Missed Cut

Baton Rouge Open, Feb. 27–March 2: 67–71–71–71—280, T-2, $1,350

Greater New Orleans Open, March 9–11: 73–67–71–70—281, T-3, $1,300

Pensacola Open, March 13–16: 70–75–72–69—286, T-12, $475

St. Petersburg Open, March 20–23: 70–69–72–65—276, 1st, $2,000

Azalea Open, March 28–30: 66–73–75–68—282, 2nd, $1,500, lost playoff to Howie Johnson, 77–78

Masters Tournament, April 3–6: 70–73–68–73—284, 1st, $11,250

Tournament of Champions, April 24–27: 72–68–72–70—282, T-6, $1,310

Colonial National Invitation, May 1–4: 65–77–73–74—289, T-12, $662.50

Arlington Hotel Open, May 8–11: 69–71–76–76—292, T-51, No Money

Memphis Invitational, May 15–18: 69–70–66–68—273, 7th, $900

Western Open, May 29–June 1: 66–73–72–70—281, T-7, $815

U.S. Open, June 13–15: 75–75–77–72—299, T-21, $200

Buick Open, June 19–23: 76–71–70–69—286, T-2, $3,800

Pepsi Championship, June 26–29: 66–69–67–71—273, 1st, $9,000

Rubber City Open, July 3–6: 72–68–68–68—276, T-12, $630

Insurance City Open, July 10–13: 66–68–70–70—274, T-8, $900

PGA Championship, July 17–20: 76–71–77–74—298, T-40, $110

Gleneagles-Chicago Open, Aug. 1–4: 72–73–71–67—283, T-30, $256.67

Miller Open, Aug. 7–11: 70–73—143, Withdrew

St. Paul Open, Aug. 14–17: 67–75–65–68—275, T-22, $290

Canadian Open, Aug. 20–23: 67–66–70–69—272, T-12, $680

Vancouver Open, Aug. 28–30, Sept. 1: 72–73–71–69—285, T-27, $350

Utah Open, Sept. 5–8: 65–69–68–66—268, T-2, $1,350

Denver Centennial Open, Sept. 11–14: 67–68–66–69—270, T-3, $1,300

Carling Open, Nov. 5–9: 70–76–75–73—294, T-18, $510

West Palm Beach Open, Nov. 20–23: 70–66–67–74—277, T-6, $725

Mayfair Inn Open, Dec. 11–14: 72–66–73–70—281, T-17, $245

PGA Tour summary: Official events entered 32, money $42,608, scoring average 70.66

1959

Los Angeles Open, Jan. 2–5: 72–69–72–72—285, T-9, $1,062.50

Tijuana Open, Jan. 9–12: 69–69–71–72—281, T-18, $356

Bing Crosby National Pro-Am, Jan. 15–18: 69–77–67–73—286, T-8, $1,025

Thunderbird Invitational, Jan. 22–25: 67–70–67–62—266, 1st, $1,500

San Diego Open, Jan. 29–Feb. 1: 72–67–73–76—288, T-52, No Money

Phoenix Open, Feb. 5–8: 68–68–73–69—278, T-11, $495.72

Tucson Open, Feb. 12–15: 70–68–64–66—268, T-4, $900

Baton Rouge Open, Feb. 27–March 1: 67–76–75–73—291, T-21, $170

Greater New Orleans Open, March 6–9: 74–70–72–75—291, 30th, $100

Pensacola Open, March 12–15: 68–69–69–72—278, T-7, $725

St. Petersburg Open, March 20–23: 69–72–72–72—285, T-11, $475

Seminole Pro-Amateur, March 24–25: 71–70—141, T-1, $900

Masters Tournament, April 2–5: 71–70–71–74—286, 3rd, $4,500

Houston Classic, April 16–19: 66–68–71–73—278, T-3, $1,850

Tournament of Champions, April 23–26: 70–73–74–76—293, T-13, $1,250

Colonial National Invitation, April 30-May 3: 73–74–69–75—291, T-17, $331.25

Oklahoma City Open, May 7–11: 73–64–67–69—273, 1st, $3,500

Eastern Open, June 4–7: 73–73–69—215, Withdrew

U.S. Open, June 11–14: 71–69–72–74—286, T-5, $2,100

Gleneagles-Chicago Open, June 25–28: 67–69–70–75—281, T-11, $1,230

Buick Open, July 2–5: 72–74–69–71—286, T-8, $1,650

Western Open, July 9–12: 67–66–69–71—273, 2nd, $2,500

Insurance City Open, July 16–19: 68–71–68–72—279, T-8, $950

PGA Championship, July 30–Aug. 2: 72–72–71–71—286, T-14, $1,050

Carling Open, Aug. 6–9: 75–71–73–76—295, T-52, No Money

Motor City Open, Aug. 13–16: 69–66–71–73—279, T-4, $1,333.34

Rubber City Open, Aug. 20–23: 66–69–68–69—272, T-4, $1,100

Miller Open, Aug. 27–30: 73–69–66–65—273, T-12, $900

Lafayette Open, Nov. 12–15: 74–69–73–67—283, T-7, $700

Mobile Sertoma Open, Nov. 19–22: 72–68–74–73—287, T-17, $225

West Palm Beach Open, Nov. 26–29: 72–67–66–76—281, 1st, $2,000, defeated Gay Brewer and Pete Cooper in four-hole, sudden-death playoff

Coral Gables Open, Dec. 3–6: 69–72–66–72—279, T-3, $1,233.33

PGA Tour summary: Official events entered 31, money $32,462, scoring average 70.51

1960

Los Angeles Open, Jan. 8–9, 11–12: 72–74–70–73—289, T-25, $395

Yorba Linda Open, Jan. 15–18: 72–71–70–73—286, T-12, $610

Bing Crosby National Pro-Am, Jan. 21–24: 78–70–73–75—296, T-15, $670

San Diego Open, Jan. 28–31: 71–69–65–70—275, T-7, $850

Palm Springs Desert Classic, Feb. 3–7: 67–73–67–66–65—338, 1st, $12,000

Phoenix Open, Feb. 11–15: 70–71–66–71—278, T-12, $725

Tucson Open, Feb. 18–21: 65–74–69–68—276, T-5, $872.86

Texas Open, Feb. 25–28: 69–65–67–75—276, 1st, $2,800

Baton Rouge Open, March 3–6: 71–71–69–68—279, 1st, $2,000

Pensacola Open, March 10–13: 68–65–73–67—273, 1st, $2,000

St. Petersburg Open, March 19–21: 70–72–70–72—284, 5th, $900

DeSoto Open, March 24–27: 71–71–70–72—284, 5th, $1,475

Masters Tournament, April 7–10· 67–73–72–70—282, 1st, $17,500

Houston Classic, April 28, 30–May 2: 66–71–70–73—280, 2nd, $3,400,
    lost playoff to Bill Collins, 69–71

Tournament of Champions, May 5–8: 72 65 70 69—276, T-5, $1,650

Colonial National Invitation, May 12–15: 71–70–73–75—289, T-22,
    $243.33

"500" Festival Open, May 26–29: 70–71–73—214, Missed Cut

Oklahoma City Open, June 9–12: 68–66–75–67—276, 3rd, $2,000

U.S. Open, June 16–18: 72–71–72–65—280, 1st, $14,400

British Open, July 6–9: 70–71–70–68—279, 2nd, $2,520

PGA Championship, July 21–24: 67–74–75–70—286, T-7, $2,125

Insurance City Open, Aug. 4–7: 70–68–66–66—270, 1st, $3,500, defeated
    Bill Collins and Jack Fleck in three-hole, sudden-death playoff

Milwaukee Open, Aug. 25–28: 69–65–70–70—274, 3rd, $1,850

Carling Open, Sept. 15–18: 71–68–70–72—281, T-24, $250

Portland Open, Sept. 22–25: 66–70–67–67—270, T-4, $1,150

Mobile Sertoma Open, Nov. 24–27: 68–67–74–65—274, 1st, $2,000

West Palm Beach Open, Dec. 1–4: 71–72–69–76—288, T-5, $816.66

Coral Gables Open, Dec. 8–11: 68–72–68–73—281, T-10, $730

PGA Tour summary: Official events entered 27, money $75,263, scoring
average 69.95

1961

Los Angeles Open, Jan. 6–9: 77–72—149, Missed Cut

San Diego Open, Jan. 12–15: 69–68–69–65—271, 1st, $2,800, defeated Al Balding in one-hole, sudden-death playoff

Bing Crosby National Pro-Am, Jan. 19–22: 70–68–71–75—284, T-4, $1,625

Lucky International Open, Jan. 26–29: 66–69–72–70—277, T-8, $1,500

Palm Springs Golf Classic, Feb. 1–5: 69–68–70–72–69—348, 3rd, $2,200

Phoenix Open, Feb. 9–12: 69–65–66–70—270, 1st, $4,300, defeated Doug Sanders, 67–70, in playoff

Baton Rouge Open, Feb. 24–26: 65–67–68–66—266, 1st, $2,800

Greater New Orleans Open, March 2–5: 70–71–72–70—283, T-6, $1,300

Pensacola Open, March 9–12: 73–65–72–71—281, 7th, $900

Sunshine Open, March 23–26: 68–70–70–66—274, 2nd, $2,300

Seminole Pro-Am, March 27–28: 71–67—138, T-1, $900

Masters Tournament, April 6–8, 10: 68–69–73–71—281, T-2, $12,000

Houston Classic, April 20–23: 68–69–73–73—283, T-9, $1,200

Texas Open, April 27–30: 67–63–72–68—270, 1st, $4,300

Tournament of Champions, May 4–7: 69–76–73–78—296, T-21, $1,160

Colonial National Invitation, May 11–14: 68–73–69–76—286, 6th, $1,700

Sam Snead Festival, May 18–21: 70–67–68–66—271, T-4, $525

"500" Festival Open, May 25–28: 67–70–70–66—273, 2nd, $4,600, lost to Doug Ford in two-hole, sudden-death playoff

U.S. Open, June 15–17: 74–75–70–70—289, T-12, $900

Western Open, June 22–25: 65–70–67–69—271, 1st, $5,000

British Open, July 12–15: 70–73–69–72—284, 1st, $3,920

PGA Championship, July 27, 29–30: 73–72–69–68—282, T-5, $2,208.34

Insurance City Open, Aug. 10–13: 68–67–73–73—281, T-30, $106.25

American Golf Classic, Aug. 24–27: 70–70–69–72—281, 4th, $2,600

Dallas Open, Sept. 1–4: 67–69–72–71—279, T-2, $2,233.33

Mobile Sertoma Open, Nov. 23–26: 72–70–70–69—281, T-3, $1,100

West Palm Beach Open, Nov. 30–Dec. 3: 73–67–70–68—278, 2nd,
  $1,900

Coral Gables Open, Dec. 7–10: 73–70–71–68—282, T-17, $358.57

Wills Masters, Australia, 80–76–69–69—294, 8th

Yomiuri Shimbun Open, Japan, Nov. 5 (final day): 73–72–76–75—296,
  3rd, $600

PGA Tour summary: Official events entered 26, money $61,091, scoring
average 69.78

1962

Los Angeles Open, Jan. 5–8: 73–71–70–69—283, T-18, $825

San Diego Open, Jan. 11–14: 72–69–72–70—283, T-21, $275

Bing Crosby National Pro-Am, Jan. 18–20, 22: 76–71–72–76—295, T-21,
  $555

Lucky International Open, Jan. 25–28: 70–72–74–71—287, T-34, $170

Palm Springs Golf Classic, Jan. 31–Feb. 4: 69–67–66–71–69—342, 1st,
  $5,300

Phoenix Open, Feb. 8–11: 64–68–71–66—269, 1st, $5,300

Baton Rouge Open, March 2–4: 70–70–71–69—280, T-9, $753.33

Pensacola Open, March 8–11: 66–71–68–69—274, T-5, $1,000

Doral Country Club Open, March 22–25: 70–72–73–77—292, T-11,
  $1,230

Masters Tournament, April 5–8: 70–66–69–75—280, 1st, $20,000, won in
  playoff with 68 versus Gary Player (71) and Dow Finsterwald (77)

Greater Greensboro Classic, April 12–15: 71–76–68–69—284, T-5, $1,600

Texas Open, April 26–29: 67–69–70–67—273, 1st, $4,300

Tournament of Champions, May 3–6: 69–70–69–68—276, 1st, $11,000

Colonial National Invitation, May 10–13: 67–72–66–76—281, 1st, $7,000,
  defeated Johnny Pott in playoff, 69–73

Memphis Open, May 21–June 3: 71–71–66–70—278, T-21, $563.33

Thunderbird Classic, June 7–10: 73–74–72–71—290, T-35, $460

U.S. Open, June 14–16: 71–68–73–71—283, 2nd, $8,000, lost in playoff,
  71–74, to Jack Nicklaus

Western Open, June 28–July 1: 73–74–72–69—288, 7th, $1,900

British Open, July 11–13: 71–69–67–69—276, 1st, $4,200

PGA Championship, July 19–22: 71–72–73–72—288, T-17, $966.67

American Golf Classic, Aug. 9–12: 67–69–70–70—276, 1st, $9,000

Seattle World's Fair Open, Sept. 13–16: 70–65–68–68—271, T-6, $1,250

Transvaal, South Africa: 71–79–70–71—291, 6th, $120

PGA Tour summary: Official events entered 21, money $81,448, scoring
average 70.27

1963

Los Angeles Open, Jan. 4–7: 69–69–70–66—274, 1st, $9,000

Bing Crosby National Pro-Am, Jan. 17–20: 70–70—140, Disqualified

Lucky International Open, Jan. 24–27: 73–69–69–74—285, T-19, $800

Palm Springs Golf Classic, Jan. 30–Feb. 3: 71–72–71–68–67—349, T-6,
  $2,000

Phoenix Open, Feb. 7–12: 68–67–68–70—273, 1st, $5,300

Greater New Orleans Open, March 1–4: 74–73–72–71—290, T-14, $825

Pensacola Open, March 7–10: 69–68–69–67—273, 1st, $3,500

Doral Country Club Open, March 21–24: 71–71–75–73—290, T-7, $1,800

Masters Tournament, April 4–7: 74–73–73–71—291, T-9, $1,800

Texas Open, April 25–28: 71–68–70–67—276, T-9, $1,050

Tournament of Champions, May 2–5: 66–71–73–68—278, T-2, $5,300

Colonial National Invitation, May 9–12: 74–75–75–75—299, T-41, $170

Thunderbird Classic, June 13–16: 67–70–68–72—277, 1st, $25,000,
  defeated Paul Harney in one-hole, sudden-death playoff

U.S. Open, June 20–23: 73–69–77–74—293, 2nd, $7,000, lost in playoff
  (76) to Julius Boros (70) and Jacky Cupit (73)

Cleveland Open, June 27–July 1: 71–68–66–68—273, 1st, $22,000, shot
  67 to defeat Tony Lema (70) and Tommy Aaron (70) in playoff

British Open, July 10–13: 76–71–71–76—294, T-26, $168

PGA Championship, July 18–21: 74–73–73–73—293, T-40, $410

Western Open, July 25–29: 73–67–67–73—280, 1st, $11,000, shot 70 to
defeat Julius Boros (71) and Jack Nicklaus (73) in playoff

American Golf Classic, Aug. 22–25: 70–71–66–73—280, 2nd, $4,600

Whitemarsh Open, Oct. 3–6: 70–71–66–74—281, 1st, $26,000

Sahara Invitational, Oct. 17–20: 71–71–70–73—285, T-26, $675

Wills Masters, Australia: 68–77–71–69—285, 1st, $2,240

PGA Tour summary: Official events entered 20, money $128,230, scoring average 70.63

1964

Los Angeles Open, Jan. 3–6: 70–70–72–70—282, T-3, $2,775

San Diego Open, Jan. 9–12: 73–69–73–66—281, T-15, $725

Bing Crosby National Pro-Am, Jan. 16–19: 72–73–76—221, Missed Cut

Lucky International Open, Jan. 23–26: 67–66–72–70—275, T-3, $3,100

Palm Springs Golf Classic, Jan. 29–Feb. 2: 78–71–72–69–73—363, T-41,
No Money

Phoenix Open, Feb. 6–9: 70–72–69–67—278, T-9, $1,450

Greater New Orleans Open, Feb. 27–March 2: 76–71–72–70—289, 10th,
$1,500

Pensacola Open, March 5–8: 69–68–68–69—274, T-2, $2,300, lost in
playoff (72) to Gary Player (71) with Miller Barber (74)

Doral Country Club Open, March 19–22: 72–72–73–70—287, T-18,
$793.75

Greater Greensboro Open, April 2–5: 70–75–70–71—286, T-13, $845

Masters Tournament, April 9–12: 69–68–69–70—276, 1st, $20,000

Tournament of Champions, April 30–May 3: 72–72–70–70—284, 9th,
$1,850

Colonial National Invitation, May 7–10: 75–71–69–72—287, T-4, $3,160

Oklahoma City Open, May 14–18: 72–69–69–67—277, 1st, $5,800

Memphis Open, May 21–24: 66–73–68–69—276, T-17, $815

Thunderbird Classic, June 4–7: 68–71–74–72—285, T-25, $787.50

U.S. Open, June 18–20: 68–69–75–74—286, T-5, $3,750

Cleveland Open, June 25–28: 67–64–71–68—270, 2nd, $12,000, lost to
    Tony Lema in one-hole, sudden-death playoff

Whitemarsh Open, July 2–5: 68–70–67–73—278, 3rd, $10,042.12

PGA Championship, July 16–19: 68–68–69–69—274, T-2, $9,000

Canadian Open, July 30–Aug. 2: 71–67–71–70—279, 2nd, $4,000

Western Open, Aug. 6–9: 68–66–67–68—269, 2nd, $5,750

American Golf Classic, Aug. 20–23: 68–73–71–69—281, 3rd, $3,300

Carling World Open, Aug. 27–30: 70–71–67–71—279, 2nd, $17,000

Piccadilly World Match Play, Wentworth West, Oct. 9–11: Quarterfinals,
    defeated Peter Butler, 1 up; Semifinal, defeated Gary Player, 8 and 6;
    Final, defeated Neil Coles, 2 and 1. $14,000 (36-hole matches)

Sahara Invitational, Oct. 15–18: 67–72–69–76—284, T-19, $960

Cajun Classic, Nov. 19–22: 68–74–71–71—284, 4th, $1,500

Australian Wills Masters: 67–70–73–72—282, T-4, $503

PGA Tour summary: Official events entered 26, money $113,203, scor-
ing average 70.24

1965

Los Angeles Open, Jan. 8–11: 72–73–70–69—284, T-9, $1,975

Bing Crosby National Pro-Am, Jan. 21–24: 73–72–77–80—302, T-63, No
    Money

Bob Hope Desert Classic, Feb. 3–7: 70–70–72–67–70—349, T-2, $6,600

Pensacola Open, March 4–7: 71–73–73–67—284, T-11, $1,600

Greater Jacksonville Open, March 18–21: 74–70–72–76—292, T-29,
    $515

Greater Greensboro Open, April 1–4: 72–74–70–67—283, T-14, $1,450

Masters Tournament, April 8–11: 70–68–72–70—280, T-2, $10,200

Tournament of Champions, April 29–May 2: 66–69–71–71—277, 1st, $14,000

Colonial National Invitation, May 6–11: 73–74–70–70—287, T-17, $1,300

Greater New Orleans Open, May 13–16: 73–70–70–71—284, T-44, $258

Buick Open, June 3–6: 73–72–73–73—291, T-20, $996.87

Cleveland Open, June 10–13: 71–70–70–71—282, T-10, $2,505

U.S. Open, June 17–20: 76–76—152, Missed Cut

St. Paul Open, June 24–27: 66–69–70–72—277, T-7, $3,050

British Open, July 7–9: 70–71–75–79—295, 16th, $322

Canadian Open, July 14–17: 70–69–68–76—283, 23rd, $1,000

Thunderbird Classic, July 29–Aug. 1: 68–71–72–69—280, T-11, $2,125

Philadelphia Golf Classic, Aug. 5–8: 69–77–146, Withdrew

PGA Championship, Aug. 12–15: 72–75–74–73—294, T-33, $737.50

Carling World Open, Aug. 19–23: 69–73–70–69—281, 2nd, $17,000

American Golf Classic, Aug. 26–29: 70–70–74–70—284, 2nd, $12,000

Oklahoma City Open, Sept. 2–5: 75–70–78–70—293, T-16, $1,058.34

Piccadilly World Match Play, Wentworth West, Oct. 14–16: Quarterfinal, defeated Kel Nagle, 3 and 2; Semifinal, lost to Peter Thomson, 1 down. $5,600 (36-hole matches)

PGA National Four-Ball Championship, Dec. 8–11: 67–66–65–68—266, T-7, $2,100 (with Jack Nicklaus)

PGA Tour summary: Official events entered 22, money $57,770, scoring average 71.42

1966

Los Angeles Open, Jan. 6–9: 72–66–62–73—273, 1st, $11,000

Bing Crosby National Pro-Am, Jan. 20–23: 70–70–73–71—284, 2nd, $6,200

Lucky International Open, Jan. 27–31: 73–66–68–68—275, T-3, $3,037.50

Bob Hope Desert Classic, Feb. 2–6: 71–70–71–67–70—349, 2nd, $8,000, lost to Doug Sanders in one-hole, sudden-death playoff

Phoenix Open, Feb. 10–14: 71–74–72–74—291, T-34, $375

Doral Open, March 10–13: 69–70–71–71—281, T-4, $3,920

Florida Citrus Open, March 17–20: 75–70–72–71—288, T-36, $502.15

Greater Greensboro Open, March 31–April 3: 71–71–68–69—279, T-6, $3,433.33

Masters Tournament, April 7–11: 74–70–74–72—290, T-4, $5,700

Tournament of Champions, April 14–18: 74–70–70–69—283, 1st, $20,000, shot 69 to defeat Gay Brewer (73) in playoff

Greater New Orleans Open, May 12–16: 71–71—142, Withdrew

Buick Open, June 9–12: 73–74–72–70—289, T-8, $2,950

U.S. Open, June 16–20: 71–66–70–71—278, 2nd, $12,500, lost in playoff, 69–73, to Billy Casper

Western Open, June 23–26: 72–70–75–72—289, T-9, $2,400

British Open, July 6–9: 73–72–69–74—288, T-8, $924

PGA Championship, July 21–24: 75–73–71–68—287, T-6, $5,000

Cleveland Open, Aug. 4–7: 69–71–66–74—280, T-25, $800

Thunderbird Classic, Aug. 11–14: 72–72–70–72—286, T-11, $2,000

Insurance City Classic, Aug. 18–21: 68–67–70–77—282, T-56, No Money

Philadelphia Golf Classic, Aug. 25–28: 71–71–65–74—281, T-3, $6,100

Piccadilly World Match Play, Wentworth West, Oct. 6–8: Quarterfinal, defeated Roberto De Vicenzo, 10 and 8; Semifinal, lost to Gary Player, 2 and 1. $5,600 (36-hole matches)

Sahara Invitational, Oct. 12–15: 71–80–67–67—285, T-2, $9,750

Australian Open, Oct. 27–30: 67–70–66–73—276, 1st, $1,792

Dunlop International, Kensington, Australia, Nov. 3–6: 78–75–73–68—294, 2nd, $1,120, lost to Bob Stanton in two-hole, sudden-death playoff

Houston Champions International, Nov. 17–20: 70–68–68–69—275, 1st, $21,000

PGA National Team Championship, Dec. 7–10: 63–66–63–64—256, 1st, $25,000 (with Jack Nicklaus)

PGA Tour summary: Official events entered 22, money $110,468, scoring average 70.69

1967

Bing Crosby National Pro-Am, Jan. 19–22: 74–75–67–75—291, 3rd, $6,000

Los Angeles Open, Jan. 26–29: 70–64–67–68—269, 1st, $20,000

Bob Hope Desert Classic, Feb. 1–5: 73–72–68–76–73—362, T-32, $539

Tucson Open, Feb. 16–19: 66–67–67–73—273, 1st, $12,000

Doral Open, March 2–5: 67–72–69–71—279, T-10, $2,085.71

Florida Citrus Open, March 9–12: 67–69–71–68—275, T-2, $11,212.50

Greater Jacksonville Open, March 16–19: 75–73—148, Missed Cut

Greater Greensboro Open, March 30–April 2: 69–68–68–66—271, 3rd, $9,375

Masters Tournament, April 6–9: 73–73–70–69—285, 4th, $6,600

Tournament of Champions, April 13–16: 68–73–74–64—279, 2nd, $12,000

Greater Dallas Open, April 20–24: 76—76, Withdrew (illness)

Houston Champions International, May 4–7: 68–66–70–71—275, 2nd, $13,800

Colonial National Invitation, May 18–21: 73–73–67–71—284, T-6, $4,140

U.S. Open, June 15–18: 69–68–73–69—279, 2nd, $15,000

Cleveland Open, June 22–25: 67–68–70–73—278, T-9, $2,691

Canadian Open, June 29–July 2: 72–70–70–70—282, T-7, $6,032

PGA Championship, July 20–23: 70–71–72–74—287, T-14, $2,360

Western Open, Aug. 3–6: 72–70–70–71—283, T-23, $893.75

American Golf Classic, Aug. 10–13: 70–67–72–67—276, 1st, $20,000

Pennsylvania Open, Laurel Valley Golf Club, August: 75–69—144, 2nd, $500 (donated)

Westchester Classic, Aug. 24–27: 69–69–67–71—276, 5th, $10,750

Carling World Open, Sept. 1–4: 75–75—150, Missed Cut

Philadelphia Golf Classic, Sept. 14–17: 70–72–72–68—282, T-6, $3,454

Thunderbird Classic, Sept. 21–24: 71–71–72–69—283, 1st, $30,000

Piccadilly World Match Play, Wentworth West, Oct. 12–14: Quarterfinal, defeated George Knudson, 5 and 4; Semifinal, defeated Billy Casper, 3 and 2; Final, defeated Peter Thomson, 2 up. £5,000 (36-hole matches)

Sahara Invitational, Oct. 25–29: 76–68–68–72—284, T-34, $521.11

Hawaiian Open, Nov. 2–5: 72–74–74–72—292, T-19, $1,150

PGA Tour summary: Official events entered 25, money $184,065, scoring average 70.19

1968

Bing Crosby National Pro-Am, Jan. 11–14: 76–70–77–71—294, T-24, $622.22

Kaiser International, Jan. 18–21: 70–73–74–69—286, T-25, $906.25

Los Angeles Open, Jan. 25–28: 69–71–69–68—277, 2nd, $12,000

Bob Hope Desert Classic, Jan. 31–Feb. 4: 72–70–67–71–68—348, 1st, $20,000, defeated Deane Beman in two-hole, sudden-death playoff

Andy Williams San Diego Open, Feb. 8–11: 72–72–71–67—282, T-19, $1,725

Tucson Open, Feb. 22–25: 74–69–73–67—283, T-30, $625

Florida Citrus Open, March 14–17: 71–76—147, Missed Cut

Greater Jacksonville Open, March 28–31: 70–65–68–73—276, T-7, $3,100

Greater Greensboro Open, April 4–7: 69–71–66–67—273, T-5, $5,270.83

Masters Tournament, April 11–14: 72–79—151, Missed Cut

Byron Nelson Golf Classic, April 25–28: 71–68–69–70—278, T-6, $3,275

Memphis Open, May 23–26: 69–65–68–70—272, T-8, $2,620

Atlanta Classic, May 30–June 2: 76–70–73–75—294, T-45, $226.71

U.S. Open, June 13–16: 73–74–79–75—301, 59th, $720

Canadian Open, June 20–23: 76–73—149, Missed Cut

Cleveland Open, June 27–30: 75–71–71–71—288, T-39, $457.42

British Open, July 10–13: 77–71–72–77—297, T-10, $964

PGA Championship, July 18–21: 71–69–72–70—282, T-2, $12,500

Western Open, Aug. 1–4: 74–70–73–71—288, T-40, $544.37

American Golf Classic, Aug. 8–11: 70–70–68–76—284, T-14, $2,000

Westchester Classic, Aug. 15–18: 71–71–66–70—278, T-11, $5,500

Thunderbird Classic, Aug. 29–Sept. 1: 71–70–74–71—286, T-10, $3,450

Kemper Open, Sept. 12–15: 69–70–70–67—276, 1st, $30,000

PGA Team Championship, Sept. 19–22: 64–72–69–68—273, T-15, $1,600
(with Jack Nicklaus)

Piccadilly World Match Play, Wentworth West, Oct. 10–13: Quarterfinal,
defeated Brian Huggett, 2 up; Semifinal, lost to Bob Charles, 7 and 6.
£2,000 (36-hole matches)

Australian Open, Oct. 24–27: 69–70–69–68—276, 5th

Australian PGA, Oct. 31–Nov. 3: 70–77–75–71—293, T-6

Hawaiian Open, Nov. 7–10. 71 71 71 69   282, T 11, $2,575

PGA Tour summary: Official events entered 23, money $114,603, scoring
average 70.19

1969

Los Angeles Open, Jan. 9–12: 72–68–71–73—284, T-17, $1,065.45

Kaiser International, Jan. 16–19: 69–68—137, 3rd, $4,785 (rain shortened)

Bing Crosby National Pro-Am, Jan. 23–26: 74–72–74–73—293, T-37,
$556.71

Bob Hope Desert Classic, Feb. 5–9: 72–73–69–72–70—356, T-26, $755

Doral Open, Feb. 27–March 2: 68–69–73–73—283, T-10, $3,450

Greater Jacksonville Open, March 20–23: 70–68–72–71—281, T-6, $3,400

National Airlines Open, March 27–30: 69–73–69–72—283, T-12, $3,428.57

Masters Tournament, April 10–13: 73–75–70–74—292, T-27, $1,450

Tournament of Champions, April 17–20: 69–74–75–71—289, T-3, $10,000

Byron Nelson Golf Classic, April 24–27: 69–75–69–69—282, T-8, $2,825

Colonial National Invitation, May 15–18: 73–68–80–69—290, T-37,
$574.50

Atlanta Classic, May 22–25: 68–73–74–72—287, T-25, $851.14

U.S. Open, June 12–15: 70–73–69–72—284, T-6, $5,000

Kemper Open, June 19–22: 73–71–70–66—280, T-5, $5,193.75

Cleveland Open, June 26–29: 74–69–66–70—279, T-9, $2,438.33

IVB-Philadelphia Classic, July 17–20: 73–69–73–71—286, T-20, $1,345.50

American Golf Classic, July 24–27: 75–68–68–71—282, T-14, $2,062.50

Westchester Classic, July 31–Aug. 3: 71–74–70–74—289, T-53, $476.19

Greater Milwaukee Open, Aug. 7–10: 76–71–68–72—287, T-23, $910

PGA Championship, Aug. 14–17: 82—82, Withdrew (right hip)

Sahara Invitational, Oct. 16–19: 69–75–68–73—285, T-34, $493.33

San Francisco Open, Oct. 23–26: 70–67–73–67—277, T-27, $681.43

Kaiser International, Oct. 30–Nov. 2: 71–69–68–69—277, T-8, $3,803.33

Hawaiian Open, Nov. 6–9: 70–71–72–73—286, T-27, $817.85

Heritage Golf Classic, Nov. 27–30: 68–71–70–74—283, 1st, $20,000

Danny Thomas–Diplomat Classic, Dec. 4–7: 68–67–70–65—270, 1st, $25,000

PGA Tour summary: Official events entered 26, money $105,128, scoring average 70.99

1970

Los Angeles Open, Jan. 8–11: 67–72–72–73—284, T-39, $390

Bing Crosby National Pro-Am, Jan. 22–25: 69–72–72–79—292, T-44, $328.78

Bob Hope Desert Classic, Feb. 4–8: 68–71–70–69–70—348, 4th, $5,850

Doral-Eastern Open, Feb. 26–March 1: 71–73–73–75—292, T-23, $1,266

Florida Citrus Invitational, March 5–8: 64–72–64–72—272, T-2, $13,875

Monsanto Open, March 12–15: 74–70–71–69—284, T-11, $2,850

Greater Jacksonville Open, March 19–22: 70–77–71–73—291, T-32, $600

Greater Greensboro Open, April 2–5: 64–67–74–71—276, T-5, $6,540

Masters Tournament, April 9–12: 75–73–74–73—295, T-36, $1,575

Tournament of Champions, April 23–26: 70–72–69–70—281, 5th, $7,400

Byron Nelson Golf Classic, April 30–May 3: 66–71–68–69—274, 2nd,
$11,400, lost to Jack Nicklaus in one-hole, sudden-death playoff

Atlanta Classic, May 21–24: 69–70–70–68—277, T-3, $6,081.25

Kemper Open, June 4–7: 69–69–74–71—283, T-11, $2,940

Western Open, June 11–14: 67–69–71–72—279, 8th, $3,830

U.S. Open, June 18–21: 79–74–75–77—305, T-54, $850

British Open, July 8–11: 68–72–76–74—290, 12th, $2,880

National Four-Ball Championship, July 23–26: 61–67–64–67—259, 1st,
$20,000 (with Jack Nicklaus)

Westchester Classic, July 30–Aug. 2: 72–69–69–68—278, T-6, $6,910.72

PGA Championship, Aug. 13–16: 70–72–69–70—281, T-2, $18,500

Dow Jones Open, Aug. 27–30: 73–70–77–75—295, T-69, $480

Lancôme Tournament of Champions, Paris, Oct. 16–18: 68–71–68—207,
T-2, $4,320

Dunlop International, Australia: 71–72–72–72—287, T-12

Heritage Golf Classic, Nov. 26–29: 73–70–72–71—286, T-3, $7,733.33

Coral Springs Open, Dec. 3–6: 72–70–68–66—276, T-6, $3,890

Bahama Islands Open, Dec. 10–13: 68–69–75–69—281, 8th, $3,830

PGA Tour summary: Official events entered 22, money $128,853, scoring average 70.9

1971

Los Angeles Open, Jan. 7–10: 71–71–69–71—282, 1-19, $1,265

Bing Crosby National Pro-Am, Jan. 14–17: 72–68–69–71—280, 2nd,
$15,400

Phoenix Open, Jan. 21–24: 68–67–66–66—267, T-16, $1,625

Hawaiian Open, Feb. 4–7: 67–69–68–73—277, T-4, $8,266

Bob Hope Desert Classic, Feb. 10–14: 67–71–66–68–70—342, 1st,
$28,000, defeated Ray Floyd in one-hole, sudden-death playoff

PGA Championship, Feb. 24–28: 75–71–70–73—289, T-18, $2,700

Doral-Eastern Open, March 4–7: 75–72–70–70—287, T-28, $1,000

Florida Citrus Invitational, March 11–14: 66–68–68–68—270, 1st, $30,000

Greater Jacksonville Open, March 18–21: 71–77–71–72—291, T-19, $1,277

National Airlines Open, March 25–28: 70–69–71–69—279, T-6, $6,225

Masters Tournament, April 8–11: 73–72–71–73—289, T-18, $2,650

Tournament of Champions, April 22–25: 71–74–77–73—295, T-14, $3,100

Byron Nelson Golf Classic, May 6–9: 70–71–68–72—281, T-10, $2,482

Houston/Champions International, May 13–16: 71–75–73–75—294, T-48, $260

Kemper Open, June 10–13: 70–71–68–72—281, T-12, $2,900

U.S. Open, June 17–20: 73–68–73–74—288, T-24, $1,500

Canadian Open, July 1–4: 70–76–70–71—287, T-11, $3,150

Westchester Classic, July 22–25: 64–70–68–68—270, 1st, $50,000

National Team Championship, July 29–Aug. 1: 62–64–65–66—257, 1st, $20,000 (with Jack Nicklaus)

American Golf Classic, Aug. 5–8: 70–73–72–67—282, T-6, $4,875

U.S. Match Play Championship, Aug. 25–29: Round 1, defeated Bruce Devlin, 68–71; Round 2, defeated Mike Hill, 68–71; Round 3, defeated Dave Eichelberger, 69–72; Quarterfinals, lost to Bruce Crampton, 69–72. $5,000

Piccadilly World Match Play, Wentworth West, Oct. 7–9: Quarterfinal, defeated by Bob Charles, 37 holes. £1,500 (36-hole match)

Lancôme Trophy, Paris, Oct. 15–17: 66–65–71—202, 1st, $20,000

Sahara Invitational, Oct. 28–31: 74–74–69–73—290, T-20, $1,269

Rolex Watch Classic, Tokyo, Nov. 5–6: 70–73—143, T-2, $616

Sea Pines Heritage Golf Classic, Nov. 25–28: 69–74–69–74—286, 5th, $4,500

Walt Disney World Open, Dec. 2–6: 71–66–71–70—278, T-3, $8,850

PGA Tour summary: Official events entered 24, money $209,604, scoring average 70.6

1972

Glen Campbell Los Angeles Open, Jan. 6–9: 69–71–71–70—281, T-23, $1,012.86

Hawaiian Open, Feb.3–6: 67–76–70–66—279, T-11, $3,800

Bob Hope Desert Classic, Feb. 9–13: 69–68–76–66–69—348, 6th, $5,220

Jackie Gleason Inverrary Classic, Feb. 24–27: 74–68–80–79—301, 75th, $400

Florida Citrus Invitational, March 9–12: 72–75—147, Missed Cut

Greater Jacksonville Open, March 16–19: 71–72–75–69—287, T-7, $3,842.50

Greater Greensboro Open, March 30-April 2: 69–66–68–70—273, T-3, $9,750

Masters Tournament, April 6–9: 70–75–74–81—300, T-33, $1,675

Tournament of Champions, April 20–23: 74–74–70–71—289, T-9, $5,033.34

Byron Nelson Golf Classic, April 27–May 1: 70–71–67–68—276, 6th, $4,500

Danny Thomas Memphis Classic, May 18–21: 71–71–74–73—289, T-10, $4,025

Kemper Open, June 1–4: 70–75–71–72—288, T-51, $233.34

U.S. Open, June 15–18: 77–68–73–76—294, 3rd, $10,000

Canadian Open, July 6–9: 71–71–71–72—285, T-23, $1,293.75

British Open, July 12–15: 73–73–69–71—286, T-7, $4,322

American Golf Classic, July 20–23: 68–70–70–74—282, T-10, $3,600

National Team Championship, July 27–30: 66–72–67–70—275, T-30, $710 (with Jack Lewis)

PGA Championship, Aug. 3–6: 69–75–72–73—289, T-16, $3,262.50

Westchester Classic, Aug. 10–13: 73–73—146, Missed Cut

U.S. Match Play Championship, Aug. 26–27: Round 1, lost to Don Bies, 5 and 4, $5,000

John Player Classic, Turnberry, Scotland, Sept. 27–30: 71–73–73–74—291, T-7

Lancôme Trophy, Paris, Oct. 5–8: 74–68–73–70—285, 4th, $2,500

Kaiser International, Oct. 19–22: 66–67–75–74—282, T-11, $2,681.25

Sahara Invitational, Oct. 26–29: 65–69–71–69—274, 2nd, $15,400

Rolex Golf Classic, Kawasaki City, Nov. 10–11: 76–78—154, 19th, $130

Walt Disney World Open, Nov. 30–Dec. 3: 69–77—146, Missed Cut

PGA Tour summary: Official events entered 22, money $84,181, scoring average 71.4

1973

Glen Campbell Los Angeles Open, Jan. 4–7: 75–71–71–69—286, T-24, $1,129.33

Bing Crosby National Pro-Am, Jan. 25–28: 72–73–76–76—297, T-49, $442.80

Hawaiian Open, Feb. 1–4: 70–75–69–70—284, T-22, $1,740

Bob Hope Desert Classic, Feb. 7–11: 71–66–69–68–69—343, 1st, $32,000

Jackie Gleason Inverrary Classic, Feb. 22–25: 74–71–74–73—292, T-49, $663

Florida Citrus Open, March 1–4: 70–74—144, Missed Cut

Greater New Orleans Open, March 22–25: 72–75–73–72—292, T-56, $256.14

Greater Greensboro Open, March 29–April 2: 69–68–70–69—276, T-18, $2,092.37

Masters Tournament, April 5–9: 77–72–76–70—295, T-24, $2,100

Tournament of Champions, April 19–22: 70–71–77–75—293, T-19, $3,646.50

Byron Nelson Golf Classic, April 26–29: 71–70–71–77—289, T-44, $441.42

Kemper Open, May 31–June 3: 68–73–71–72—284, T-34, $905.45

U.S. Open, June 14–17: 71–71–68–72—282, T-4, $9,000

American Golf Classic, June 21–24: 68–71–71–70—280, T-9, $3,680

Western Open, June 28–July 1: 66–71–68–71—276, T-7, $5,381.50

British Open, July 11–14: 72–76–70–72—290, T-14, $2,470

Canadian Open, July 26–29: 70–75–70–70—285, T-10, $4,025

Westchester Classic, Aug. 2–5: 71–70–69–69—279, T-19, $2,515.63

PGA Championship, Aug. 9–12: 76–74—150, Missed Cut

Sammy Davis Jr. Greater Hartford Open, Aug. 31–Sept. 3: 68–65–67–
66—266, T-3, $9,750

Sea Pines Heritage Classic, Sept. 13–16: 70–73–71–70—284, T-10, $3,300

John Player Classic, Turnberry, Scotland, Sept. 26–29: 71–76–80–74—301,
T-9

Lancôme Trophy, Paris, Oct. 4–7: 74–71–73–70—288, 8th

Sahara Invitational, Oct. 25–28: 71–67–72–73—283, T-20, $1,338.66

World Open, Nov. 8–11, 14–17: 73–70–77–75–73–68–74–76—586, T-25,
$2,867.43

ABC Cup, U.S. vs. Japan, Osaka, Nov. 22–25: 75–72–74—221, 3rd,
$4,326

PGA Tour summary: Official events entered 22, money $89,457, scoring
average 71.33

1974

Hawaiian Open, Jan. 31–Feb. 3: 72–72–76–72—292, T-71, No Money

Bob Hope Desert Classic, Feb. 6–10: 76–70–74–69–73—362, T-49,
$381.58

Glen Campbell Los Angeles Open, Feb. 14–17: 68–73–74–76—291, T-32,
$849

Florida Citrus Open, Feb. 28–March 3: 68–73–72–74—287, T-41, $540

Greater Jacksonville Open, March 14–17: 70–69–77–71—287, T-25, $1,110

Sea Pines Heritage Classic, March 21–24: 73–74–67–73—287, T-14, $3,100

Greater Greensboro Open, April 4–7: 74–72—146, Missed Cut

Masters Tournament, April 11–14: 76–71–70–67—284, T-11, $3,375

Chunichi Crowns, Nagoya Prefecture, Japan, April 26–29: 69–74–66–
75—284, T-23, $733

Byron Nelson Golf Classic, May 2–5: 71–74—145, Missed Cut

Colonial National Invitation, May 16–19: 74–73—147, Missed Cut

Kemper Open, May 30–June 2: 70–76—146, Missed Cut

U.S. Open, June 13–16: 73–70–73–76—292, T-5, $8,000

American Golf Classic, June 20–23: 70–73–73–69—285, T-13, $2,975

Western Open, June 27–30: 74–72–74–74—294, T-5, $6,925

Canadian Open, July 25–28: 69–71–68–69—277, T-13, $3,400

PGA Championship, Aug. 8–11: 72–75–70–72—289, T-28, $1,565

Westchester Classic, Aug. 22–25: 68–73–71–80—292, T-67, $406.50

Tournament Players Championship, Aug. 30–Sept. 2: 73–78—151, Missed
Cut

World Open, Sept. 12–15: 78–72—150, Missed Cut

Lancôme Trophy, Paris, Oct. 3–6: 73–71–71–77—298, 4th, $3,000

Walt Disney World National Team, Oct. 31–Nov. 3: 67–63–66–67—263,
T-25, $1,115 (with Lanny Wadkins)

ABC Cup, U.S. vs. Japan, Osaka, Nov. 28–Dec 1: 74–75–73—222, 11th,
$1,500

PGA Tour summary: Official events entered 21, money $36,293, scoring
average 73.37

1975

Dean Martin Tucson Open, Jan. 16–19: 72–71–67–70—280, 10th, $5,000

Hawaiian Open, Jan. 30–Feb. 2: 69–67–69–71—276, 3rd, $15,620

Bob Hope Desert Classic, Feb. 5–9: 68–72–71–72–70—353, T-20, $1,638.40

Glen Campbell Los Angeles Open, Feb. 20–23: 70–78–73–69—290, T-25,
$1,155

Jackie Gleason Inverrary Classic, Feb. 27–March 2: 68–66–71–74—279,
T-7, $7,995

Florida Citrus Open, March 6–9: 72–69–75–73—289, T-42, $660

Greater Jacksonville Open, March 20–23: 68–68–73–75—284, T-17,
$1,808.57

Sea Pines Heritage Classic, March 27–30: 74–75–71–68—288, T–23, $1,688

Greater Greensboro Open, April 3–6: 77–73–72–66—288, T–20, $2,305

Masters Tournament, April 10–13: 69–71–75–72—287, T–13, $3,250

Spanish Open, April 16–19: 72–69–69–73—283, 1st, $9,000

Houston Open, May 1–4: 74–70–76–69—289, T–53, $322.56

British PGA Championship, May 23–26: 71–70–73–71—285, 1st, $24,000

Atlanta Golf Classic, May 29–June 1: 75–79—154, Missed Cut

Kemper Open, June 5–8: 72–77—149, Missed Cut

U.S. Open, June 19–22: 69–75–73–73—290, T–9, $5,000

Western Open, June 26–29: 68–79–73–72—292, T–21, $1,960

British Open, July 9–12: 74–72–69–73—288, T–16, $2,760

Canadian Open, July 24–27: 68–73–69–67—277, 4th, $9,400

PGA Championship, Aug. 8–10: 73–72–73–73—291, T–33, $1,215

Tournament Players Championship, Aug. 21–24: 71–78—149, Missed Cut

World Open, Sept. 11–14: 73–74—147, Missed Cut

Lancôme Trophy, Paris, Oct. 9–12: 69–74–75–70—288, 5th, $2,000

Walt Disney World National Team, Oct. 23–26: 68–67—135, Missed Cut
   (with Leonard Thompson)

PGA Tour summary: Official events entered 20, money $59,017, scoring average 71.8

1976

Tucson Open, Jan. 8–11: 77–73—150, Missed Cut

Hawaiian Open, Jan. 29–Feb. 1: 68–71–69–71—279, T–21, $2,185

Bob Hope Desert Classic, Feb. 4–8: 74–64–76, Withdrew (Deacon's death)

Glen Campbell Los Angeles Open, Feb. 19–22: 72–69–76–74—291, T–41, $647.29

Tournament Players Championship, Feb. 26–March 1: 72–73–68–76—289, T–51, $705

Florida Citrus Open, March 4–7: 74–72—146, Missed Cut

Greater Jacksonville Open, March 18–21: 75–72—147, Missed Cut

Masters Tournament, April 8–11: 74–81—155, Missed Cut

Tallahassee Open, April 15–18: 71–72–72–69—284, T-15, $1,160

Houston Open, April 29–May 2: 71–75—146, T-68, $196.54

Byron Nelson Golf Classic, May 6–9: 71–72–73–72—288, T-44, $565.56

British PGA Championship, May 28–31: 72–68–71–71—282, T-5, $3,000

Kemper Open, June 10–13: 74–70–74–71—289, T-47, $657.60

U.S. Open, June 17–20: 75–75–75–75—300, T-50, $1,090

British Open, July 7–10: 75–72–76–77—300, T-55, $325

Westchester Classic, July 15–18: 69–67–72–77—285, T-58, $600

Canadian Open, July 22–25: 66–71–74–70—281, T-18, $2,162.50

PGA Championship, Aug. 12–15: 71–76–68–72—287, T-15, $3,400

Sammy Davis Jr. Greater Hartford Open, Aug. 19–22: 68–70–74–66—278, T-21, $1,995

American Golf Classic, Aug. 26–29: 71–74–73–68—286, T-23, $1,653.33

Piccadilly World Match Play, Wentworth West, Oct. 7–9: Quarterfinal, defeated by Gary Player, 5 and 4. £5,000 (36-hole match)

Lancôme Trophy, Paris, Oct. 14–17: 75–70–69–70—284, 2nd, $9,000

Walt Disney World National Team, Nov. 4–7: 65–71—136, Missed Cut (with Leonard Thompson)

Pepsi-Cola Mixed Team Championship, Dec. 16–19: 73–73–67–71—284, T-7, $2,016.67 (with Sandra Palmer)

PGA Tour summary: Official events entered 19, money $17,017, scoring average 72.0

1977

Bing Crosby National Pro-Am, Jan. 20–23: 74–71–74—219, Missed Cut

Andy Williams San Diego Open, Jan. 27–30: 74–71—145, Missed Cut

Hawaiian Open, Feb. 3–6: 73–71–66–74—284, T-30, $1,490.40

Bob Hope Desert Classic, Feb. 9–13: 73–68–69–74–71—355, T-25, $1,570

Glen Campbell Los Angeles Open, Feb. 17–20: 76–78—154, Missed Cut

Florida Citrus Open, March 3–7: 71–72–69–75—287, T-48, $494.28

Tournament Players Championship, March 17–20: 78–75–74–75—302, T-40, $1,110

Heritage Golf Classic, March 24–27: 75–74—149, Missed Cut

Masters Tournament, April 7–10: 76–71–71–70—288, T-24, $2,200

Houston Open, April 28–May 1: 72–74–71–67—284, T-17, $2,700

Byron Nelson Golf Classic, May 5–8: 73–72–71–73—289, T-42, $680

Memorial Tournament, May 19–22: 79–74–70–73—296, T-35, $1,111

British PGA Championship, May 25–28: 73–71–77–73—294, T-20, £623.33

Kemper Open, June 2–5: 71–73–71–69—284, T-19, $2,675

U.S. Open, June 16–19: 70–72–73–72—287, T-19, $1,887.50

Western Open, June 23–26: 77–73–73–73—296, T-43, $660

British Open, July 6–9: 73–73–67–69—282, 7th, $6,375

Canadian Open, July 21–24: 72–78–81—231, Withdrew

PGA Championship, Aug. 11–14: 72–73–73–73—291, T-19, $2,700

Colgate Hall of Fame Classic, Aug. 25–28: 71–71–71–73—286, T-57, $525

B.C. Open, Sept. 8–11: 65–69–75–74—283, T-22, $1,780

Lancôme Trophy, Paris, Oct. 13–16: 75–73–75–69—292, 8th, $1,000

Pensacola Open, Oct. 27–30: 73–68–71–70—282, T-41, $367.26

Walt Disney World National Team, Nov. 3–6: 71–66—137, Missed Cut (with Leonard Thompson)

Australian Open, Nov. 17–20: 76–77–74–74—301, T-34, $963

Pepsi Cola Mixed Team Championship, Dec. 1–4: 69–69–70–67—275, T-3, $6,018.67 (with Sandra Palmer)

PGA Tour summary: Official events entered 20, money $21,950, scoring average 72.49

1978

Phoenix Open, Jan. 12–15: 69–68–71–67—275, 5th, $8,200

Bing Crosby National Pro-Am, Jan. 20–23: 75–77–73—225, Missed Cut

Hawaiian Open, Feb. 2–5: 75–74—149, Missed Cut

Bob Hope Desert Classic, Feb. 8–11: 69–70–75–75–74—363, T-67, $365

Florida Citrus Open, March 2–6: 65–73–71–71—280, T-14, $3,400

Tournament Players Championship, March 16–19: 74–78–76–85—313, T-77, $750

Masters Tournament, April 6–9: 73–69–74–77—293, T-37, $1,900

Houston Open, April 20–23: 70–74–68–72—284, T-49, $492

Byron Nelson Golf Classic, May 4–7: 66–77–74–74—291, T-63, $360

Memorial Tournament, May 18–21: 77–71–75–76—299, T-46, $910

Kemper Open, June 1–4: 67–70–75–71—283, T-20, $3,300

U.S. Open, June 15–18: 76–75—151, Missed Cut

Canadian Open, June 22–25: 70–76–73–68—287, T-8, $5,803.58

British Open, July 12–15: 71–71–75–75—292, T-34, $900

PGA Championship, Aug. 3–6: 78–74—152, Missed Cut

Labatt's Canadian PGA, Aug. 17–20: 72–68–68–77—285, 6th, $3,900

Colgate Hall of Fame Classic, Aug. 24–27: 71–75–69–75—290, T-28, $1,592.25

PGA Tour summary: Official events entered 15, money $27,073, scoring average 72.87

1979

Bob Hope Desert Classic, Jan. 10–14: 72–74–77–71—294, Missed Cut

Bing Crosby National Pro-Am, Feb. 1–4: 74–76–77—227, Missed Cut

Hawaiian Open, Feb. 8–11: 73–74—147, Missed Cut

Joe Garagiola Tucson Open, Feb. 15–18: 72–75—147, Missed Cut

Bay Hill Citrus Classic, March 1–4: 70–74–70–80—294, 59th, $555

Tournament Players Championship, March 22–25: 72–75–79–77—303, T-50, $950.86

Sea Pines Heritage Classic, March 29–April 1: 73–70–71–75—289, T-38, $1,230

Masters Tournament, April 12–15: 74–72—146, Missed Cut

Houston Open, May 3–6: 73–67–73–73—286, 70th, $600

Byron Nelson Golf Classic, May 10–13: 68–72–76–73—289, T-45, $903

Memorial Tournament, May 24–27: 75–81–74–73—303, T-42, $1,270

Kemper Open, May 31–June 3: 70–73–74–69—286, T-47, $899

U.S. Open, June 14–17: 76–73–75–81—305, T-59, $1,235

Canadian Open, June 21–24: 73–80—153, Missed Cut

PGA Championship, Aug. 2–5: 81–74—155, Missed Cut

German Open, Aug. 16–19: 75–73–73–72—292, T-34, £245.69

Southern Open, Oct. 11–14: 74–69–68–71—282, T-25, $1,633.34

Lancôme Trophy, Oct. 25–28: 72–75–73–72—292, 8th, £758.29

Brazilian Open, Nov. 29–Dec. 2: 67–69–70–66—272, T-3, $3,300

Sun City Classic, Bophuthatswana, South Africa, Dec. 12–15: 69–76–73–
71—289, 11th, 2,450 rand

PGA Tour summary: Official events entered 16, money $9,276, scoring average 73.96

1980

Bob Hope Desert Classic, Jan. 9–13: 70–71–75–78—294, Missed Cut

Bing Crosby National Pro-Am, Jan. 31–Feb. 3: 75–72–77—224, Missed Cut

Hawaiian Open, Feb. 7–10: 71–70–71–69—281, T-35, $1,532.15

Bay Hill Classic, Feb. 28–March 2: 76–71–74–85—306, T-69, $600

Sea Pines Heritage, March 27–30: 75–69–71–78—293, T-46, $874

Masters Tournament, April 10–13: 73–73–73–69—288, T-24, $3,025

Michelob Houston Open, May 1–4: 71–69–72–64—276, T-19, $4,242

Memorial Tournament, May 21–25: 77–75—152, Missed Cut

Kemper Open, May 29–June 1: 74–70–73–73—290, T-42, $1,287

U.S. Open, June 12–15: 73–73–77–78—301, 61st, $1,300

British Open, July 17–20: 76–74—150, Missed Cut

PGA Championship, Aug. 7–10: 74–74–78–76—302, T-72, $700

Canadian PGA Championship, Aug. 14–17: 68–68–64–71—271, 1st, $20,000

Southern Open, Oct. 2–5: 66–69–73–72—280, T-13, $3,029.09

Pensacola Open, Oct. 9–12: 70–77—147, Missed Cut

Disney World National Team Championship, Oct. 16–19: 68–67–65—200, Missed Cut (with Larry Nelson)

U.S. vs. Japan ABC Cup Matches, Hyogo, Nov. 6–9: 72–76–78–78—304, 17th, 1,050,000 yen

Rolex World Mixed Classic, Yokohama: Nov. 10–11: 75–70–73–75—293, 7th, 1.5 million yen (United States team with Laura Baugh)

PGA Tour summary: Official events entered 14, money $16,589

1981

Bob Hope Desert Classic, Jan. 14–18: 72–70–73–70–76—361, 71st, $545

Phoenix Open, Jan. 21–24: 69–72–74–70—285, T-69, $585

Hawaiian Open, Feb. 11–14: 73–75—148, Missed Cut

Bay Hill Classic, Feb. 26–March 1: 73–72–73–76—294, T-63, $639

Tournament Players Championship, March 19–22: 75–74–74–73—296, T-45, $1,144

Masters Tournament, April 9–12: 75–78—153, Missed Cut

Michelob Houston Open, April 30–May 2: 73–69–76—218, T-74, $501.37 (rain shortened)

Atlanta Classic, June 4–7: 75–73—148, Missed Cut

U.S. Open, June 18–21: 77–78—155, Missed Cut

Canadian PGA Championship, June 25–28: 78–73–78–77—306, T-49, $190

British Open, July 16–19: 72–74–73–71—290, T-23, $2,437

PGA Championship, Aug. 6–9: 74–73–74–77—298, 76th, $750

Buick Open, Aug. 20–23: 77–75—152, Missed Cut

Southern Open, Oct. 8–11: 74–76—150, Missed Cut

Disney World National Team Championship, Oct. 22–25: 64–63–68—195, Missed Cut (with Larry Nelson)

PGA Tour summary: Official events entered 13, money $4,164

1982

Bob Hope Desert Classic, Jan. 13–17: 75–72–71–71—289, Missed Cut

Phoenix Open, Jan. 21–25: 74–73—147, Missed Cut

Hawaiian Open, Feb. 11–14: 71–73–69–72—285, T-22, $2,853.75

Australian Masters, Feb. 18–21: 76–73–74–77—300, T-31, $690 (Aus.)

Bay Hill Classic, March 4–7: 76–74—150, Missed Cut

Tournament Players Championship, March 18–21: 72–77—149, Missed Cut

Sea Pines Heritage, March 25–28: 76–74—150, Missed Cut

Masters Tournament, April 8–11: 75–76–78–80—309, 47th, $1,500

Colonial National Invitation, May 13–16: 68–73–78–76—295, T-76, $654.50

Memorial Tournament, May 27–30: 72–72–73–78—295, T-58, $1,612.50

U.S. Open, June 17–20: 81–75—156, Missed Cut

British Open, July 15–18: 71–73–78–74—296, T-27, $2,736

PGA Championship, Aug. 5–8: 74–76—150, Missed Cut

Lancôme Trophy, Oct. 21–24: 73–72–68–68—281, T-4, £3,384.10

Johnnie Walker Trophy, Oct. 28–31: 71–75–77–74—297, 10th, $1,300

PGA Tour summary: Official events entered 11, money $6,621

1983

Glen Campbell Los Angeles Open, Jan. 13–16: 66–69–68–72—275, T-10, $7,800

Bob Hope Desert Classic, Jan. 19–23: 71–74–73–73—291, Missed Cut

Hawaiian Open, Feb. 10–13: 77–70—147, Missed Cut

Isuzu–Andy Williams San Diego Open, Feb. 17–20: 73–70–69–70—282, T-32, $1,624.29

Bay Hill Classic, March 10–13: 78–85—163, Missed Cut

Tournament Players Championship, March 25–28: 77–72–76–74—299, T-54, $1,617

Masters Tournament, April 7–10: 68–74–76–78—296, T-36, $2,450

Memorial Tournament, May 26–29: 73–81—154, Missed Cut

U.S. Open, June 16–19: 74–75–78–76—303, T-60, $1,907

Canadian PGA, July 7–10: 73–74–69–70—286, T-12, $2,000

British Open, July 14–17: 72–74–68–75—289, T-56, $1,087

PGA Championship, Aug. 4–7: 74–73–74–73—294, T-67, $1,505.80

Panasonic Las Vegas Pro Celebrity Classic, Sept. 14–18: 75–76–72–79—
    302, Missed Cut

Suntory World Match Play, Wentworth West, Oct. 6–9: Round 1, Seve
    Ballesteros defeated Arnold Palmer, 21 holes. £5,000

Kapalua Invitational, Nov. 2–5: 70–71–71–75—287, T-25, $2,700

Skins Game, Desert Highlands, Nov. 26–27: 2nd, 8 skins, $140,000

World Mixed Championship, Dec. 15–18: 145–65–71—281, T-6, $3,250
    (with Laura Baugh)

PGA Tour summary: Official events entered 11, money $16,904

1984

Bob Hope Classic, Jan. 11–15: 75–77–72–69—293, Missed Cut

Bay Hill Classic, March 15–18: 72–71–74–78—295, T-68, $812

Tournament Players Championship, March 29–April 1: 72–76–76–77—
    301, T-66, $1,640

Masters Tournament, April 12–15: 77–76—153, Missed Cut

Memorial Tournament, May 24–27: 75–79—154, Missed Cut

Anheuser-Busch Golf Classic, July 12–15: 76–73—149, Missed Cut

British Open, July 19–22: 76–77—153, Missed Cut

PGA Championship, Aug. 16–19: 79–73—152, Missed Cut

Walt Disney World Golf Classic, Oct. 18–21: 71–71–74—216, Missed Cut

Skins Game, Desert Highlands, Nov. 24–25: T-3, 0 skins, $0

PGA Tour summary: Official events entered 8, money $2,452

1985

Bob Hope Classic, Jan. 9–13: 70–70–72–74—286, Missed Cut

Hawaiian Open, Feb. 7–10: 74–74—148, Missed Cut

Hertz Bay Hill Classic, March 7–10: 78–73—151, Missed Cut

Tournament Players Championship, March 28–31: 74–72–75–76—297,
    T-69, $1,791

Masters Tournament, April 11–14: 83–72—155, Missed Cut

PGA Championship, Aug. 8–11: 75–72–75–76—298, T-65, $1,536

Skins Game, Bear Creek, Nov. 30–Dec. 1: 3rd, 4 skins, $80,000

   PGA Tour summary: Official events entered 6, money $3,327

1986

Bob Hope Chrysler Classic, Jan. 15–19: 74–74–69–71—288, Missed Cut

Hertz Bay Hill Classic, March 13–16: 78—78, Missed Cut (rain
    shortened)

Tournament Players Championship, March 27–30: 75–77—152, Missed Cut

Masters Tournament, April 10–13: 80–76—156, Missed Cut

PGA Championship, Aug. 7–10: 75–77—152, Missed Cut

The International, Aug. 14–18: Stableford format, Missed Cut, First
    Round

Fred Meyer Challenge, Aug. 18–19: Semifinals (Best-Ball): Greg
    Norman–Gary Player defeat Arnold Palmer–Tom Watson, 64–72.
    3rd-place match, Palmer-Watson defeat Fuzzy Zoeller–Fred Couples,
    66–68, $50,000.

Skins Game, TPC at PGA West, Nov. 29–30: 3rd, 1 skin, $25,000

   PGA Tour summary: Official events entered 6, money $0

1987

Bob Hope Chrysler Classic, Jan. 14–18: 73–70–71–77—291, Missed Cut

Hertz Bay Hill Classic, March 12–15: 77–79—156, Missed Cut

Masters Tournament, April 9–12: 83–77—160, Missed Cut

British Open, July 16–19: 75–78—153, Missed Cut

PGA Championship, Aug. 6–9: 76–75–79–76—306, T-65, $1,650

Fred Meyer Challenge, Aug. 17–18: 68–67—135, 7th (with Greg Norman, Best-Ball)

Skins Game, TPC at PGA West, Nov. 28–29: 4th, 0 skin, $0

JCPenney Classic, Dec. 3–6: 67–74–70–69—280, T-31, $1,962 (with Tammie Green)

PGA Tour summary: Official events entered 4, money $1,650

1988

Bob Hope Chrysler Classic, Jan. 20–24: 71–74–71–70—286, Missed Cut

Hertz Bay Hill Classic, March 17–20: 72–74—146, Missed Cut

Masters Tournament, April 7–10: 80–77—157, Missed Cut

GTE Byron Nelson Golf Classic, May 12–15: 70–75—145, Withdrew (rib cage pull)

PGA Championship, Aug. 11–14: 74–76—150, Missed Cut

Fred Meyer Challenge, Aug. 22–23: 64–65—129, T-3 (with Peter Jacobsen, Best-Ball)

PGA Tour summary: Official events entered 5, money $0

1989

Bob Hope Chrysler Classic, Jan. 11–15: 73–77–74–77—301, Missed Cut

Nestle Invitational, March 9–12: 83–74—157, Missed Cut

Masters Tournament, April 6–9: 81–80—161, Missed Cut

British Open, July 20–23: 82–82—164, Missed Cut

PGA Championship, Aug. 10–13: 68–74–81–70—293, T-63, $2,290

Fred Meyer Challenge, Aug. 21–22: 65–62—127, 3rd, $35,000 (with Peter Jacobsen)

RMCC Invitational/Greg Norman, Nov. 17–19: 75–68–61—204, T-9, $31,000 (with Peter Jacobsen)

PGA Tour summary: Official events entered 4, money $2,290

1990

Bob Hope Chrysler Classic, Jan. 17–21: 73–70–70–70—283, Missed Cut

Nestle Invitational, March 22–25: 74–77—151, Missed Cut

Masters Tournament, April 6–9: 76–80—156, Missed Cut

British Open, July 19–22: 73–71—144, Missed Cut

PGA Championship, Aug. 9–12: 81–81—162, Missed Cut

Fred Meyer Challenge, Aug. 20–21: 63–65—128, 6th, $25,500 (with Peter
    Jacobsen)

RMCC Invitational/Greg Norman, Nov. 16–18: 61–66–60—187, 2nd,
    $70,000 (with Peter Jacobsen)

PGA Tour summary: Official events entered 4, money $0

1991

AT&T Pebble Beach National Pro-Am, Jan. 31–Feb. 3: 73–78–79—230,
    Missed Cut

Bob Hope Chrysler Classic, Feb. 6–10: 75–71–75–69— 290, Missed Cut

Nestle Invitational, March 14–17: 72–71–70—213, T-24, $7,737.50 (rain
    shortened)

Masters Tournament, April 11–14: 78–77—155, Missed Cut

PGA Championship, Aug. 8–11:77–78—155, Missed Cut

Fred Meyer Challenge, Aug. 19–20: 66–65—131, T-8, $24,125 (with Peter
    Jacobsen)

Shark Shootout, Nov. 22–24: 68–70–60—198, T-7, $35,250 (with Peter Jacobsen)

JCPenney Classic, Dec. 5–8: 72–68–72–72—284, T-48, $2,675 (with
    Tammie Green)

PGA Tour summary: Official events entered 5, money $7,738

1992

Bob Hope Chrysler Classic, Jan. 15–19: 66–74–70–76—286, Missed
    Cut

AT&T Pebble Beach National Pro-Am, Jan. 30–Feb. 2: 71–78–72—221, Missed Cut

Nestle Invitational, March 19–22: 74–77—151, Missed Cut

Masters Tournament, April 9–12: 75–73—148, Missed Cut

PGA Championship, Aug. 13–16: 79–83—162, Missed Cut

Fred Meyer Challenge, Aug. 24–25: 70–63—133, T-6, $25,000 (with Peter Jacobsen)

Franklin Funds Shark Shootout, Nov. 20–22: 63–70–65—198, T-9, $31,000 (with Peter Jacobsen)

PGA Tour summary: Official events entered 5, money $0

1993

Bob Hope Chrysler Classic, Feb. 10–14: 72–76–68–76—292, Missed Cut

Nestle Invitational, March 18–21: 73–76–78–75—302, T-71, $1,970

Masters Tournament, April 8–11: 74–78—152, Missed Cut

Memorial Tournament, June 3–6: 77–81—158, Missed Cut

PGA Championship, Aug. 12–15: 77–76—153, Missed Cut

Fred Meyer Challenge, Aug. 23–24: 65–68—133, T-6, $25,000 (with Peter Jacobsen)

Franklin Funds Shark Shootout, Nov. 19–21: 69–70–64—203, 10th, $30,000 (with Peter Jacobsen)

Skins Game, Bighorn Golf Club, Nov. 27–28: T-3, 0 skins, $0

PGA Tour summary: Official events entered 5, money $1,970

1994

AT&T Pebble Beach National Pro-Am, Feb. 3–6: 69–75–78—222, Missed Cut

Bob Hope Chrysler Classic, Feb. 16–20: 74–73–71–68—286, Missed Cut

Nestle Invitational, March 17–20: 80–78—158, Missed Cut

Masters Tournament, April 7–10: 78–77—155, Missed Cut

U.S. Open, June 16–20: 77–81—158, Missed Cut (Final U.S. Open)

PGA Championship, Aug. 11–14: 79–74—153, Missed Cut (Final PGA
Championship)

Fred Meyer Challenge, Aug. 22–23: 64–62—126, 3rd, $35,000 (with Peter
Jacobsen)

Franklin Funds Shark Shootout, Nov. 18–20: 73–64–59—196, 6th,
$39,000 (with Peter Jacobsen)

JCPenney Classic, Dec. 1–4: 72–72–66–71—281, 51st, $2,300 (with
Tammie Green)

Diners Club Matches, Dec. 8–11: Senior PGA Tour, Quarterfinals, Arnold
Palmer–Jack Nicklaus defeat Tom Weiskopf–Simon Hobday, 19 holes;
Semifinal, Palmer–Nicklaus defeat Jim Dent–Chi Chi Rodriguez, 4
and 3; Final, Dave Eichelberger–Ray Floyd defeat Palmer Nicklaus, 19
holes

PGA Tour summary: Official events entered 6, money $0

1995

AT&T Pebble Beach National Pro-Am, Feb. 2–5: 77–70–74—221, Missed
Cut

Bob Hope Chrysler Classic, Feb. 16–19: 76–72–75–74—297, Missed Cut

Nestle Invitational, March 16–19: 73–78—151, Missed Cut

Masters Tournament, April 6–9: 79–73—152, Missed Cut

British Open, July 20–23: 83–75—158, Missed Cut (Final Open
Championship)

Fred Meyer Challenge, Aug. 21–22: 69–68—137, 11th, $22,500 (with
Peter Jacobsen)

Franklin Templeton Shark Shootout, Nov. 17–19: 66–67–59—192, 8th,
$34,000 (with Peter Jacobsen)

Diners Club Matches, Dec. 7–10: Senior PGA Tour, Quarterfinals, Ray
Floyd–Dave Eichelberger defeat Arnold Palmer–Jack Nicklaus, 3 and 2

Lexus Challenge, La Quinta Citrus Club Course, Dec. 13–17: 68–66–134, T-7, $60,833 (Best-Ball, with Grant Show)

PGA Tour summary: Official events entered 5, money $0

1996

Bob Hope Chrysler Classic, Jan. 17–21: 75–76–74–72—297, Missed Cut

AT&T Pebble Beach National Pro-Am, Feb. 1–4: 74–72—146, Canceled by weather

Bay Hill Invitational, March 14–17: 75–74—149, Missed Cut

Masters Tournament, April 11–14: 74–76—150, Missed Cut

Fred Meyer Challenge, Aug. 19–20: 66–67—133, T-10, $22,917 (with Peter Jacobsen)

Lexus Challenge, La Quinta Resort, Dec. 18–21: 68–64—132, T-8 (Best-Ball, with Chris O'Donnell)

PGA Tour summary: Official events entered 4, money $0

1997

Bay Hill Invitational, March 20–23: 81—81, Withdrew before completion of delayed second round

Masters Tournament, April 10–13: 89–87—176, Missed Cut

Fred Meyer Challenge, Aug. 4–5: 63–65—128, 4th, $30,000 (with Peter Jacobsen)

PGA Tour summary: Official events entered 2, money $0

1998

Bob Hope Chrysler Classic, Jan. 14–18: 75–77–77–74—303, Missed Cut

Bay Hill Invitational, March 19–22: 78–78—156, Missed Cut

Masters Tournament, April 9–12: 79–87—166, Missed Cut

Fred Meyer Challenge, Aug. 24–25: 67–68—135, T-11, $30,250 (with Peter Jacobsen)

PGA Tour summary: Official events entered 3, money $0

1999

Bob Hope Chrysler Classic, Jan. 20–24: 76–76–78–75—305, Missed Cut

Bay Hill Invitational, March 11–14: 78–74—152, Missed Cut

Masters Tournament, April 8–11: 83–78—161, Missed Cut

Fred Meyer Challenge, Aug. 23–24: 68–66—134, 12th, $30,000 (with Peter Jacobsen)

PGA Tour summary: Official events entered 3, money $0

2000

Bob Hope Chrysler Classic, Jan. 19–23. 82–79–76–77—314, Missed Cut

Bay Hill Invitational, March 16–19: 82–76—158, Missed Cut

Masters Tournament, April 6–9: 78–82—160, Missed Cut

Fred Meyer Challenge, Aug. 7–8: 65–65—130, T-7, $36,250 (with Peter Jacobsen)

Franklin Templeton Shootout, Nov. 17–19: 76–70–62, 12th, $42,500 (with Peter Jacobsen)

PGA Tour summary: Official events entered 3, money $0

2001

Bob Hope Chrysler Classic, Feb. 14–18: 81–79–75–71—306, Missed Cut

Bay Hill Invitational, March 15–18: 85–78—163, Missed Cut

Masters Tournament, April 5–8: 82–76—158, Missed Cut

CVS Charity Classic, July 9–10: 61–65—126, 7 shots back of first (with Billy Andrade)

Fred Meyer Challenge, Aug. 6–7: 68–67—135, 11th (with Peter
    Jacobsen)

Marconi Pennsylvania Classic, Sept. 20–23: Withdrew after two rounds

UBS Warburg Cup, Nov. 16–18: Day 1, Foursomes, Gary Player (ROW
    captain)–Des Smyth defeat Arnold Palmer (U.S. captain)–Mark
    O'Meara, 3 and 2; Day 2, Four-Ball, Player-Smyth (ROW) defeat
    Palmer–Dana Quigley, 2 up; Day 3, Singles, Palmer defeated Player,
    2 and 1. Final team score U.S. 12½, Rest of the World 11½. Winners
    $150,000 each.

Hyundai Team Matches, Champions Tour, Dec. 8–9: Semifinals, Tom
    Watson–Andy North defeat Arnold Palmer–Bruce Fleisher, 5 and 3.
    Third-place match: Palmer-Fleisher defeat Gary McCord–Tom Kite,
    1–up

PGA Tour summary: Official events entered 4, money $0

2002

Bob Hope Chrysler Classic, Jan. 16–20: 78–77–80–88—323, Missed
    Cut

Bay Hill Invitational, March 14–17: 86, Withdrew

Masters Tournament, April 11–14: 89–85—174, Missed Cut

Fred Meyer Challenge, Aug. 5–6: 67–65—132, 11th (with Peter
    Jacobsen)

UBS Warburg Cup, Nov. 15–17: Day 1, Foursomes, Nick Faldo–Gary
    Player (ROW captain) defeat Arnold Palmer (U.S. captain)–Curtis
    Strange, 1 up; Day 2, Four-Ball, Palmer-Tom Watson (U.S.) defeat
    Player–Bernhard Langer, 3 and 2; Day 3, Singles, Player defeated
    Palmer, 6 and 5. Final score, United States 14½, Rest of the World 9½.
    Winner's share: $150,000 per player.

PGA Tour summary: Official events entered 3, money $0

2003

Bay Hill Invitational, March 20–23: 87–85—172, Missed Cut

Masters Tournament, April 10–13: 83–83—166, Missed Cut

UBS Warburg Cup, Nov. 21–23: Day 1, Foursomes, Nick Faldo–Tony Jacklin (ROW captain) defeat Arnold Palmer (U.S. captain)–Rocco Mediate, 1 up; Day 2, Four-Ball, Palmer–Curtis Strange (U.S.) defeat Jacklin-Faldo, 4 and 3; Day 3, Singles, Jacklin (ROW) defeated Palmer, 1 up. Final score, United States 12, Rest of the World 12, U.S. retains cup.

Office Depot Father-Son Challenge, Dec. 6–7: 65–67—132, 12th, $44,000 (with grandson Sam Saunders)

PGA Tour summary: Official events entered 2, money $0

2004

Bay Hill Invitational, March 18–21: 88–79—167, Missed Cut (Final Bay Hill event)

Masters Tournament, April 8–11: 84–84—168, Missed Cut (Final Masters)

CVS Charity Classic, June 28–29: 64–65—129, 8th, $95,000 (with Billy Andrade)

UBS Warburg Cup, Nov. 18–21: Day 1, Foursomes, Arnold Palmer (U.S. captain)–Jay Haas halve with Gary Player (ROW captain)–Mark McNulty; Day 2, Four-Ball, Palmer-Haas (U.S.) halve with Player-McNulty; Day 3, Singles, Player (ROW) defeated Palmer, 6 and 5. Final score, United States 14, Rest of the World 10. Winning team $150,000 each.

Office Depot Father-Son Challenge, Dec. 4–5: 65–65—130, T-12, $43,000 (with grandson Sam Saunders)

PGA Tour summary: Official events entered 2, money $0

2005

CVS Charity Classic, June 27–28: 67–67—134, 10th, $90,000 (with Billy Andrade)

MBNA WorldPoints Father-Son Challenge, Dec. 3–4: 67–65—132, T-14, $42,250 (with grandson Sam Saunders)

PGA Tour summary: Official events entered 0, money $0

2006

Del Webb Father-Son Challenge, Dec. 2–3: 64–68—132, 15th, $42,000 (with grandson Sam Saunders)

PGA Tour summary: Official events entered 0, money $0

2007

Del Webb Father-Son Challenge, Dec. 1–2: 62–64—126, T-6 (with grandson Sam Saunders)

PGA Tour summary: Official events entered 0, money $0

2008

Del Webb Father-Son Challenge, Dec. 6–7: 64–64—128, T-7, $52,000 (with grandson Sam Saunders)

PGA Tour summary: Official events entered 0, money $0

2011

Umpqua Bank Challenge (formerly Fred Meyer Challenge), Aug. 29–30: 71–68—139, 6th (with Peter Jacobsen)

PGA Tour summary: Official events entered 0, money $0

2012

PNC Father-Son Challenge, Dec. 15–16: 80–76—156, 18th, $40,000
(with grandson Will Wears)

PGA Tour summary: Official events entered 0, money $0

PLAYING HIGHS AND LOWS

Lowest 18-hole score all-time: 60, Latrobe Country Club, September 12, 1969

First 18-hole score on PGA Tour: 78, Miami Open, Miami Springs Country Club, Dec. 9, 1954

Lowest 18-hole score PGA Tour: 62, Jan. 25, 1959, fourth round Thunderbird Invitational; Jan. 8, 1966, third round, Los Angeles Open

Best first round: 64, 1955 Canadian Open (Aug. 17); 1962 Phoenix Open (Feb. 8); 1970 Citrus Open (March 5); 1970 Greensboro Open (April 2); 1971 Westchester Classic (July 22)

Best second round: 63, 1961 Texas Open (April 28)

Best third round: 62, 1966 Los Angeles Open (Jan. 8)

Best fourth round: 62, 1959 Thunderbird Classic (Jan. 29)

Lowest score, first 36 holes: 67–63—130, 1961 Texas Open (April 27–28)

Lowest score, first 54 holes: 64–67–64—195, 1955 Canadian Open (Aug. 17–19)

Lowest score, 72 holes: 265, came at his first tour victory, Aug. 17–20, 1955, Canadian Open (64–67–64–70—265)

Largest margin of victory: 12 shots, Phoenix Open 1962

Most consecutive birdies: 7, 1966 Los Angeles Open, third round, January 8

Holes in one: 20, including one in Japan, four on the Champions Tour and three in PGA Tour events. Last ace was on Tuesday, November 8, 2011, a 5-iron shot on the 163-yard seventh hole of the Charger Course at Bay Hill. His first hole in one was as a high schooler at Latrobe Country Club.

PROFESSIONAL PLAYOFF RECORD (15–11)

1956—Panama Open, defeated Sam Snead on sixth hole of sudden death;
   Insurance City Open, defeated Ted Kroll with a birdie on second hole
   of sudden death

1957—Rubber City Open, defeated Doug Ford with birdie on sixth hole
   of sudden death

1958—Azalea Open, lost to Howie Johnson, 77–78

1959—West Palm Beach Open, defeated Gay Brewer and Pete Cooper
   with par on fourth hole of sudden death

1960—Houston Classic, lost to Bill Collins, 69–71; Insurance City Open,
   defeated Bill Collins and Jack Fleck with birdie on third hole of sudden
   death

1961—San Diego Open, defeated Al Balding with birdie on first hole of
   sudden death; Phoenix Open, defeated Doug Sanders, 67–70; "500"
   Festival Open, lost to Doug Ford's birdie on second hole of sudden death

1962—Masters Tournament, won with 68 versus Gary Player (71) and
   Dow Finsterwald (77); Colonial National Invitation, defeated Johnny
   Pott, 69–73; U.S. Open, lost 71–74 to Jack Nicklaus

1963—Thunderbird Classic, defeated Paul Harney with a par on first hole
   of sudden death; U.S. Open, shot 76 to lose to Julius Boros (70) and
   Jacky Cupit (73); Cleveland Open, shot 67 to defeat Tony Lema (70)
   and Tommy Aaron (70); Western Open, shot 70 to defeat Julius Boros
   (71) and Jack Nicklaus (73)

1964—Pensacola Open, lost in playoff (72) to Gary Player (71) with Miller
   Barber (74); Cleveland Open, lost to birdie by Tony Lema on first hole
   of sudden death

1966—Bob Hope Desert Classic, lost to birdie by Doug Sanders on first
   hole of sudden death; Tournament of Champions, shot 69 to defeat Gay
   Brewer (73); U.S. Open, lost 69–73 to Billy Casper; Dunlop International,
   Kensington, Australia, lost to Bob Stanton on second hole of sudden death

1968—Bob Hope Desert Classic, defeated Deane Beman with par on
   second hole of sudden death

1970—Byron Nelson Golf Classic, lost to Jack Nicklaus with birdie on first hole of sudden death

1971—Bob Hope Desert Classic, defeated Ray Floyd with birdie on first hole of sudden death

VARDON TROPHY

Won four times for lowest scoring average on PGA Tour:

1961, 69.859, 99 rounds, 6,916 strokes; 1962, 70.271, 85 rounds, 5,973 strokes
1964, 70.010, 96 rounds, 6,721 strokes; 1967, 70.188, 85 rounds, 5,966 strokes

PALMER IN THE RYDER CUP

Two-time Captain, 2–0 Record:

Playing Captain, 1963, East Lake Country Club, Atlanta, Ga., United States 23, Great Britain 9

Nonplaying, 1975, Laurel Valley Golf Club, Ligonier, Pa., United States 21, Great Britain & Ireland 11

Six-time Player, 6–0 Team Record, His Play:

1961–OCT. 13–14, ROYAL LYTHAM & ST. ANNES, ST. ANNES, ENGLAND. UNITED STATES 11½, GREAT BRITAIN 9½

Day 1

Morning Foursomes, Arnold Palmer–Billy Casper (U.S.) defeat Dai Rees–Ken Bousfield, 2 and 1

Afternoon Foursomes, Palmer-Casper (U.S.) defeat John Panton–Bernard Hunt, 5 and 4

Day 2

Morning Singles, Palmer (U.S.) and Peter Alliss halve
Afternoon Singles, Palmer (U.S.) defeats Tom Haliburton, 2 and 1
This Match, Palmer won–loss–tied record 3–0–1.

1963–OCT. 11–13, EAST LAKE COUNTRY CLUB, ATLANTA, GA., UNITED STATES 23, GREAT BRITAIN 9

Day 1

Morning Foursomes, Brian Huggett–George Will (GB) defeat Arnold
    Palmer–Johnny Pott, 3 and 2
Afternoon Foursomes, Palmer–Billy Casper (U.S.) defeat Huggett-Will, 5
    and 4

Day 2

Morning Four-Ball, Palmer–Dow Finsterwald (U.S.) defeat Huggett–Dave
    Thomas, 5 and 4
Afternoon Four-Ball, Palmer-Finsterwald (U.S.) defeat Neil Coles–
    Christy O'Connor Sr., 3 and 2

Day 3

Morning Singles, Peter Alliss (GB) defeats Palmer, 1 up
Afternoon Singles, Palmer (U.S.) defeats Will, 3 and 2
This Match, Palmer won–loss–tied record 4–2–0; two-match composite
    record 7–2–1.

1965—OCT. 7–9, ROYAL BIRKDALE GOLF CLUB, SOUTHPORT,
ENGLAND, UNITED STATES 19½, GREAT BRITAIN 12½

Day 1

Morning Foursomes, Dave Thomas–George Will (GB) defeat Arnold
Palmer–Dave Marr, 6 and 5
Afternoon Foursomes, Palmer-Marr (U.S.) defeat Thomas-Will, 6 and 5

Day 2

Morning Four-Ball, Palmer-Marr (U.S.) defeat Peter Alliss–Christy
O'Connor Sr., 6 and 4
Afternoon Four-Ball, Alliss–O'Connor Sr. (GB) defeat Palmer-Marr, 2 up

Day 3

Morning Singles, Palmer (U.S.) defeats Jimmy Hitchcock, 3 and 2
Afternoon Singles, Palmer (U.S.) defeats Peter Butler, 2 up
This Match, Palmer won-loss-tied record 4–2–0; three-match composite
record 11–4–1.

1967—OCT. 20–22, CHAMPIONS GOLF CLUB, HOUSTON, UNITED
STATES 23½, GREAT BRITAIN 8½

Day 1

Morning Foursomes, Arnold Palmer–Gardner Dickinson (U.S.) defeat
Peter Alliss–Christy O'Connor Sr., 2 and 1
Afternoon Foursomes, Palmer-Dickinson (U.S.) defeat Malcolm Gregson–
Hugh Boyle, 5 and 4

Day 2

Afternoon Four-Ball, Palmer–Julius Boros (U.S.) defeat George Will–
Boyle, 1 up

Day 3

Morning Singles, Palmer (U.S.) defeats Tony Jacklin, 3 and 2
Afternoon Singles, Palmer (U.S.) defeats Brian Huggett, 5 and 3
This Match, Palmer won-loss-tied record 5–0–0; four-match composite
record 16–4–1.

1971–SEPT. 16–18, OLD WARSON COUNTRY CLUB, ST. LOUIS, UNITED STATES 18½, GREAT BRITAIN 13½

Day 1

Morning Foursomes, Arnold Palmer–Gardner Dickinson (U.S.) defeat
Peter Townsend–Peter Oosterhuis, 2 up
Afternoon Foursomes, Palmer-Dickinson (U.S.) defeat Townsend-
Oosterhuis, 1 up

Day 2

Morning Four-Ball, Palmer-Dickinson (U.S.) defeat Oosterhuis–Bernard
Gallacher, 5 and 4
Afternoon Four-Ball, Palmer–Jack Nicklaus (U.S.) defeat Townsend–
Harry Bannerman, 1 up

Day 3

Morning Singles, Palmer (U.S.) and Bannerman halve

Afternoon Singles, Oosterhuis (GB) defeats Palmer, 3 and 2

This Match, Palmer won–loss–tied record 4–1–1; five-match composite
record 20–5–2.

1973–SEPT. 20–22, MUIRFIELD, SCOTLAND, UNITED STATES 19, GREAT BRITAIN & IRELAND 13

Day 1

Morning Foursomes, Arnold Palmer–Jack Nicklaus (U.S.) defeat Maurice
Bembridge–Eddie Polland, 6 and 5

Afternoon Four-Ball, Bembridge–Brian Huggett (GBI) defeat Palmer–
Nicklaus, 3 and 1

Day 2

Morning Foursomes, Peter Oosterhuis–Tony Jacklin (GBI) defeat Palmer–
Dave Hill, 2 up

Afternoon Four-Ball, Palmer–J. C. Snead (U.S.) defeat Brian Barnes–Peter
Butler, 2 up

Day 3

Afternoon Singles, Oosterhuis (GBI) defeats Palmer, 4 and 2

This Match, Palmer won–loss–tied record 2–3–0.

Full six-match record: 32 matches played, 22–8–2 record (best all-time
winning percentage), singles 6–3–2, Foursomes 9–3–0, Four-Ball
7–2–0, Total Points 23.

CANADA CUP/WORLD CUP/INTERNATIONAL TROPHY

JUNE 23–26, 1960, PORTMARNOCK GOLF CLUB, DUBLIN,
IRELAND
Individual: 69–71–75–69—284, T-3
U.S. Team with Sam Snead: 140–139–142–144—565, 1st

NOVEMBER 8–11, 1962, JOCKEY CLUB, BUENOS AIRES,
ARGENTINA
Individual: 68–72–69–69—278, T-2
U.S. Team with Sam Snead: 136–137–141–143—557, 1st

OCTOBER 24–28, 1963, GOLF DE SAINT-NOM-LA-BRETÈCHE,
PARIS, FRANCE
Inclement weather shortened final round to nine holes
Individual: 69–70–72–34—245, T-5
U.S. Team with Jack Nicklaus: 136–142–138–66—482, 1st

DECEMBER 3–6, 1964, ROYAL KA'ANAPALI GOLF COURSE, MAUI,
HAWAII
Individual: 66–67–67–78—278, 2nd
U.S. Team with Jack Nicklaus: 138–136–132–148—554, 1st

NOVEMBER 10–13, 1966, YOMIURI COUNTRY CLUB,
TOKYO, JAPAN
Individual: 66–67–69–73—275, 5th
U.S. Team with Jack Nicklaus: 135–135–136–142—548, 1st

NOVEMBER 9–12, 1967, CLUB DE GOLF MEXICO, MEXICO CITY,
MEXICO
Individual: 68–70–71–67—276, 1st
U.S. Team with Jack Nicklaus: 140–141–140–136—557, 1st

WORLD SERIES OF GOLF

Palmer played in three WSOGs, an unofficial 36-hole event involving the winners of the year's major championships, held at Firestone Country Club, par-70, 7,165-yard South Course, Akron, Ohio.

September 8–9, 1962—Jack Nicklaus 66–69—135, $50,000; Arnold Palmer 65–74—139, $12,500; Gary Player 69–70—139, $12,500

September 7–8, 1963—Jack Nicklaus 70–70—140, $50,000; Julius Boros 72–69—141, $15,000; Arnold Palmer★ 71–72—143, $5,000; Bob Charles 70–77—147, $5,000.

September 12–13, 1964—Tony Lema 70–68—138, $50,000; Ken Venturi 69–74—143, $15,000; Bobby Nichols 77–70—147, $5,000; Arnold Palmer 74–74—148, $5,000

★Won playoff Aug. 20 to be fourth contestant.

PGA SENIOR TOUR (CHAMPIONS)

CAREER SUMMARY

Events started, 319; cuts made, 294; firsts, 10; seconds, 7; thirds, 9; top-10 finishes, 67; top-25 finishes, 123; total money won, $1,765,795; money by year: 1980—$20,000; 1981—$55,100; 1982—$73,848; 1983—$106,590; 1984—$184,582; 1985—$137,024; 1986—$99,056; 1987—$128,910; 1988—$185,373; 1989—$119,907; 1990—$66,519; 1991—$143,967; 1992—$70,815; 1993—$106,232; 1994—$34,471; 1995—$51,526; 1996—$48,192; 1997—$29,052; 1998—$20,454; 1999—$8,185; 2000—$15,338; 2001—$4,384; 2002—$5,596; 2003—$19,311; 2004—$14,812; 2005—$15,701; 2006—$850. Note: 10 victories rank him T-30 on senior victory list, tied with five others, among them Jack Nicklaus

VICTORIES (10)

1980 Senior PGA Championship
1981 U.S. Senior Open

1982 Marlboro Classic, Denver Post Champions of Golf

1983 Boca Grove Classic

1984 Senior PGA Championship, Senior Tournament Players
      Championship, Quadel Senior Classic

1985 Senior Tournament Players Championship

1988 Crestar Classic

SENIOR TOUR (NON-CHAMPIONS)

VICTORIES (2)

1984 Doug Sanders Celebrity Pro-Am

1986 Unionmutual Classic

CHRYSLER CUP (RYDER CUP-STYLE SENIOR EVENT, U.S. VERSUS INTERNATIONALS)

Palmer was the U.S. captain for the five years it was played, 1986–1990, and
had a 4–1 record. It was during the inaugural event at the TPC at Avenel
course in Potomac, Md., that he aced the 187-yard number three hole two
days in a row using the same 5-iron. Palmer's match results:

1986 (Sept. 4–7): Final score, United States 68½, International 31½. Day
1, Four-Ball, Arnold Palmer (U.S. captain)–Gene Littler defeat Gary Player
(International captain)–Bob Charles, 1 up; Day 2, Singles Match, Palmer
(U.S.) defeated Harold Henning, 1 up; Day 3, Singles Stroke, Palmer (U.S.)
defeated Peter Thomson, 71–73; Day 4, Stroke Play, Palmer 35–34–69, T-1.
Winning team members $50,000 each.

1987 (April 2–5): Final score, International 59.5, United States 40.7. Day
1, Four-Ball, Arnold Palmer (U.S. captain)–Chi Chi Rodriguez defeated
Peter Butler–Christy O'Connor, 5 and 4; Day 2, Singles Stroke, Harold
Henning defeated Palmer, 72–73; Day 3, Best-Ball Stroke, Palmer–Don
January 36–35—71, T-6; Day 4, Stroke Play, Palmer 74, T-12. Losing team
members $25,000 each.

1988 (April 21–24): Final score, United States 55, International 45.

Round 1, Four-Ball Match, Arnold Palmer (U.S. captain)–Chi Chi Rodriguez defeat Gary Player (International captain)–Bob Charles, 1-up; Round 2, Singles Match, Bruce Crampton defeats Palmer, 2 and 1; Round 3, Four-Ball Stroke, Crampton–Harold Henning defeat Palmer–Miller Barber, 64–65; Round 4, Singles Stroke, Gary Player defeated Palmer, 72–74. Winning team members $50,000 each.

1989 (April 20–23): Final score, United States 71, International 29. Round 1, Four-Ball Match, Arnold Palmer (U.S. captain)–Miller Barber halved with Gary Player–Doug Dalziel; Round 2, Singles Match, Palmer (U.S.) halved with Roberto De Vicenzo; Round 3, Four-Ball, Palmer–Dave Hill (U.S.) defeat De Vicenzo–Dalziel, 65–68; Round 4, Singles Stroke, Palmer (U.S.) defeated Bruce Devlin, 70–74. Winning team members $50,000 each.

1990 (Feb. 22–25): Final score, United States 53½, International 30½. Round 1, Four-Ball, Arnold Palmer (U.S. captain)–Orville Moody defeat Roberto De Vicenzo–Peter Thomson, 1 up; Round 2, Singles Match, canceled, weather; Round 3, Four-Ball Stroke, De Vicenzo–Harold Henning (International) defeat Palmer–Don Bies, 69–70; Round 4, Singles Stroke, Henning defeated Palmer, 70–74. Winning team members $50,000 each.

CHAMPIONS TOUR SKINS GAME
Played 20 events, 1988–1996, 1998–2008

Three-time winner: 1990, 8 skins, $240,000; 1992, 7 skins, $205,000; 1993, 6 skins, $190,000. Total money of all events: $1,265,000

DISTINCTIONS
PGA Tour leading money winner: 1958, 1960, 1962, 1963
PGA Player of Year: 1960, 1962
Vardon Trophy winner (lowest stroke average): 1961, 1962, 1964, 1967
First player on PGA Tour to win $100,000 in a season
First player on PGA Tour to win $1 million in a career
One loss as U.S. team captain (10–1–1): 2–0 Ryder Cup 1963, 1975; 1–0

Presidents Cup 1996; 3–0–1 UBS Warburg Cup 2001, 2002, 2003, 2004; 4–1 Chrysler Cup, 1986–1990 (lost in 1987).

Byron Nelson Award (most tour victories 1957, 1960, 1961, 1962, 1963)

Sixth all-time in top-10 finishes in professional major championships with 38, comprising 12 in the Masters, 13 U.S. Open, 7 Open Championship and 6 in the PGA Championship. His first top-10 was in the 1955 Masters and final was the 1977 Open Championship.

CAREER ACHIEVEMENT

Halls of Fame: World Golf Hall of Fame (1974 charter member); PGA Hall of Fame (Palm Beach Gardens, Fla., 1980); American Golf (Foxburg, Pa.); Ohio Golf Hall of Fame (1992); All-American Collegiate Golf Hall of Fame—Man of Year (1984); Wake Forest; Pennsylvania; Phoenix Open; Western Pennsylvania Golf (inaugural class 2013); Northern Ohio Golf Association (2003); Southern Conference (2009 inaugural class); Westmoreland County; North Carolina; Florida Sports; Cambria County; Western Pennsylvania Interscholastic Athletic League (2007 inaugural class); National High School Sports; North Florida PGA (2010); Tri-State PGA (2002)

Presidential Medal of Freedom from President George W. Bush, 2004

Congressional Gold Medal, passed by Congress and signed by President Obama in 2009

Bob Jones Award (1971, U.S. Golf Association)

Gold Tee Award (1965, Metropolitan Golf Writers Association)

William D. Richardson Award (1969, Golf Writers Association of America)

Charles Bartlett Award (1976, GWAA)

Sportsman of the Year (1960, *Sports Illustrated*)

Rae Hickok Belt Award for Professional Athlete of the Year 1960

Athlete of the Decade (1960s, Associated Press)

Lowman Humanitarian Award

Dapper Dan Man of Year (1960, Pittsburgh)

Wake Forest Distinguished Alumni Award (1962)

Golf Digest "Man of the Silver Era," 1950–1975

Arthur J. Rooney Award, Catholic Youth Association (1977)

Francis Ouimet Award for Lifelong Contributions to Golf (1997 inaugural winner)

Partner in Science Award, March of Dimes Birth Defects Foundation

Herb Graffis Award (1978, National Golf Foundation)

Distinguished Pennsylvanian (1980)

Walter Hagen Award (1981)

Golf Course Superintendents Association of America's Old Tom Morris Award (1983)

Golfer of Century from the New York Athletic Club (1985)

Ellis Island Medal of Honor (1986)

Golf Digest Commemorative Tournament honoree (1987)

Order of Eagle Exemplar, U.S. Sports Academy (1989)

American Senior Golf Association National Award (1989)

Chicago District Golf Association Distinguished Service Award (1989)

Atlanta Athletic Club Sports Appreciation Trophy (1990)

World Series of Golf Ambassador of Golf Award (1991)

Bing Crosby Tournament Sponsor Award, Bay Hill Classic (1992, MGWA)

Theodore Roosevelt Award, National Collegiate Athletic Association

Outstanding American Award, Los Angeles Philanthropic Foundation (1992)

Memorial Tournament honoree (1993)

Sports Legends Award, Juvenile Diabetes Association (1993)

National Sports Award (1993)

"Good Guy" Award, American Legion National Commanders (1993)

Humanitarian Award, Variety Club International (1993)

Ford Achievement Award (1994)

PGA of America Distinguished Service Award (1994)

Latrobe Chamber of Commerce Community Service Award (1995)

Distinguished Service Award (PGA of America Tri-State Section, 1996)

Reagan Distinguished American Award (1996)

Golf Associations of Philadelphia Centennial Award (1996)

PGA Tour's Lifetime Achievement Award (1998)

University of Pittsburgh Cancer Institute Spirit of Hope Award (1998)

Lifetime Achievement Award, March of Dimes Athletic Awards (1998)

Western Pennsylvania Golf Association's Golfer of the Century (1998)

Lifetime Achievement Award (1998, PGA Tour)

Golf World magazine's Newsmaker of Century (1999)

American Society of Golf Course Architects Donald Ross Award (1999)

James Ewing Layman's Award, Society of Surgical Oncology (1999)

Athletes Who Changed Game, *Sports Illustrated*'s 20th-Century Sports
    Awards (1999)

Novell Utah Showdown Dave Marr Award (2000)

Golden Anniversary Award (MGWA), presented to the Big Three—
    Arnold Palmer, Gary Player, Jack Nicklaus—as the players who had the
    greatest influence on golf during the half century 1952–2001

Ike Grainger Award (USGA, 2000)

National Golf Foundation Golf Family of Year (2000)

Patriot Award, Congressional Medal of Honor Society (2000)

Payne Stewart Award (PGA Tour, 2000)

Great Ones Award, Jim Murray Memorial Foundation (2001)

National Golf Course Owners Association Award of Merit (2001)

George Bush Three Amigos Inspiration Award (2001)

Great American Award, Starkey Hearing Foundation (2003)

ASAP Sports/Jim Murray Award (2003, GWAA)

Top 10 Male Athletes of Atlantic Coast Conference 50th anniversary (2003)

Dave Marr Shell Award (2004)

Dapper Dan Lifetime Achievement Award (2005)

Portugal Order of Merit (2005)

Adelphoi USA Spirit of Hope Award (2006)

Will F. Nicholson Award for "a lifetime of dedication and commitment to
   the game" (2007)

Golf Coaches Association of America Lifetime Achievement Award, Hall
   of Fame (2008)

Northern California Section Langley Award (2008)

Woodlands Foundation Spirit of Golf Award (2008)

Boy Scout Eagle Award (2008, Central Florida Council)

Byron Nelson Prize (2009)

Golf Business Forum Lifetime Achievement Award (2009)

Children's Miracle Network Lifetime Legacy Award (2009)

Wright Brothers Master Pilot Award (2010)

American Cancer Society Premiere Award (2010, Latrobe Country Club)

National Business Aviation Association Meritorious Service Award
   (2010)

Ranked by GQ magazine "one of the 25 coolest athletes of all time"
   (February 2011)

Champions for Babies, March of Dimes (2012)

Cessna Jet Pilots Association Hall of Honor (2014)

DeMolay International Legion of Honor (2015)

Stan Musial Lifetime Achievement Award for Sportsmanship (2015)

HONORARY DEGREES

Honorary Doctor of Humane Letters, St. Vincent College

Honorary Doctor of Humane Letters, Allegheny College

Honorary Doctor of Humane Letters, Florida Southern University

Honorary Doctor of Laws, National College of Education

Honorary Doctor of Humane Letters, Seton Hill University

Honorary Doctor of Humanities, Thiel College

Honorary Doctor of Law, University of St. Andrews

Honorary Doctor of Laws, Wake Forest University

Honorary Doctor of Public Service, Washington & Jefferson College

ARNOLD PALMER LANDMARKS

PLAQUES

Cherry Hills, Denver, first tee, in honor of his 1960 U.S. Open victory

Country Club of Detroit, in honor of his 1954 U.S. Amateur win

Royal Birkdale, 16th hole, to recognize a famous shot he hit during the 1961 Open Championship

Ignominiously, Rancho Park Golf Course, for the 12 he took on the 18th hole on January 6, 1961, in the Los Angeles Open

At Augusta National, one of the many landmarks is a Palmer plaque attached to a drinking fountain behind the 16th tee

STATUES

Laurel Valley Golf Course, Ligonier, Pa., unveiled on September 10, 2009, in honor of his 80th birthday

Wake Forest has a statue on campus at its practice facility in front of the Haddock House that depicts him posed in his follow-through.

A Palmer statue also stands at the Arnold Palmer Regional Airport and Georgia Golf Hall of Fame.

FACILITIES

The Latrobe airport is named the Arnold Palmer Regional Airport in Latrobe; it was formerly known as the Westmoreland County Airport.

The U.S. Golf Association in New Jersey has named part of its facility the United States Golf Association Museum and Arnold Palmer Center for Golf History.

When Palmer was 85, the Latrobe High School athletic building was named the Arnold Palmer Field House.

In Orlando, next to the Winnie Palmer Hospital for Women & Babies is the Arnold Palmer Hospital for Children.

In La Quinta, Calif., there is the Arnold Palmer Restaurant, and a Wake Forest University residence hall is named after him.

ROADS

There are Arnold Palmer Boulevards in Louisville, Ky., and Norton, Mass., and Arnold Palmer Drives in Orlando; Raleigh, N.C.; Haymarket, Va.; Belleville, Ill.; Tucson, Ariz.; Blaine, Minn.; Gibsonia, Pa.; and Virginia Beach, Va.

The most famous Arnold Palmer Drive is in Latrobe, Pa., which is where the high school is located: 131 Arnold Palmer Drive. Off of Arnold Palmer Drive is 123 Legends Lane, the address of Arnold Palmer Enterprises. As for bodies of water, at Sedgefield Country Club, the creek on the then 16th hole in the 1972 Greater Greensboro Open was unofficially called "Arnie's Creek" due to the triple bogey he took from it, which wiped out his two-shot lead and sent him to a tie for third.

ARNOLD PALMER COURSE DESIGN

With his main associate Ed Seay, designed more than 300 courses world-wide, including in 1981 designing Chung Shan Hot Springs, the first golf course in mainland China since World War I. According to *Golf Digest*, these are the top 10 Palmer–designed courses:

Tralee Golf Club, County Kerry, Ireland, 1984

Musgrove Mill Golf Club, Clinton, S.C., 1988

Old Tabby Links, Spring Island, S.C., 1992

Adios Golf Club, Coconut Creek, Fla., 1984

Tradition Golf Club, La Quinta, Calif., 1997

Dakota Dunes Country Club, S.D., 1991

Lonnie Poole Golf Course at North Carolina State, Raleigh, 2009

Aviara Golf Club, Carlsbad, Calif., 1991

Arborlinks Golf Course, Nebraska City, Neb., 2002

The Bluffs on Thompson Creek, St. Francisville, La., 1988

INDEX

ABOUT THE AUTHOR

Tom Callahan, a former senior writer at *Time* magazine and sports columnist at the *Washington Post*, is the author of *Johnny U*, *In Search of Tiger*, *The Bases Were Loaded (and So Was I)*, *The GM*, and *His Father's Son: Earl and Tiger Woods*. He lives in Williamsburg, Virginia.